OXFORD STUDIES IN AFRICAN AFFAIRS

General Editors

JOHN D. HARGREAVES *and* GEORGE SHEPPERSON

COCOA, CUSTOM, AND SOCIO-ECONOMIC CHANGE IN RURAL WESTERN NIGERIA

COCOA, CUSTOM, AND SOCIO-ECONOMIC CHANGE IN RURAL WESTERN NIGERIA

BY

SARA S. BERRY

CLARENDON PRESS · OXFORD
1975

Oxford University Press, Ely House, London W.1

GLASGOW NEW YORK TORONTO MELBOURNE WELLINGTON
CAPE TOWN IBADAN NAIROBI   DAR ES SALAAM LUSAKA ADDIS ABABA
DELHI BOMBAY CALCUTTA   MADRAS KARACHI LAHORE DACCA
KUALA LUMPUR SINGAPORE HONG KONG TOKYO

ISBN O 19 821697 1

© OXFORD UNIVERSITY PRESS 1975

PRINTED IN GREAT BRITAIN
BY BUTLER & TANNER LTD
FROME AND LONDON

TO MY PARENTS

Acknowledgements

THE research on which this study is based was made possible by grants from the Centre for Research on Economic Development at the University of Michigan and the Midwest Universities Consortium for International Activities. During my visits to Nigeria, I enjoyed the hospitality of the Nigerian Institute of Social and Economic Research and the Department of Agricultural Economics at the University of Ife, both of which helped in numerous ways to facilitate my research. The staff of the National Archives at Ibadan and librarians at the Universities of Ibadan and Ife were unfailingly helpful, and I also received much assistance from staff members at the Public Record Office and the Royal Commonwealth Society Library in London.

I am grateful to the John Holt Company, Liverpool, for permission to consult the Holt Archives; to the Secretary of the Ibadan City Council for granting me access to historical records in Mapo Hall, Ibadan; to the family of the late Chief J. Akinpelu Obisesan for permission to read the Obisesan papers in the University of Ibadan Library; to the Revd. E. A. Lijadu, who showed me a number of his grandfather's private papers; and to E. S. Munger, whose Africana collection at the California Institute of Technology I consulted frequently while writing the manuscript. The Western Nigeria Marketing Board, the Ministry of Agriculture and Natural Resources, and the Customary Courts in Ibadan, Ife, and Ondo were also most generous in allowing me to consult their records and in helping me to obtain information.

This study would not have been possible without the capable and untiring efforts of my research assistants: Adebayo Adeyanju, 'Soga Alomilagba, Francis Ige, and Olajiri Ogundeji, who helped me collect oral evidence in Nigeria, and Gary S. Shea, who assisted in analysing the evidence after I returned to the United States. The International Development Research Centre and the Department of Economics at Indiana University provided financial and clerical assistance in preparing the manuscript.

It is impossible to thank individually all of the people who have contributed to this study with their time, their knowledge, and their hospitality. The farmers of Western Nigeria, whose accomplishments I have attempted to set down here, assisted me in every way to understand their story; I hope I have rendered it fairly. Of the many others who helped me to gather evidence or to clarify my ideas, I will mention only two: Professor Wolfgang F. Stolper, who first got me involved in studying the economic history of Nigeria, and Chief J. A. Ayorinde, who introduced me to the history of cocoa farming there. Neither is, of course, responsible for the uses I have made of their teachings.

Contents

List of Maps

List of Figures

List of Tables

Abbreviations

CSO	Chief Secretary's Office, Lagos
CMS	Church Missionary Society
CMS (Y)	Church Missionary Society (Yoruba Mission)
CRIN	Cocoa Research Institute of Nigeria
CSNRD	Consortium for the Study of Nigerian Rural Development
MANR	Ministry of Agriculture and Natural Resources
NAI	National Archives, Ibadan
NISER	Nigerian Institute of Social and Economic Research
UAC	United Africa Company
WALC	West African Lands Committee

Introduction

COCOA cultivation was introduced into Western Nigeria towards the end of the nineteenth century and has expanded steadily ever since. By the 1930s the level of economic activity throughout Western Nigeria generally rose and fell with the world price of cocoa and, by and large, it continues to do so today. Despite Western Nigeria's long dependence on cocoa there has been no systematic study of the history of cocoa farming there or of its impact on the rural economy. Galletti, Baldwin, and Dina's massive study, *Nigerian Cocoa Farmers*, contains no historical dimension: it presents much information about farmers' productive activities and household accounts in 1951–2, but makes no attempt to compare this year with earlier ones or to assess the long-term impact of cocoa farming on the pattern of rural life in Western Nigeria.[1] Apart from a few statistical investigations of the 'determinants' of trends in Nigerian cocoa output, which have been uniformly hampered by lack of data, most other studies discuss cocoa incidentally, in the course of examining some other aspects of Western Nigerian social organization or economic change.[2]

Export Growth and Economic Development in West Africa

In the literature on West African economic development cocoa is often lumped together with other agricultural commodities in discussions of the economic causes and consequences of increased primary production for export. Much of this discussion follows Hla Myint in applying Adam Smith's notion—that external trade sometimes serves as a 'vent for surplus production' in economies with limited domestic markets—to the growth of export production in West Africa.[3] In particular, the vent-for-surplus hypothesis

---

[1] R. Galletti, K. D. S. Baldwin, and I. O. Dina, *Nigerian Cocoa Farmers*, published on behalf of the Nigerian Cocoa Marketing Board by Oxford University Press (London, 1956).

[2] The writings of P. C. Lloyd, for example, contain much information on cocoa farming in Western Nigeria, although they deal primarily with other topics. See especially *Yoruba Land Law* (London, 1962) and *Africa in Social Change* (New York, 1968).

[3] Hla Myint, 'The "Classical Theory" of International Trade and the Underdeveloped Countries', *Economic Journal*, 68 (June 1958), pp. 317–37. This article has

has formed the analytical basis for several case studies of export growth and economic development in particular West African economies.[4]

Basically, these studies argue that the 'essentially static' economies of West Africa were galvanized in the latter half of the nineteenth century by 'the appearance of European trading firms, missionaries sowing new ideas and bringing education, and later an externally imposed government.... Most significant of all was the offering by traders of rewards for the sale of particular crops which were in demand abroad—principally palm oil and palm kernels, and later cocoa, rubber and groundnuts.'[5] This author is discussing Nigeria, but the same line of argument occurs in studies of Ghana and Sierra Leone.[6] These new market opportunities raised the opportunity cost of leisure, thereby inducing West African farmers to sacrifice some of it in order to expand output. Since uncultivated land was abundantly available in West Africa, agricultural production could be substantially increased without significantly altering traditional techniques of production or modes of productive organization. In the Nigerian case, Helleiner argues that

Beyond offering peasant farmers a vent for their potential surplus production the foreigner did next to nothing to alter the technological backwardness of the economy. Since production functions were left largely untouched, he cannot be accused of introducing an export bias to the economy. All that he did was to dangle sufficiently attractive prizes before the producers' noses to persuade them to convert potential into actual surpluses by increasing their inputs.[7]

The vent-for-surplus model correctly identifies the crucial importance of an abundant supply of land[8] for export growth and economic development in West Africa and has also helped to focus

---

since become part of orthodox international trade theory by virtue of its inclusion in R. E. Caves and H. G. Johnson, eds., *Readings in International Economics*, published for the American Economic Association by R. D. Irwin (Homewood, Ill., 1968).

[4] See, e.g., G. K. Helleiner, *Peasant Agriculture, Government and Economic Growth in Nigeria* (Homewood, Ill., 1966); R. Szereszewski, *Structural Changes in the Economy of Ghana, 1891–1911* (London, 1965).

[5] Helleiner, p. 3.

[6] Szereszewski; C. M. Elliott, 'Agriculture and Economic Development in Africa: Theory and Experience 1880–1914', in E. L. Jones and S. J. Woolf, eds., *Agrarian Change and Economic Development* (London, 1969).

[7] Helleiner, p. 12.

[8] Helleiner has coined the term 'land surplus economy' to describe the situation encountered in many parts of West Africa in which the supply of cultivable land exceeds the effective demand for it. 'Typology in Development Theory: The Land Surplus Economy', *Food Research Institute Studies*, 6, 2 (1966).

attention on African farmers' responsiveness to market incentives.[9] It has also raised the issue of the elasticity of the agricultural labour supply in West African economies—although to what extent increases in export production were due to aggregate increases in labour input rather than to the reallocation of labour from alternative activities cannot be determined from presently available evidence.[10] However, as I shall argue in more detail below, the model neglects the role of capital formation in the growth of West African agricultural exports and, in so far as it implies that expanded export production entailed little or no change in the traditional organization of productive activity or structure of the rural economy, it is positively misleading.

The shortcomings of the vent-for-surplus model can in part be traced to its proponents' almost exclusive reliance on the limited statistical information available for West African economies in the late nineteenth and early twentieth centuries. Researchers who have gone beyond these data to collect oral evidence and observe the activities of African farmers and traders directly have put much greater emphasis on the role of local initiative and enterprise in the

[9] In this respect the vent-for-surplus model is consistent with the argument that African farmers are 'economically rational' in the sense that their output decisions are positively associated with changes in costs and returns to different productive activities. This argument also receives apparent support from several statistical studies of cocoa supply functions in Ghana and Nigeria. Peter Ady, 'Trends in Cocoa Production in British West Africa', *Bulletin of the Oxford University Institute of Statistics*, 2 (1940), pp. 389–404; M. J. Bateman, 'Aggregate and Regional Supply Functions for Ghanaian Cocoa, 1946–1962', *Journal of Farm Economics*, 47, 2 (May 1965), pp. 384–401; Dean Sanders, 'The Price Responsiveness of Nigerian Cocoa Farmers', University of Michigan Ph.D. thesis, 1968; R. M. Stern, 'The Determinants of Cocoa Supply in West Africa', in I. G. Stewart and H. W. Ord, eds., *African Primary Products and International Trade* (Edinburgh, 1965). Some of the evidence used in these studies is open to question, however, and it is by no means clear that cocoa farmers' behaviour over the long run can be satisfactorily explained by means of conventional types of economic data alone.

[10] Since scholars are not even agreed on what constitutes full-time employment in African societies, it is difficult to make precise statements about the amount of 'unused' labour available at any point in time. See, e.g., D. Turnham, *The Employment Problem in Less Developed Countries: A Review of Evidence*, O.E.C.D. Development Centre Studies, Employment Series 1 (Paris, 1971). Certainly the amount of time spent on agricultural tasks varies enormously, on a seasonal and daily basis, in most West African economies. Also, most farmers who grow crops for export also grow crops for domestic markets and for their own consumption; many engage in non-agricultural pursuits as well. (See Chapter VI, below). However, it does not necessarily follow that because farmers have not specialized completely in export crop production, they have therefore achieved all or even most of the increase in their output of export crops by sacrificing leisure rather than by devoting less time to other income-earning pursuits. Cf. J. S. Hogendorn, 'The Origins of the Groundnut Trade in Northern Nigeria', in C. K. Eicher and C. Liedholm, eds., *Growth and Development of the Nigerian Economy* (East Lansing, Mich., 1970), pp. 44–5.

growth of export production.[11] In a pioneering study of the development of cocoa growing in southern Ghana, Polly Hill showed that
Akwapim and other Ghanaian farmers not only engineered the
rapid growth of cocoa production around the turn of the century
by themselves (almost in spite of the influence of 'foreigners'), but
that they did so on distinctly capitalist lines.[12] They formed companies to raise money to purchase the necessary land, ploughed the
proceeds of their first farms back into further purchases, and often
managed several sizeable farms worked by hired labour. Although
her findings are widely quoted,[13] they have not been used systematically to modify economists' theories of the causes and consequences of economic change in West Africa. Indeed, one study
actually cites Hill's work in support of the notion that foreign investment, government propaganda, and missionary schools were
largely responsible for the rapid early development of the Ghanaian
cocoa industry—a conclusion which runs almost directly contrary
to the argument of *Migrant Cocoa Farmers*.[14]

Part of the difficulty which economists have experienced in
integrating Hill's and other fieldworkers' findings into their analyses
of West African economic development stems from the very specific
and institutionalist orientation of their work. Hill, for example,
has mostly studied individual communities (e.g. Batagarawa in
Katsina Province) or particular groups of producers or traders
(e.g. Akan cocoa farmers, Ewe fishermen, or northern Ghanaian
cattle traders). Although her writings provide a wealth of detail
on the economic activities and organizations of each group, she has
on the whole been so reluctant to generalize (or even propose
hypotheses) on the basis of single cases, that it has been difficult
for economists, especially those who are not West African specia-
lists, to appreciate the broader significance of her work on indigenous forms of economic organization.[15] Even a sympathetic reader

[11] In addition to Polly Hill's work cited below, see Hogendorn; P. Garlick, *African
Traders in Kumasi* (Accra, 1959) and *African Traders and Economic Development in
Ghana* (Oxford, 1971); M. Dupire, 'Planteurs autochtones et étrangers en Basse-Côte
d'Ivoire orientale', *Études Éburnéennes*, 8 (1960); A. J. F. Köbben, 'Le Planteur noir',
ibid. 5 (1956).
[12] Polly Hill, *Migrant Cocoa Farmers of Southern Ghana* (Cambridge, 1963).
[13] Hill has also done several short studies of African producers and traders, reported in *Studies in Rural Capitalism in West Africa* (Cambridge, 1970) and a detailed
survey of a Hausa village economy—*Rural Hausa: A Village and a Setting* (Cambridge,
1972)—and is beginning to inspire similar attempts by others, including the present
study.   [14] Elliott, pp. 145–7.
[15] These criticisms do not apply to *Rural Hausa* in which Hill uses her findings on
Batagarawa to suggest some very interesting hypotheses about the sources and effects
of economic inequality in rural African communities.

such as Stephen Hymer, who purports to explain the economic
implications of Hill's work in a foreword to *Studies in Rural Capitalism*, encounters difficulties in making such generalisations. For
example, Hymer is correct in pointing out the importance of indigenous capital formation, but there is little evidence in Hill's work
to support his conclusion that the act of capital formation has
created 'a "class" of rural capitalists' in West African societies,
whose economic behaviour is qualitatively different from that of
other producers.[16] And, confronted with the institutional variety
displayed by producers and owners of capital in different areas or
lines of production, Hymer takes refuge in the economist's familiar
notion that 'market imperfections' have inhibited the inter-sectoral
mobility of domestic capital and therefore the efficiency with which
it has been allocated to alternative uses.

This conclusion seems to me to run counter to one of Hill's main
points—namely, that indigenous institutions often serve as highly
effective mechanisms for economic enterprise and change. Hymer's
contention that, unlike industrialized Western economies, West
African economies are characterized by the accumulation of a
multitude of 'capitals', each oriented towards a specific productive
activity, with little movement of investible resources from one sector
or area to another, reflects a widespread tendency among Western
economists to treat unfamiliar institutions and cultural practices in
developing economies as impediments to the free flow of market
information and the movement of resources from less to more
productive forms of employment. To be sure, much lip-service is
paid to the desirability of examining the ways in which economic
change is affected by social and cultural variables, but in practice
most development economists assume that the effects are negative
and do not bother to examine available historical or anthropological
evidence in any detail. As a result, they rarely consider the alternative possibility—namely, that in some circumstances traditional
institutions in non-Western economies have served to facilitate
economic growth and change.

In the case of cocoa farming, for example, Hill has shown that
in Ghana the development of the crop involved capitalistic forms
of organization and investment behaviour on the one hand and,

---

[16] Hill, *Studies in Rural Capitalism*, pp. xviii, xx, Cf. Hill's discussion of economic
inequality and the lack of class formation in Batagarawa, (*Rural Hausa*, chs. XII–
XIII) and chs. IV–VI, below.

on the other, considerable mobility on the part of southern Ghanaian farmers. Her work has often been cited as evidence that African farmers do sometimes behave like capitalists, or to show that migrants have played an important role in spreading knowledge of new productive techniques, but few readers have examined the implied relationship between migration and capital formation or considered the economic significance of these farmers' mobility. Why, we may ask, should migrant farmers show a particular propensity towards capital formation, or—if the association works the other way—why should capitalist farmers be more mobile than others?

Both the ecological requirements of cocoa and the relative abundance of uncultivated land in the West African forest belt have led cocoa growers to follow extensive patterns of cultivation.[17] In both Ghana and Nigeria increases in output have usually occurred through the opening up of previously unused forest land for planting new cocoa farms. In this respect, the pattern of export growth has been consistent with the vent-for-surplus hypothesis. However, the process of combining labour with the available land in order to produce cocoa was not essentially costless, as the vent-for-surplus model implies. The establishment of a new cocoa farm requires the expenditure of resources on clearing land, planting young trees, and maintaining them for seven years or more before the farm yields enough to cover annual maintenance costs. Although little physical capital equipment is required for cocoa cultivation, the farmer must provide working capital—either to maintain himself and his dependants while they are establishing the farm, or to hire labourers. During the first two or three years food crops may be grown among the young cocoa trees, but once the canopy forms, the farm is too shady for food crops. Thus, for the latter part of the maturation period the farmer cannot even derive foodstuffs from the young cocoa farm, but must find alternative means to satisfy his subsistence requirements as well as other consumption needs. Moreover, in so far as labour must be bid away from alternative uses, the costs of employing it in cocoa cultivation are not negligible.

[17] The varieties of cocoa grown in Western Nigeria generally require lower inputs of labour and financial outlay when established on forested land than when planted on land which has recently been cultivated. R. Montgomery and A. J. Smyth, *Soils and Land Use in Central Western Nigeria* (Ibadan, 1962), p. 191; Cocoa Research Institute of Nigeria, *Annual Report*, 1962/3, and Western Nigeria Ministry of Agriculture and Natural Resources, Western Nigeria Development Project, *Cocoa* (Ibadan, n.d.).

Given the relative abundance of uncultivated forest land, the main economic problem involved in establishing cocoa farms in West Africa was one of getting labourers to the available land and supervising and maintaining them while they worked. In this economic context the process of capital formation was integrally bound up with migration, on the one hand, and with the organization and maintenance of groups of settlers on the other. Indeed, one cannot examine the process of capital formation involved in the increase in cocoa production in West African societies without studying migration. Conversely, by examining the ways in which farmers moved to uncultivated forest areas and established themselves there, one can gain insights into the means by which an important type of agricultural investment decision was made and implemented.

In addition to the fact that capital formation involved some mobility on the part of the cocoa farmer and his assistants, the labour-intensive techniques involved in producing and maintaining the capital goods (cocoa trees) meant that the chief managerial requirement for successful cocoa cultivation was the ability to mobilize and organize human resources. Thus the growth of cocoa production depended in part on the availability to farmers of institutional mechanisms through which they could maintain themselves while establishing their farms and/or command the labour services of others. In both Ghana and Nigeria some farmers mobilized the necessary resources through the market, using savings accumulated from other pursuits to finance their first cocoa farms, ploughing back the proceeds from these farms into the establishment of additional farms later on, and relying partly or entirely on hired labourers. However, cocoa cultivation has not been confined to wealthy or influential individuals who could finance their farms with cash.[18] Farmers have also been able to acquire the necessary resources through their participation in various 'traditional' institutions or relationships, which enabled them to draw on the resources and/or labour services of other people. Some of these institutions, such as domestic slavery or traditional co-operative labour groups (*owe* and *aro* among the Yoruba), were explicitly intended to serve economic ends, but others, such as the extended family, 'ethnic' group, or city-state, were principally social or political in character. Indeed, in West African cocoa farming, where the abundance of

land relative to labour and capital placed a premium on making
good use of available human resources, social and cultural institutions have often provided particularly appropriate mechanisms for
mobilizing and organizing economic resources.

In so far as the development of cocoa production in West African
economies has depended on non-economic institutions and relationships, as well as on market mechanisms for exchanging information
and productive services, it is not likely that market data alone will
be sufficient to explain long-run trends in investment and production.
This suggests, in turn, that efforts to estimate long-run supply functions for Ghanaian or Nigerian cocoa solely from market data are
not likely to be especially successful—as indeed, they have not been,
except for the period since World War II.[19] It also calls into question the hypothesis that the growth of cocoa production occurred
through the absorption of previously idle land and labour under
given technical and institutional conditions. Not only does this
argument neglect the process of capital formation involved in
creating the capacity to produce cocoa, but also it ignores the interactions between the growth of cocoa production *per se* and the
institutional context in which it occurred. One of the main conclusions of the present study is that only by taking these interactions
into account can one (a) accurately demonstrate changes over time
in the costs of establishing and maintaining cocoa trees and thereby
assess the extent to which they influenced changes in plantings and
output, and (b) show whether or not the spread of cocoa cultivation
left the 'traditional' agricultural economy 'unchanged'.[20]

The Development of Cocoa Farming in Western Nigeria

In this study I shall examine the development of cocoa farming in
Western Nigeria since the late nineteenth century as a process of
capital formation in a land surplus economy. In Nigeria, as in
Ghana, cocoa was not a 'traditional' crop. It was introduced to

[19] See below, pp. 54–6.
[20] In an economy where cultivable land is abundant relative to available supplies of
labour and capital, one would expect farmers to prefer labour- or capital-saving innovations to those whose primary effect is to increase yields from a given supply of land.
Thus, before concluding that the growth of cocoa output had no effect on methods of
production in West African economies, we need to know whether or not there have been
changes in the methods whereby farmers have mobilized and combined labour and
capital in the cocoa economy. In so far as proponents of the vent-for-surplus model
have implicitly identified technical progress with yield-increasing innovations, they
may have failed to notice changes in methods of labour employment or financial
organization—the more so because these changes have often involved institutions or
practices normally considered to be beyond the scope of economic analysis.

Yorubaland through Lagos in the latter part of the nineteenth century and was developed as an export crop (there is virtually no domestic consumption of cocoa products in Nigeria) through the initiative and enterprise of African farmers and traders. Far from dangling 'prizes' before the noses of Yoruba farmers to induce them to grow the new crop, foreign traders and colonial officials found themselves obliged, in the early years of this century, to 'respond' to the fact that these farmers were reluctant to follow European advice to plant cotton because they did not wish to divert resources from the lucrative and expanding business of growing cocoa. Thus, my concern is not to document Yoruba farmers' 'response' to new economic opportunities 'opened up' to them by Europeans, but rather to discover when and how farmers decided to incur the risks of investing in an unfamiliar crop with a long gestation period; by what means they combined productive resources to establish and maintain cocoa farms; and how the spread of cocoa cultivation affected not only the volume of output and income in the Western Nigerian economy, but also its distribution among different groups in rural society and the structure and organization of productive activities in the rural economy.

Cocoa farming began in Western Nigeria at a time when the economic opportunities open to the bulk of the Yoruba population were undergoing considerable change—both because of external forces and because of internal political developments. These changes are briefly described in Chapter I; Chapter II considers their significance for the beginnings of cocoa cultivation in several Yoruba communities. On the whole I argue that, although there were some similarities in the personal backgrounds of early cocoa planters in each of the communities I studied, the rate at which farmers in different communities adopted cocoa depended primarily on changes in the structure of local economic opportunities and their effects on people's incentives to experiment with an unfamiliar crop.

Chapters III to V are concerned basically with patterns of interaction between expanding cocoa production in Western Nigeria and the institutional context in which it occurred. Chapter III considers the long-run trend of investment in new cocoa trees in relation to patterns of migration and settlement involved in opening up new areas for cocoa cultivation. Previous efforts to explain long-run trends in plantings or output in Nigeria in terms of changes in market prices only have not been especially successful; I argue that we can explain theses trends more clearly by taking into account the ways in which Yoruba farmers used 'traditional' institutions, such as kinship and ethnic groups, to organize the migratory process and to mobilize savings for investment in cocoa farms.

In Chapters IV and V, I examine in detail cocoa farmers' methods of mobilizing and employing land and labour respectively, and show how the development of cocoa farming has tended to commercialize the operation of rural markets for productive services, without completely disrupting related patterns of social interaction. Farmers with mature cocoa plots relied increasingly on hired labour to maintain their existing farms and plant new ones and, as uncultivated forest land became scarce in some areas, the costs of acquiring various rights to land tended to rise also. At the same time, methods of exchanging productive services and the relationships between, for example, landowners and land-users, or farm owners and farm workers, continued to reflect traditional practices— particularly in cases where traditional relationships had been used to mobilize resources for cocoa production. Moreover, the markets for productive services have not been characterized by sizeable concentrations of economic power on one side or the other, and hence have not contributed to the stratification of rural society along economically defined lines. Within the rural sector, at least, landowners, tenant farmers, and farm labourers have all participated in the gains from cocoa production, and individuals frequently move from one category to another or even participate simultaneously in more than one.

As cocoa plantings spread and farmers' incomes from mature plots increased, productive activity in the rural areas became increasingly diversified and commercialized. In Chapter VI I examine this process, using data collected in four villages in different parts of the cocoa belt, where cocoa growing began at different times and is presently at different stages of development. In general, increased demand has led to the growth of trade in foodstuffs and other consumer goods and services. The cocoa belt as a whole has become a food-importing area, and some of the larger villages in older cocoa-growing areas have attracted traders and craftsmen who do little or no farming but specialize in trade or the production of non-agricultural goods and services demanded by the local farming population. At the same time, although the growing accumulation of capital in the rural sector and the general diversification and commercialization of economic activity accompanying the spread of cocoa cultivation have generated considerable inequalities in individual or household income and wealth, these do not appear to be associated with a stratified system of socio-economic classes in rural areas. As in the case of factor markets mentioned above, differences in occupation (e.g. between farmers, traders, and craftsmen) are not clearly related to apparent differences in wealth or social position; nor do farmers with relatively large holdings necessarily differ significantly from their neighbours in either the organization of their economic activities or their social position.

On the other hand, the relative social and economic mobility I have observed within the cocoa-farming sector of Western Nigeria does not necessarily extend to relationships between that sector and others—particularly the urban-based commercial and (nowadays) industrial part of the economy. Although it is beyond the scope of this study to trace in detail the historical development of relationships between the cocoa-growing sector and the rest of the Nigerian economy,[21] I have collected some information on the subject (admittedly largely from the farmers' point of view) which may contribute to the assessment of the current needs and future development prospects of the cocoa economy itself. Accordingly, in the seventh and final chapter, I shall present what evidence I have on the farmers' position *vis-à-vis* the purchasers of their crops, and also on the flow of financial and human resources from the cocoa-farming sector into commerce, crafts, and other urban facilities, and point out some of the implications of my findings for the future growth and diversification of the rural economy.

Methodology

The fieldwork for this study was carried out in two stages. I originally intended to investigate the early history of cocoa farming in Nigeria as an example of a successful innovation in a developing economy. Published and archival material on this subject was scarce and I had to collect much of my material in the field. Since it was obviously not possible for me to cover all parts of the cocoa belt—an area some 200 miles long and 50 miles wide in central Western Nigeria—I decided to select two of the traditional Yoruba

---

[21] In particular, I have not undertaken a detailed investigation of the organization of cocoa marketing in Western Nigeria, or of the changing character of economic and social relationships between farmers and traders.

city-states for intensive study. Having ascertained, from preliminary inquiries and the few statistical sources available, that cocoa growing had developed twenty to thirty years earlier in Ibadan than in Ondo, I decided to study its spread in these two city-states and, by comparing both the personal backgrounds of early planters and the general social and economic conditions in each state, to formulate conclusions about factors which influence the timing and rate of adoption of an economic innovation.

In the course of this initial investigation, I not only traced the extensive pattern of cultivation by which cocoa spread within Ibadan and Ondo before 1940, but also became aware of the fact that after the war many farmers had migrated from older cocoa areas and savannah communities to parts of the cocoa belt where uncultivated land was still available. Further inquiry indicated that most of these migrants had gone first to Ife, where they planted thousands of new farms in the late 1940s and the 1950s. In order to assess the impact of this movement on the recent development of the cocoa economy, I decided to collect information on the history of the migration to Ife and the migrants' current status there, and also to interview stranger farmers in Ibadan and Ondo for purposes of comparison.

Since one of the main purposes of the earlier study was to trace the historical and geographical spread of cocoa planting and related patterns of migration and settlement in Ibadan and Ondo, I made no attempt to interview a representative sample of today's cocoa farmers. Instead, I began by collecting information, from colonial archives and local historians and agricultural officials, on areas or families in each state who were important in the early development of cocoa growing, and on the spread of cocoa planting from these focal points to other parts of the state. I then interviewed farmers in these focal families or villages about their own histories, and used this information to select further villages and individuals to interview. In making these further selections, I attempted (1) to track down the earliest cocoa planters in each city-state, and (2) to corroborate (or disprove) the importance of various determinants of the rate and pattern of cocoa planting which seemed important in the first interviews.[22]

In my second period of fieldwork, in which I sought to compare

<hr/>

[22] Altogether I interviewed about 150 individuals in thirty-one Ibadan villages and as many people again in Ondo, although I visited only nineteen villages and subordinate towns there.

patterns of migration and relations between stranger and local farmers in the areas where cocoa farming is today at different stages of development, it would in principle have been desirable to select some kind of 'representative' sample of farmers or at least farm villages in each area. In practice, however, this was not possible. For one thing, there were no reliable sampling frames to use in selecting villages to study. Moreover, the success of my investigations depended on securing the co-operation of the entire village (since I wished to take a census of the village and then feel free to select individuals from that census for more detailed questioning), and this in turn depended largely on how I was introduced to the community and by whom. Thus, for practical purposes, it would have been pointless to try to select villages randomly, since I would have had to keep selecting and rejecting individual villages until I found some where I could make good contacts, in which case the 'randomness' of the selection would have been vitiated. Accordingly, I began by visiting about twenty villages in Ife where either I had good contacts or I had reason to believe I could meet some of the earliest migrants from the savannah communities or older cocoa-growing areas. I then selected four villages—Araromi-Aperin in Ibadan, Abanata in Ife, and Orotedo and Omifon in Ondo—for more detailed study. These selections were based entirely on local contacts; for the most part they, in effect, volunteered themselves for my project.[23] (See Map 1.)

In carrying out most of my fieldwork, I used very open-ended interviewing methods. My reason for doing so was that basically very little is known about either the organization of indigenous

[23] *Araromi-Aperin* was recommended to me by the Western Nigeria Ministry of Agriculture and Natural Resources (MANR). I had been there in 1966 and the Bale (village head) remembered me. Through the good offices of the Bale and other members of the Aperin family, whom I had met separately, I readily secured the co-operation of the entire village in my project. *Abanata*, a village founded by farmers from the town of Ifetedo, was suggested to me by one of its residents whom I had originally met through the Western State Farmers' Union in Ifetedo. I had already held a number of interviews in Ifetedo and this man had had several opportunities to observe my work in Ifetedo and to discuss it with his neighbours there. Nevertheless, I visited Abanata several times and discussed my project with the Bale and other community leaders before obtaining general consent for my project. I was introduced to *Orotedo* by a prominent Ondo citizen who had extensive farms in the vicinity and who kindly offered me the use of his farmhouse during my fieldwork. My relations with the residents of Orotedo were not, however, entirely satisfactory. Many of the immigrant farmers thought, apparently because of my initial contacts, that I represented the interests of the land-holders in the area who might use information I collected to deprive the immigrants of their land usage rights. One group of immigrants refused to discuss with me any details of their land acquisition or farm management methods.

economic activity in rural Western Nigeria, or how it has changed
over time. There is little use in trying, for example, to estimate the
costs of establishing and maintaining a cocoa farm for x years at
various points in time, unless one knows what the relevant inputs
are and what institutional mechanisms were available to farmers
for obtaining and employing these inputs. As I have already indicated, these facts are not so obvious as previous researchers have

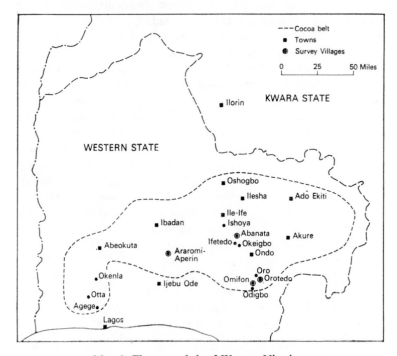

Map 1. The cocoa belt of Western Nigeria

assumed. It is easy, especially for foreign observers, to misinterpret
the economic significance of unfamiliar cultural practices and social
institutions, and one must be constantly prepared to revise one's
preconceptions about what constitutes 'relevant' material. In my
early interviews I soon realized that the more carefully I determined
in advance what I wanted people to tell me, the more likely informants were to say what they thought I wanted to hear rather than
what was important to them. Consequently, I tried to avoid asking
questions with predetermined answers and instead to encourage

my informants to describe and discuss their experiences in their own way.[24] Such methods did not, of course, yield much quantitative evidence on the growth of cocoa production and its economic effects, but they were responsible for my 'discovering' such basic facts as the migration of northern Yorubas to the cocoa belt.

In most of the villages I visited, I met farmers singly or in groups, generally interviewing those individuals whom the community designated as best qualified to supply the kind of historical information I wanted. In the case of the four villages selected for detailed study, however, I followed a somewhat different procedure. In three of them, I took a house-by-house census and then selected a number of individuals (mostly adult men in different occupational categories) for further interviews. I also conducted individual interviews, but did not take a census, in the fourth village—Omifon.[25] In the longer interviews, I asked questions about the informants' histories of migration and occupations, their personal and family backgrounds, and, finally, detailed questions about their current occupations—especially farming. While collecting this material, I lived in the village itself and thus had an opportunity to meet people informally and observe various economic and social activities, as well as to question people about them in the interviews. The resulting data give a picture of the socio-economic organization of villages established at different periods in the history of cocoa farming and thus help to illustrate various stages in the development of the cocoa economy.

Three Yoruba City-states[26]

My evidence and conclusions in this study are, of course, influenced by the particular communities in which I worked. Although all Yoruba-speaking peoples share a common cultural and historical heritage, each city-state has its own history and customs; not only

---

[24] Cf. Hill, *Studies in Rural Capitalism*, p. 12; Dupire, pp. 26–7.

[25] I originally visited Omifon to do a single group interview, but the people were so receptive to my interest that I decided to take the opportunity to interview farmers and farm labourers individually, especially since my work in the other Ondo immigrant village—Orotedo—was not entirely successful. Eventually, one of the leaders of the migrants settled at Omifon, Mr. Joseph Adedoyin, took me to his home town, Isanlu Isin in Kwara State, where I had the opportunity to discuss the history of the inhabitants' migration to the West with the Olusin and Chiefs of Isanlu. However, I did not attempt to take a census at Omifon, partly because the 'village' was actually a series of migrant camps spread over a considerable area and I did not have the time or resources to make arrangements to study all of them.

[26] It is customary among historians and ethnographers to refer to pre-colonial Yoruba states as 'kingdoms', but this term implies a type of political structure which

did cocoa farming begin at different times and develop at different rates in different states, but the pattern of socio-economic change associated with the spread of cocoa cultivation also varied from one state to another, in accordance with local differences in circumstance and institution. In order to help the reader place my findings in perspective, therefore, I shall conclude this introductory chapter with a brief sketch of the history and social organization of the three city-states in which I collected most of my material.

Ibadan. This is the youngest of the three states I worked in, having been founded *c.* 1830 by warriors and refugees from several other Yoruba communities who had been displaced during the break-up of the Oyo empire.[27] Chosen initially for the defensive advantages of the site, Ibadan soon became a large settlement.[28] The Oyo warriors and their followers soon gained ascendency over the other groups, and organized the first successful Yoruba stand aganist the Fulani, defeating the latter at Oshogbo in 1839.[29] Thereafter the Ibadan army turned to conquering its neighbours and, by 1854, had established hegemony over a number of smaller states, including most of Ekiti.[30] Many of these vassal states chafed under Ibadan dominion and others, like Ijebu and Egba, grew increasingly alarmed at the growth of Ibadan's power. Eventually, the Ekitis rebelled and, in 1877, formed a confederation with the Ijeshas (known as the Ekitiparapo) against Ibadan.[31] The Ekitiparapo soon received the support of the Ijebus, Egbas, and (tacitly) the Ifes and, from 1877 until the arrival of a British pacification force in 1892, the Ibadan

---

did not in fact exist in some states—e.g. Ibadan—and whose form varied considerably among others. I have chosen instead to employ the term 'city-state' which emphasizes the unique urban character of pre-colonial Yoruba settlements, without implying a uniform political structure.

[27] There were also Egba, Ife, and Ijebu settlers, but the Oyos soon took control of the emerging town government and have remained the dominant group ever since. R. Smith, *Kingdoms of the Yoruba* (London, 1969), p. 158.

[28] In 1851 Hinderer estimated the population at between 60,000 and 100,000; a century later it was thought to be close to 1,000,000. P. C. Lloyd, A. L. Mabogunje, and B. Awe, eds., *The City of Ibadan* (Cambridge, 1967), pp. 3, 15.

[29] Smith, p. 161; J. F. A. Ajayi and R. Smith, *Yoruba Warfare in the Nineteenth Century* (Cambridge, 1964), ch. 5; S. Johnson, *History of the Yorubas* (Lagos, 1921), pp. 285–9.

[30] B. Awe, 'The Ajele System', *Journal of the Historical Society of Nigeria*, 3, 1 (Dec. 1964), and 'Ibadan, its Early Beginnings', in Lloyd *et al.*, *The City of Ibadan*. A number of towns did not wait to be conquered by Ibadan but voluntarily put themselves under her protection.

[31] S. A. Akintoye, *Revolution and Power Politics in Yorubaland, 1840–1893*, Ibadan History Series (London, 1971); B. Awe, 'The End of an Experiment: The Collapse of the Ibadan Empire, 1877–1893', *Journal of the Historical Society of Nigeria*, 3, 2 (Dec. 1965); Johnson, chs. XXIII ff.

army withstood (but could not overcome) the combined military opposition of most of its neighbours.

The internal political structure of Ibadan reflects her military origins. The town was not governed in the typical Yoruba fashion— by an *oba* (king) chosen from a royal descent group—but by a *bale* (ruler of a small town or village) and council of chiefs, of whom the *bale* was the senior member, having been promoted systematically through the other chiefly ranks. The chiefs were divided into a military and a civilian line. Since most free adult males were often involved in wars and raids, chiefs frequently died in battle, and were replaced by others who had risen to prominence through their military exploits and ability to attract followers in the town. Thus, both military and civilian chiefs attained their titles through demonstrating leadership ability; moreover, although the *bale* was, theoretically, the head of the civilian line, he was likely to have proved himself initially as a warrior and was sometimes chosen directly from the military line.[32] This system is still formally in existence today, although economic and political achievement have replaced military exploit as the main avenues to chiefly titles. In general, the authority of the traditional chiefs was seriously undermined during the colonial period—both because British administrators failed to understand the peculiar character of Ibadan's political structure and because of the growing influence of educated men and, eventually, of regional and national political parties.[33]

The fluid political system and emphasis on military strength and achievement in Ibadan were associated with a social and legal system based on agnatic lineages and patrilineal succession.[34] The opportunities to accumulate wealth, influence, and power open to anyone who could command a following tended, if anything, to reinforce the importance of the agnatic descent group in Ibadan. Men rose to prominence through the support of their kinsmen[35] and sought, in

[32] Johnson, e.g. pp. 365 ff.; cf. G. D. Jenkins, 'Government and Politics in Ibadan', in Lloyd *et al.*, *The City of Ibadan*, pp. 213–14.

[33] Jenkins, pp. 223–33.

[34] Agnatic descent groups and patrilineal inheritance are characteristic of most but not all Yoruba states. P. C. Lloyd, 'Agnatic and Cognatic Descent Among the Yoruba', *Man*, n.s. 1, 4 (1966); C. D. Forde, *The Yoruba-Speaking Peoples of South-Western Nigeria*, Ethnographic Survey of Africa: Western Africa, Part IV (London, 1951); W. B. Schwab, 'Kinship and Lineage Among the Yoruba', *Africa*, 25, 4 (Oct. 1955), pp. 352–74.

[35] *Mogaji*, or heads of powerful lineages, selected by the members of their own descent group, formed the group from which all Ibadan chiefs were recruited. Johnson, p. 69; Jenkins, p. 213.

turn, to promote the interests of their lineage and pass on their wealth and titles to their descendants. Indeed, Johnson states that in 1858 the Ibadans decided to modify the old system of sibling inheritance in favour of a man's children: 'if the children are minors the uncle may act for them until they are of age, otherwise the eldest surviving issue of the head of the house must succeed as the head of the house in rotation...',[36] and Fadipe suggests that this change was associated with the tendency of successful warriors to accumulate large amounts of property.[37] Similarly, rights of land ownership were vested in lineages or lineage segments, most of them having simply staked out claims to vacant rural land as they settled in the town. Once such a claim had been made, the land belonged corporately to the entire descent group, who had the right to grant usufructuary rights to non-members. Personal property, such as houses or, later, economic trees, were inherited by a man's children and were often held by them jointly, thus becoming 'family property' over time.[38]

Ile-Ife. According to Yoruba tradition, Ile-Ife is the cradle of civilization. All Yoruba sub-groups have a tradition of descent from Ife. It is an ancient kingdom, although little is known of its history prior to the nineteenth century. Whether the golden age of Ife art was also a time of extensive power, we do not know, but from the fifteenth century on Ife was probably overshadowed by the Oyo and Benin empires.[39] During the nineteenth century, the Ifes were involved in several of the inter-Yoruba wars and the town itself was apparently deserted for some time, people taking refuge in smaller towns such as Ishoya and Okeigbo.[40] A large group of refugees fled there after the break-up of the Oyo empire. Known as the Modakekes, after the name of their quarter, the Oyos maintained an uneasy coexistence with the Ifes until well into the twentieth century.[41] During the latter part of the nineteenth century Ife felt directly threatened by Ibadan—which tended to side with the Modakekes in their disputes with Ife—and sympathized with the Ekitiparapo, although it did not openly join forces with them,

[36] Johnson, pp. 326–7.
[37] N. A. Fadipe, *Sociology of the Yoruba*, eds. F. O. and O. O. Okediji (Ibadan, 1970), p. 143.
[38] For a detailed discussion of inheritance by siblings and by children see Lloyd, *Yoruba Land Law*, pp. 292–300.
[39] Smith, pp. 16 ff.; Lloyd, *Yoruba Land Law*, pp. 51 ff.
[40] Johnson, p. 232.
[41] See below, pp. 114–16.

preferring instead indirect measures such as interference with Ibadan's supply routes to the coast.[42]

The Oni of Ife is chosen from among four royal houses (or lineage segments), and governs with the advice of a council of chiefs.[43] The chiefs most closely associated with the Oni hold hereditary titles; the others are heads of different wards in the town and are selected from within their respective wards on the basis of ability and reputation. During the nineteenth century Ife was not an especially powerful state, nor—judging from the unsettled state of its internal affairs—does it seem likely that the Oni wielded much effective power at home. During the colonial period, however, the Oni received strong support from the British administration, whose policy of Indirect Rule rested on the assumption that African societies were hierarchically structured and governed by virtually autocratic rulers. As the titular spiritual head of all the Yorubas, the Oni was assumed by the British to possess extensive authority and it was their policy to support that authority at all times.[44] As a result, the power of the Oni and chiefs was probably strengthened during the early years of colonial rule—a historical accident which may in part account for the Ifes' subsequent reputation for conservatism.[45] In other respects, the social organization of Ife is similar to that of the Oyo and Ekiti states: descent groups are agnatic, with corporate rights to land and a patrilineal system of inheritance.

Much of my work in the Ife area, in 1970-1, involved residents of Ifetedo, a town on the Ife–Ondo border about thirty miles southeast of Ife itself. Ifetedo was founded in 1931 by people of Ife descent who had been living in Okeigbo, just across the Oni river in Ondo territory.[46] Founded as a military camp during the nineteenth century with a largely Ife (rather than Ondo) population, Okeigbo has maintained an arm's-length relationship with Ondo.[47] The people of Okeigbo have farmed on both Ondo and Ife territory since the nineteenth century. Land is held corporately by agnatic

[42] Johnson, p. 452.　　　[43] Fadipe, pp. 199 ff.; Forde, pp. 20 ff.
[44] See below, pp. 122-3.
[45] This view was expressed not only in colonial administrators' reports, especially those written towards the end of the colonial era, but also by many Yorubas I met—including a number of Ifes.
[46] See discussion of Ondo, below; also A. F. B. Bridges, 'Intelligence Report, Ondo District, etc', 1935, CSO 26/30172 (NAI). I held a number of interviews in Okeigbo in 1966, since it was one of the earliest centres of cocoa growing in Ondo.
[47] In some respects, Okeigbo's experiences in the nineteenth century have more in common with those of Ibadan and the Ekitiparapo, than with those of Ife and Ondo, which were less oriented toward warfare. I shall develop this point further in Chapter II.

E C R W N—B

descent groups, as in Ife. The town has its own set of chiefs chosen from among five royal lineage segments in rotation.

In 1931 a dispute arose between the Ife and Ondo Native Administrations over the right to collect taxes from Okeigbo cocoa farmers.[48] A compromise was reached which included an agreement to refund part of the taxes already paid to the Ife Native Authority by Okeigbo farmers, but the refund never materialized. The farmers blamed a clerk in the Ondo Native Authority for their losses and a number of them became so enraged with the Ondo authorities that they decided to return to their ancestral state and establish a new town on the Ife side of the river, where many of them already had farms. The new town was named Ifetedo (Ife dwells here) and considers itself subject to the Oni, although it retains close ties with its 'sister town' of Okeigbo.[49]

Ondo. Like Ife, Ondo is an ancient state, governed by an *oba* (the Oshemawe) who traces his descent from Oduduwa, the mythical first ruler of Ife. In many other respects, however, Ondo's social and political structure is quite different from that of Ife or the Ekiti and Oyo states. Descent groups in Ondo are cognatic; they trace their ancestors back only a few generations and engage in relatively few corporate activities.[50] Traditionally, there is no lineage ownership of rural land in Ondo; an Ondo may farm anywhere in Ondo territory as long as he does not encroach on other cultivators. Because of this system, the advent of cocoa farming affected rural land tenure rather differently in Ondo than it did in Ife or Ibadan.[51]

Chieftancy titles are numerous in Ondo. In addition to the most senior (*iwarefa*) chiefs who advise the *oba* in all affairs, there are hundreds of other chiefly titles associated with the *oba*'s palace, with different quarters in Ode Ondo, or with the subordinate towns. It has been suggested that at one time nearly every free-born adult male in Ondo was titled.[52] Very few of these titles are claimed by particular descent groups. Most chiefs attain their titles on the basis of their reputation in the community and their ability to finance the expensive ceremonies involved. For many Ondo men, title-taking is a major form of investment.

[48] This account is based on interviews and also on a district officer's records of the dispute in OYOPROF 3/644 (NAI).

[49] Many Ifetedos have close kinsmen living in Okeigbo, and vice versa.

[50] There is an excellent account of the social and political organization of Ondo in P. C. Lloyd, *Yoruba Land Law*, pp. 98–110, which I have largely followed here.

[51] Lloyd, *Yoruba Land Law*, pp. 110 ff., and 'Agnatic and Cognatic Descent', pp. 498–9.   [52] Lloyd, *Yoruba Land Law*, p. 106.

During the nineteenth century Ondo was not directly involved in the inter-Yoruba wars. Ife soldiers were called in to aid an internal uprising during the 1840s; they and the dissidents from Ondo scattered the town's inhabitants and then established a camp at Okeigbo, from which they apparently prevented the Ondos from returning to their capital until 1872, when a British official intervened. During the Sixteen Years War between Ibadan and the forces of the Ekitiparapo, when the Egbas and Ijebus frequently closed their roads, the trade route through Ondo became important both to the belligerents and to peace-making missions from Lagos.[53] Ondo was an early centre of Christian missionary activity in Yorubaland and the population is predominantly Christian today (unlike Ibadan, where the majority are Muslim). This may in part account for the Ondos' receptivity to Western education and ideas.[54]

There are several subordinate towns in Ondo, in addition to Okeigbo, some of which are quite old and claim considerable political independence from Ondo. The head chiefs (*oloja*) of these towns often claim exclusive right to allocate farmland under their jurisdiction, although various Oshemawes have disputed this claim.[55] In the two Ondo villages (Omifon and Orotedo) which I surveyed in detail, farmers have acquired cultivation rights from the leaders of two subordinate towns (Odigbo and Oro, respectively) rather than from the Oshemawe.

[53] Johnson, pp. 452 ff.; Akintoye, pp. 78–9, 110–11, 123 ff.
[54] Cf. Lloyd, *Yoruba Land Law*, p. 100.
[55] Ibid., pp. 126–8, 132; cf. paragraph on Ipaiye in Appendix I.

CHAPTER I

The Economic Background

WEST AFRICAN peoples have a long history of participation in
international trade. Communities on the coast of West Africa
exported slaves, ivory, gold, and other commodities to Europe and
the Americas from the sixteenth century; before that, West African
products were conveyed to North Africa and the Mediterranean
by trans-Saharan caravans. The Yoruba-speaking peoples of present-
day Dahomey and Western Nigeria apparently participated in the
slave trade from at least 1670.[1] During the nineteenth century
Lagos became one of the major slave ports on the West African
coast.[2] In the 1840s, however, the external slave trade began to
decline and was gradually replaced by so-called 'legitimate commerce' in primary products. For the rest of the nineteenth century,
palm oil and kernels made up the bulk of the goods exported from
Lagos, but in the 1890s some new items appear in the trade figures—
notably rubber. (See Table I.1 opposite.)

Detailed study of the economic history of nineteenth-century
Yorubaland is only beginning, but there is already sufficient evidence
to indicate that changes in the level and structure of productive
activity and exports during this period were the product of a more
complex historical process than the 'opening up' of overseas trade.

[1] P. Morton-Williams, 'The Oyo Yoruba and the Atlantic Slave Trade, 1670–1830',
Journal of the Historical Society of Nigeria, 3, 1 (Dec. 1964), p. 25.
[2] C. W. Newbury, *The Western Slave Coast and Its Rulers* (Oxford, 1961), p. 36.

Notes and Sources: Prices are export unit values except for the figures in paren-
theses which are average prices in the U.K.
[a] 1856–65: Newbury, pp. 58, 211.
[b] 1866–1900: Lagos, *Bluebooks*. 1 ton = 300 gallons.
[c] Derived from values given in the *Bluebooks*.
[d] Lagos, *Bluebooks*.
[e] 1856–60: Newbury, p. 58.
   1861–1900: *Bluebooks*.
[f] Export unit values from *Bluebooks*. U.K. prices from A. Sauerbeck's annual
articles on commodity prices in *Journal of the Royal Statistical Society*, 53
(1890) and 63 (1900)
[g] Great Britain, House of Commons, Parliamentary Papers, 'Statistical
Abstract for the Colonies', v, 100, 1900.
[h] Derived from export values, ibid.

TABLE I.1

Some Major Exports from Lagos in the Nineteenth Century

	Palm oil		Palm kernels		Cotton		Rubber	
	tons^{a,b}	£/ton^c	tons^d	£/ton^e	lbs.^{e}	d./lb.^{f}	lbs.^{g}	d./lb.^{h}
1856	3,884				34,941	(6·3)		
1857	4,942				114,848	(7·8)		
1858	4,612				236,500	(6·9)		
1859	3,730				198,305	(6·8)		
1860	2,752				1,735	(6·2)		
1861	3,865				153,754	(8·5)		
1862	1,763				—	(17·2)		
1863	4,538		2,665	—	—	(23·2)		
1864	3,878		4,511	—	—	(27·5)		
1865	3,800	22·3	2,630	8·1	433,912	19·0		
1866	6,397	22·4	7,216	8·5	761,874	15·5		
1867	5,473	—	13,619	—	796,590	(10·9)		
1868	4,869	37·5	15,498	15·5	1,029,202	10·5		
1869	5,903	37·0	20,394	15·9	893,297	12·1		
1870	5,841	34·8	15,894	13·5	1,508,961	10·0		
1871	5,961	35·5	19,375	14·9	860,876	8·5		
1872	4,337	31·5	16,870	13·3	448,366	10·5		
1873	3,208	30·0	16,410	11·8	—	(9·0)		
1874	4,610	25·5	25,192	10·9	—	(8.0)		
1875	6,009	24·7	26,455	10·8	—	(7·4)		
1876	6,641	29·0	30,306	10·9	—	(6·2)		
1877	11,016	21·7	30,876	11·4	—	(6·3)		
1878	5,133	27·0	27,873	11·4	—	(6·1)		
1879	8,231	25·3	27,839	11·5	—	(6·3)		
1880	4,988	26·7	29,632	11·7	—	(7·0)		
1881	6,024	24·4	20,801	10·6	—	(6·4)		
1882	8,791	24·9	28,591	—	—	(6·6)		
1883	6,571	28·4	25,821	10·6	411,534	(5·8)		
1884	7,942	28·5	29,802	11.0	530,413	(6·0)		
1885	8,859	24·6	30,805	—	278,850	5·6	534	6·4
1886	10,322	20·6	34,812	7·3	96,980	5·1	112	22.0
1887	8,354	18·0	35,784	7·5	121,735	5·5	92	13·8
1888	8,225	14·9	43,525	7·2	231,484	5·5	567	18.0
1889	7,830	17.0	32,715	7·3	482,950	5·9	502	13·5
1890	10,669	11·3	38,829	8·2	358,830	6·0	119	17·6
1891	14,016	18·0	42,342	8·1	379,300	4·7	104	8·8
1892	8,194	16·8	32,180	8·1	41,052	4·2	—	—
1893	13,576	18·6	51,456	8·5	71,406	4·6	56	16·5
1894	11,311	16·6	53,534	8·2	148,946	3·8	5,867	13·6
1895	12,754	16·1	46,501	6·9	19,851	3·8	5,069,577	13·1
1896	10,514	15·1	47,649	7·2	1,326	4·3	6,484,363	13·2
1897	6,196	15·8	41,299	7·2	—	3·9	4,458,327	15·6
1898	6,277	15·5	42,775	8·5	70,640	3·3	3,778,266	18·6
1899	10,976	15·3	49,501	8·3	13,659	3·5	1,993,525	19·8
1900	9,926	19·1	48,514	8·3	24,080		596,332	19·9

Not only did Yoruba participation in international trade long ante-
date the nineteenth century, but also the volume and composition
of external trade were influenced by several factors, both external
and internal. These included (1) the intermittent wars which various
Yoruba city-states fought with one another; (2) international
market conditions; and (3) the gradual encroachment of British
missionary, commercial, and political interests upon Yoruba affairs.

Historians are still debating the economic significance of the
nineteenth-century Yoruba wars. A number of contemporary
observers were inclined to regard the wars as one more unfortunate
consequence of the slave trade, which undermined the energy and
stability of West African societies by encouraging them to raid one
another endlessly for saleable captives.[3] This interpretation, which
has found advocates among later generations of historians,[4] assumes
that internal developments in West Africa were essentially responses
to external demands and pressures: when European traders offered
to buy slaves, Africans fought each other to obtain them; when, in
the latter part of the nineteenth century, Britain effectively suppressed
the slave trade and European merchants turned their attention
to palm oil instead, Africans continued to fight each other—partly
to obtain slaves to produce and transport palm produce, and partly
to gain control over the trade routes between the interior and the
coast.

More recently, students of African history have begun to investigate internal developments in African societies more directly and
systematically than hitherto and, concomitantly, to argue that
African relations with outsiders often changed in response to internal
events, as well as vice versa.[5] In the case of Yorubaland, this shift in
emphasis has sometimes been accompanied by a tendency to play
down the importance of economic factors for an understanding of

[3] Great Britain, House of Commons, Parliamentary Papers, 'Report of Select Committee on the State of the British Settlements on the West Coast of Africa', v, 412,
1865.
[4] See for example, M. Crowder, *The Story of Nigeria* (London, 1962), chs. IV, VI;
A. Burns, *History of Nigeria*, 4th ed. (London, 1948), ch. 2; B. Davidson, *Black
Mother* (London, 1961), pp. 198–202.
[5] K. O. Dike, *Trade and Politics in the Niger Delta* (Oxford, 1956) is an important
early example of this school of writing. No one has yet made a comparable study of
the political and economic history of nineteenth-century Yorubaland, but several
writers have discussed some aspects of the effects of internal political and military
events on external trade: S. A. Akintoye, *Revolution and Power Politics in Yorubaland,
1840–1893*, and 'The Economic Background of the Ekitiparapo', *Odu*, 4, 2 (1968),
pp. 31–52; J. H. Kopytoff, *Preface to Modern Nigeria* (Madison, Wis., 1965); C. W.
Newbury, *The Western Slave Coast and Its Rulers*.

THE ECONOMIC BACKGROUND 25

nineteenth-century Yoruba history.[6] Ajayi and Smith both suggest
that the rise of Lagos as a major slave port after 1820 was a consequence of the break-up of the Oyo empire and the subsequent
struggle for political supremacy among the Yoruba states. According to their interpretation, the Yoruba wars represented an attempt
to fill a power vacuum left by the collapse of Oyo; the growth of
Yoruba slave exports occurred because the belligerents required
increasing amounts of imported arms and ammunition to sustain
their military efforts.[7] S. A. Akintoye has extended this thesis to
late nineteenth-century developments in eastern Yorubaland: he
argues that the Ekitiparapo, who challenged Ibadan's political and
military pre-eminence after 1877, sold slaves to obtain arms rather
than vice versa, and attributes the depressed condition of Lagos
trade in the 1870s and 1880s to the fact that the trade routes to the
interior were rendered hazardous by military activity and sometimes closed altogether for political and/or military reasons.[8]

Recently, A. G. Hopkins has suggested that the suppression of
the slave trade in the mid-nineteenth century was responsible, if not
for the beginning of the wars, at least for their prolongation until
the advent of British rule in 1893. He has argued that the suppression
of the slave trade and concomitant growth of European demand for
vegetable oils led to 'innovations in production [which] brought
about changes in the balance of economic and social power which in
turn led to conflicts between states, between the rulers within states,
between the rulers and the ruled'.[9] On the one hand, the internal
slave trade (and therefore slave raiding) continued, as chiefs and
warriors turned to the production of palm oil and employed slave
labour for the purpose.[10] On the other hand, Hopkins also points

---

[6] J. F. A. Ajayi and R. Smith, *Yoruba Warfare in the Nineteenth Century*, pp. 50–5
and Part II; E. A. Ayandele, *The Missionary Impact on Modern Nigeria*, Ibadan
History Series (London, 1966), ch. 2; R. Smith, *Kingdoms of the Yoruba*, chs. XI, XII.

[7] Ajayi and Smith, pp. 52–3, 123–6; Smith, pp. 156–7.

[8] Akintoye, *Revolution and Power Politics*, pp. 150–1; 'The Ondo Road Eastwards
of Lagos, *c.* 1870–1895', *Journal of African History*, 10, 4 (1969), pp. 588–9.

[9] A. G. Hopkins, 'Economic Imperialism in West Africa: Lagos, 1880–1892',
Economic History Review, 21, 3 (Dec. 1968), p. 604. See also J. F. A. Ajayi and R. A.
Austen, 'Hopkins on Economic Imperialism in West Africa', ibid. 25, 2 (May 1972),
and Hopkins, 'Rejoinder', ibid., pp. 303–12. Ajayi reaffirms his position in *Yoruba
Warfare*, that economic considerations were subordinate to political ones in the
Yoruba wars, and suggests that control of trade was not essential to achieving political
power in most Yoruba states, but he does not present new evidence on the subject.

[10] Hopkins, 'Economic Imperialism', pp. 587–8; S. Johnson, *History of the Yorubas*,
p. 693. These and other sources show that there were large households with many slaves
engaged in agricultural pursuits, but we do not know what proportion of households
held many slaves or whether this proportion varied from one Yoruba state to another.

out that because there were no economies of scale in the production of palm oil and kernels, it was not necessary to own many slaves in order to produce oil and kernels. Hence, 'the ordinary African farmer, employing mainly family labour, could enter the overseas exchange economy for the first time'.[11] In response to this unwonted competition from below, Yoruba chiefs extended their efforts to acquire slaves and control trade routes through military means, which led, paradoxically, 'to the abandonment of fertile land, and to the creation of broad areas of neutral territory between hostile states. They perpetuated the very conditions that were inimical to the growth of the embryonic, rural, petty capitalism which had been fostered by legitimate commerce.'[12] As a result of these economically anachronistic conflicts, the Yoruba states were so weakened that they succumbed easily to the imposition of British rule in the 1890s. This, in turn, opened the way for the rapid development of trade and export production by small-scale producers and 'petty capitalists'.

One difficulty with this argument is that it does not distinguish very clearly between the economic requirements of export production and those of trade in exportable goods. While it is probably true that there were no economies of scale in the production of palm oil (given the techniques available in the nineteenth century and still widely employed today), it is not clear that this was equally true for the business of transporting and marketing it. Hopkins himself states that the slave trade was a labour-intensive enterprise which required considerable working capital 'for the maintenance and equipment of raiding parties, and for financing subsequent trading operations',[13] and this was presumably true of the internal slave trade as well as the external. The former did not cease simultaneously with the latter; indeed some people have argued that the internal slave trade was stimulated by the switch to 'legitimate commerce', as slave labour was employed in transporting palm produce to centres of commercial activity. Since the intermittent warfare among the Yoruba states rendered travel hazardous, trading caravans required armed protection and may well have found safety in large numbers.[14] In other words, the technical requirements of transportation may have favoured traders who could

[11] Hopkins, 'Economic Imperialism', p. 588.
[12] Ibid., p. 590.   [13] Ibid., p. 588.
[14] Akintoye, 'The Ondo Road', pp. 587–8; Ajayi and Smith, p. 3.

command the labour of large numbers of slaves even during the era of 'legitimate commerce'.

Also, much of the export trade in palm produce and other commodities was conducted on a credit basis; European merchants in Lagos advanced goods or cash to African agents or middlemen who, in turn, used them to purchase produce in the interior. We do not have much evidence of how these middlemen organized their trading activities: whether trade advances went directly to small-scale traders and even individual farmers or whether they passed from Lagos traders to relatively large-scale middlemen from Ijebu, Egbaland, and (at least after 1877) communities further inland, whose ability to obtain credit and withstand the risks of trade rested in part on the scale and reliability of their operations. On the eastern route, many traders employed the services of specialized transporters who maintained large numbers of slaves to operate canoes or headload goods overland.[15] However, we do not know the scale of operations of the traders themselves, or how many times produce changed hands between the producer and the European merchant who shipped it abroad. Without such information, one cannot say whether export trade (as opposed to the production of goods for export) began to pass from large- to small-scale middlemen when palm produce replaced slaves as the principal export from Yorubaland or, therefore, whether 'the ordinary African farmer' enjoyed a larger share of the gains from long-distance trade than he had before.[16] However, given the distances and uncertainties of travel, and the highly labour-intensive character of inland transport at this time, it seems implausible to argue (without direct supporting evidence) that individual farmers began not only to produce palm oil and kernels for sale but also to compete effectively with large slave-owners who were in a position to transport and market their produce as well.

Other evidence which Hopkins cites to show that the old order was crumbling[17] all relates to the period 1880–92 and could just as well be attributed to the depression in palm produce prices as to the

---

[15] Akintoye, 'The Ondo Road', p. 587.

[16] Certainly some of the people involved in such trade—e.g. the Ijeshas at Aiyesan who clashed frequently with Ondo and other communities over control of the eastern route—were Lagos businessmen, not 'ordinary African farmers'. See ibid., pp. 588, 595–6.

[17] He cites evidence that chiefs in Ijebu towns collected high tolls and taxes and occasionally went bankrupt in financing military activities at this time. 'Economic Imperialism', pp. 590–1.

abolition of the slave trade. Indeed, as Hopkins himself has pointed out in other contexts, the depression in world markets for palm produce and other tropical products played an important role in effecting changes in the structure of economic activity in late-nineteenth-century Yorubaland.[18] The decline in palm produce prices did not lead to a reduction in the volume of palm oil and kernels exported from Lagos,[19] but both European and African merchants suffered declining profit margins in the 1870s and 1880s because of the drop in world market prices.[20] The result was a rapid turnover of trading firms in Lagos,[21] and increased efforts by African traders and chiefs to protect their profits by gaining mono-polistic control over the trade routes to the interior.[22] Again it seems likely that traders with the largest financial resources with-stood the slump most successfully.

In many cases, however, African merchants lost heavily during the depression and were forced to look for alternative income-earning opportunities—including potential new export commodities and/or agricultural production itself. As I shall discuss in more detail in the next chapter, some of the earliest cocoa farms in Nigeria were planted around Lagos by African merchants whose businesses had suffered during the depression and who had decided to try farming instead. The incentive to develop new productive activities to replace or supplement those adversely affected by the depression may also have contributed to the rubber boom of the 1890s.

[18] A. G. Hopkins, 'The Lagos Chamber of Commerce, 1883–1903', *Journal of the Historical Society of Nigeria*, 3, 2 (Dec. 1965), pp. 241–8; 'The Currency Revolution in South-Western Nigeria in the Late Nineteenth Century', ibid. 3, 3 (Dec. 1966), pp. 471–8; 'The Lagos Strike of 1897', *Past and Present*, 35 (Dec. 1966), pp. 133–55; and 'Economic Imperialism'.

[19] Not all of the palm produce exported from Lagos came from the Yoruba states of Western Nigeria. In some years almost half of Lagos's exports came from Dahomey; unfortunately, the data are not systematic enough to show whether increased tranship-ments from Dahomey compensated for declining supplies from the interior in years when the Egba and/or Ijebu routes were blocked. Newbury, p. 125.

[20] Newbury, pp. 86–7; Hopkins, 'Economic Imperialism', p. 591.

[21] The turnover of European firms in particular was also due partly to increased competition from new firms, made possible by improvements in transportation from Europe and by changes in the currency system in West Africa. Hopkins, 'Economic Imperialism', p. 593, and 'The Currency Revolution'. Cf. Newbury, pp. 87–8.

[22] The main trading routes were those passing through Egba and Ijebu, and the eastern route, opened in 1872, over which several communities tried to exert control. Akintoye, 'The Ondo Road', pp. 592–6; Moloney to Knutsford, 30 Apr. 1890, Great Britain, Colonial Office, Confidential Print (CO 879/33, No. 399). Many towns col-lected tolls from all traders passing through their gates and could close the routes entirely if they wished. See Hopkins, 'Economic Imperialism', p. 589.

Little is known about the details of the rubber boom, although evidence for it in the trade figures is certainly dramatic. Rubber exports, which were negligible before the mid-1890s, suddenly rose, from a mere 56 lbs. in 1893 to 5,867 lbs. in 1894, to an astonishing 5,069,577 lbs. (worth £269,893) in 1895. For five years Lagos exported several thousand tons of rubber annually; then exports declined almost as dramatically as they had first risen, apparently because wild supplies near the coast were exhausted by destructive tapping measures.[23]

The technique of tapping wild *ire* trees, which grew throughout the rain-forest areas of Southern Nigeria, was apparently introduced to Lagos in 1894 by a political prisoner from the Gold Coast.[24] It spread rapidly to the interior through the efforts of traders and entrepreneurs from Lagos and other ports, some of whom brought their own labourers from the coast, and is vividly remembered in interior towns even today.[25] The Ibadan historian, Sir Isaac Akinyele records that during Bower's residency (1893–7) 'trade in Rubber was introduced into the town, by which the town became wealthier'.[26] In Ondo the Revd. Charles Phillips found it impossible to hire labourers, owing to 'the excitement caused all over the country by the rubber trade', and his colleague, E. M. Lijadu attributed rising food prices to the fact that 'the rubber trade turned the attention of farmers from the soil to itself'.[27] We do not know to what extent the rubber boom was brought about by Lagos merchants seeking to recover from the effects of the depression, but, like early experiments with cocoa growing, it does appear to have resulted from the general economic conditions prevailing in Yorubaland in the 1890s. These in turn were affected not only by external market conditions and internal military struggles, but also

[23] Lagos, *Annual Report*, 1903. The rubber trade continued for some years after this on a smaller scale, drawing on supplies further inland. In 1907 Yoruba rubber collectors were reported near Kabba, in Northern Nigeria. John Holt Company Archives, 1/6.

[24] A. G. Hopkins, 'An Economic History of Lagos, 1880–1914', University of London Ph.D. thesis, 1964, p. 264.

[25] Some of my informants in Okeigbo recalled the rubber trade of the 1890s which they said was introduced into their town by a man from Warri, who brought labourers with him from the coast to tap *ire* trees.

[26] I. B. Akinyele, *Outlines of Ibadan History* (Lagos, 1946), p. 75.

[27] Phillips to J. B. Wood, 10 May 1895, CMS (Y) 1/7/6; Lijadu, Diary, Feb. 1898. Cf. J. S. Adejumo, 'History of the Foundation of the Gospel at Ile-Ife, 1897–1939', CMS (Y) 4/1/13, who describes rubber in 1897 as 'the then only famous trade', and S. A. Akintoye, *Revolution and Power Politics*, who mentions Ekiti participation in rubber tapping, p. 227.

by the direct intervention by British authorities into internal Yoruba affairs—a subject to which we must now turn.

Pax Britannica

The advent of British colonial rule did help to accelerate some previous developments in Yoruba economic life and to retard others, although it was only one among several factors operating to produce the economic changes of the early twentieth century, and its effects were largely indirect. Before the nineteenth century, European traders purchased slaves on the coasts of West Africa, rather than venture inland to procure them, and hence had little contact with the peoples of the interior. After 1807, although traders continued to confine their activities to the coasts, the British government's campaign to abolish the slave trade led gradually to British involvement in the internal affairs of many West African societies. In Yoruba country the British intervened partly through direct military and political action—Lagos was conquered in 1851 and became a British colony ten years later—partly through negotiations, ultimately backed by the threat of force, for the protection of 'legitimate commerce'. Although jealous of their respective spheres of influence, both missionaries and traders tended to encourage official intervention.[28]

During the 1880s the government in Lagos made repeated efforts to effect a truce among the warring Yoruba states, conducting negotiations through Yoruba Christians who served as interpreters and intermediaries.[29] Finally in 1892, when numerous efforts to negotiate a lasting peace had failed and both traders and missionaries were exerting great pressure on the government to intervene, the British circulated 'peace treaties' among the various Yoruba states which marked the beginning of effective colonial rule. Even so, the extent of British authority varied from one Yoruba state to another, and British administrators were not established in some of the major Yoruba towns for another twenty years.[30]

[28] Ayandele, ch. 2, especially the account of the British expedition against Ijebu, pp. 54–69; J. F. A. Ajayi, *Christian Missions in Nigeria, 1841–1891* (Evanston, Ill., 1965), pp. 66–88; Hopkins, 'Economic Imperialism', pp 596–8.
[29] Samuel Johnson and Charles Phillips both wrote accounts of their negotiations and there is also much material on them in Phillips's Diaries (C. Phillips, Diaries, CMS (Y) 3 (NAI)). See Johnson's *History* and also Great Britain, House of Commons, Parliamentary Papers, 'Correspondence Respecting the War Between Native Tribes in the Interior . . . of Lagos', C. 4957, 1887.
[30] See, e.g., Akintoye, *Revolution and Power Politics*, pp. 216–23.

In terms of economic activity, the advent of peace and British 'protection' acted as a permissive rather than a compelling force for change.[31] Especially in the early years of the Lagos Protectorate (as much of present-day Western Nigeria was known until 1906), British economic policy was a rather haphazard affair, characterized primarily by a *laissez-faire* attitude towards African production and a reluctance to spend money. The government sought to promote trade, but not at the cost of unbalancing the budget; even for the railway, that *sine qua non* of Victorian economic progress, protracted official correspondence and some parliamentary debate were required to induce the British treasury to float a loan (which the colony had, of course, to pay back) to finance its extension beyond Ilorin.[32] And the railway alone had relatively little effect on the export trade; without a related system of feeder roads, it significantly reduced transport costs only for produce grown or collected near the railway itself.[33]

Other government policies were aimed at protecting the legal and economic rights of individual Africans, rather than directly increasing their productivity, and even these were enunciated less clearly and consistently at first than has often been assumed. For example, in 1901 the British administration announced the abolition of slave trading in the Protectorate,[34] but enforcement was perfunctory. Governor Carter wrote to Joseph Chamberlain in 1896 that the Egbas complained frequently about escaping slaves and declared that 'it has been my practice when slaves do not actually come into British jurisdiction to give assistance in recovering them. . .'[35] In some areas new employment opportunities and the presence of British officials encouraged slaves to escape or ransom themselves, but elsewhere they preferred to remain in their old occupations and often in the service of their old masters.[36]

Similarly, the government's policy of refusing to grant land con-

---

[31] Cf. discussions of the relative importance of permissive and compelling factors for economic innovation and change in A. O. Hirschman, *Strategy of Economic Development* (New Haven, Conn., 1958), pp. 143–9, and H. J. Habakkuk, *American and British Technology in the Nineteenth Century* (Cambridge, 1962), p. 2; also Chapter II, below.

[32] See, e.g., J. S. Hogendorn, 'The Origins of the Groundnut Trade in Northern Nigeria', University of London Ph.D. thesis, 1966.

[33] Newbury, p. 145.

[34] Lagos, *Annual Report*, 1901–2.

[35] Great Britain, Colonial Office, Confidential Print (CO 879/45, No. 509). Cf. Hopkins, 'The Lagos Strike', pp. 144–5.

[36] Lagos, *Annual Report*, 1901–2; Hopkins, 'The Lagos Strike', pp. 143–4.

cessions to foreign firms—a policy which probably protected Nigeria from some of the worst forms of imperialist economic exploitation— developed gradually, on grounds of expediency rather than principle. For many years no outsiders wanted land in Southern Nigeria except for trading stations or mission buildings. Actually the early British administrators were not opposed to foreign settlement which would contribute to the development of the country,[37] although they adhered to the general principle that development should not disrupt existing customs and institutions any more than necessary. The Native Lands Acquisition Proclamations of 1900 and 1903 accordingly provided that any non-Nigerian who wished to obtain land must first have written consent of the High Commissioner.[38] Presumably, the High Commissioner would see to it that the interests of the 'natives' involved were properly looked after. In practice two factors determined the effects of this policy: the 'natives'' own reluctance to grant sizeable concessions, and the complexity of traditional systems of land tenure.

The government did not hesitate to press for large concessions that it deemed beneficial to the development of trade. In 1904 the British Cotton Growing Association applied for a lease of 15,000 acres of land near Ibadan, to establish a plantation.[39] The British Resident at Ibadan put great pressure on the chiefs to grant the lease; the Governor himself came up from Lagos to urge the B.C.G.A.'s cause. After months of resistance, the chiefs finally agreed to lease 5,000 acres for thirty years at a nominal rent. However, the plantation was not economically successful and the whole experience did not encourage further foreign settlement.

In other cases, just the stipulation that foreign concessionnaires must arrange a purchase or lease with the owners of the land was enough to kill a projected plantation. In 1908 Lever Bros. applied for permission to erect palm-oil mills in Southern Nigeria and asked for sizeable concessions around the mills from which to draw supplies of palm fruit. The government agreed, on condition that

[37] Governor to Secretary of State for the Colonies, 1 Feb. 1911, Public Record Office, Southern Nigeria Correspondence. W. K. Hancock, *A Survey of Commonwealth Affairs*, II, 2 (London, 1942), p. 181.

[38] A. McPhee, *The Economic Revolution in British West Africa* (London, 1926), p. 165.

[39] This paragraph is based on records of Ibadan Town Council meetings, which are deposited in Mapo Hall, Ibadan. See also, K. Dike Nworah, 'The West African Operations of the British Cotton Growing Association, 1904–1914', *African Historical Studies*, 4, 2 (1971), pp. 318–20.

the company make the necessary arrangements with every land-
holder in the concession area. This proved entirely impracticable
and eventually the whole scheme was dropped.[40]

Even in the introduction of new crops, British efforts were largely
confined to the promotion of cotton growing, which never became
very important in Western Nigeria, and to the establishment of the
Botanical Gardens at Ebute Meta, which gave new kinds of seeds,
including cocoa, coffee and, later, kola, to farmers who came and
requested them, but which did not have the facilities to undertake
extensive propaganda and demonstration campaigns.[41] In short,
government policies and programmes did little to effect significant
changes in Yoruba economic activity during the early years of
colonial rule. On the other hand, the cessation of hostilities among
the Yoruba states did create conditions under which trade and
production could grow and change more easily than had been
possible before.[42] The greater safety of travel and the demobilization of the Yoruba armies facilitated both the growth of trade in
general and the spread of new crops in particular.

The immediate impact of the peace on external trade was not
spectacular. Some local restrictions on trade persisted after 1893: in
Oyo Province there were tollgates on the edges of most towns until
1903.[43] Moreover, considerable trading had continued throughout
the Sixteen Years War (and earlier conflicts). Although the wars
made travel risky and probably limited the distance which slaves or
freemen could go from towns or villages to farm and reap wild palm
fruit, such restraints did not operate equally in all areas or at all
times. There were several routes through Egba and Ijebu territory,
and not all of them were always closed simultaneously.[44] In the early
1870s, the British opened a route through the eastern part of Yoruba
country which bypassed the Ijebus entirely and helped to extend the
area from which Lagos drew supplies of palm oil and kernels.
Traders from Lagos, Ondo, and the Ekiti towns began to take
imported goods inland and to exchange them for palm produce in
Ondo, Okeigbo, and Ekiti, or for potash and leather goods in

[40] Great Britain, Colonial Office, Confidential Print, African 1023, 1914.
[41] Lagos, *Annual Reports*, 1900–3.
[42] See for example, Akinyele, *Outlines of Ibadan History*, p. 71.
[43] Lagos, *Annual Report*, 1903. Cf. Great Britain, Colonial Office, Confidential
Print (CO 879/62).
[44] For example, Ijebu Remo continued to trade with Ibadan during the Ijaye war
when the Egbas and other Ijebus closed their roads to the Ibadans. Ajayi and Smith,
p. 92.

Ilorin.[45] Although travellers on the eastern route were increasingly
threatened in the 1880s and 1890s by piracy and armed conflict
among Ijebu, Mahin, and Ijo traders seeking to control its southern
access, enough traffic seems to have continued along it during this
period to warrant the establishment of new trading settlements by
Lagos entrepreneurs at places such as Atijere, Aiyesan, and Ajebamidele.[46]

However, the increased freedom to trade and travel facilitated the
spread of new productive activities, such as rubber tapping, into the
interior of Yorubaland. Indeed, there appears to have been a general
increase in movement between Yoruba states during the 1890s, as
people sought new economic opportunities through trade or employment in large towns and other centres of economic activity. Although
the government in Lagos complained of a shortage of labour, this
appears to have been the result of their own unwillingness to pay
competitive wages, rather than to any lack of people looking for
employment.[47] There was never much difficulty finding men to
work on the railway[48] and 'between June 1900 and January 1902
approximately 6500 labourers left Lagos to work on the Secondi
railway and in the gold mines of the Gold Coast, where the rate of
pay was higher than in Nigeria'.[49] By 1900 some 400 'strangers' were
reported to have come to Ibadan from Lagos, Egba, and Ijebu to set
up as traders in anticipation of the railway.[50]

Meanwhile, young men from interior towns were moving towards
the coast in search of new opportunities. In 1901 the Church
Missionary Society mission at Okeigbo reported that 'the young
men [were] going to other parts of the country in search of work',[51]
and two years later the Bale of Ibadan complained that hundreds of
young men had left Ibadan 'without authority . . . to proceed to the
Coast to better themselves'.[52] During the next twenty years farmers

[45] Akintoye, 'The Ondo Road', pp. 585–6.
[46] Ibid., p. 590; Ayandele, p. 35; Kopytoff, p. 195; C. Phillips, Diaries. In 1966 I
interviewed descendants of the founder of Ajebamidele.
[47] Hopkins, 'The Lagos Strike', pp. 147–8. Cf. B. A. Agiri, 'Kola in Western Nigeria,
1890–1930: A History of the Cultivation of Cola Nitida in Egba-Owode, Ijebu-Remo,
Iwo and Ota Areas', University of Wisconsin Ph.D. thesis, 1972, pp. 46–7.
[48] J. O. Oyemakinde, 'A History of Indigenous Labour on the Nigerian Railway,
1895–1945', University of Ibadan Ph.D. thesis, 1970, pp. 24–5.
[49] Hopkins, 'The Lagos Strike', p. 148; cf. Newbury, p. 169.
[50] Lagos, Annual Report, 1900–1.
[51] Phillips, Diary, 25 Oct. 1901, and my interviews.
[52] Resident's Letter Book, 1901–3, Mapo Hall, Ibadan. Cf. West African Lands
Committee, Minutes of Evidence (printed for the use of the Colonial Office, 1916),
Question 8847.

near Lagos and Otta employed many labourers from interior Yoruba towns on their farms.[53]

This increase in the numbers of people travelling within and outside Yorubaland in quest of gainful employment was not only facilitated by the end of the fighting but was positively encouraged by the effects of demobilization, which deprived a substantial proportion of the adult males in the belligerent states of their principal occupation. We do not know, of course, how many men devoted what proportion of their time to military activities. Many slaves and ordinary freemen probably did not specialize completely in warfare, but fought during the dry season and returned home to farm when the rains fell.[54] However, some warriors did nothing else, and for many others military exploits constituted their chief opportunity to gain wealth and social prestige. Johnson describes vividly the problems of adjusting to peacetime in Ibadan:

It took the Ibadan rank and file some time to realize the fact that inter-tribal wars are forever at an end in this country . . . To be at home with nothing to do was rather irksome for those whose trade was war. Happily most of the important chiefs had huge farms wherein were engaged many of their domestics, and the majority of the men also were farmers, but a good many were warriors pure and simple. . . .

Ibadan never really settled down until after about eighteen months, when the Government of Lagos enlisted two battalions of men for military service in Northern Nigeria. This opening afforded relief to all those ardent spirits whose profession was arms, and with a wonderful celerity they imbibed and assimilated the new method of drill and discipline. . . . Again, the railway undertaking absorbed the energies of many.[55]

Similarly, the former warriors of the Ekitiparapo were left idle and restless by the coming of peace. Some continued to launch sporadic raids against their neighbours until suppressed by the British, when they turned increasingly to trade.[56]

To sum up, by the late nineteenth century most Yoruba communities had for some time been exchanging forest and agricultural products for imported European goods through a network of African traders who dealt with European merchants on the coast.

[53] J. B. Webster, *The African Churches Among the Yoruba, 1888–1922* (Oxford, 1964), pp. 105, 110, and 'Agege: Plantations and the African Church', *Nigerian Institute of Social and Economic Research Conference Proceedings*, Mar. 1962. B. A. Agiri has collected considerable evidence on the employment of northern Yorubas around Otta in the early years of the twentieth century, which confirms reports I received from Igbomina informants in Isanlu and Imokore, and from the people of Okeigbo.
[54] See below, p. 52.   [55] Johnson, pp. 643–4.
[56] Akintoye, *Revolution and Power Politics*, p. 218.

The pattern and volume of external trade were certainly affected by the political and military upheavals in which most Yoruba states were involved, but further research is necessary to untangle the question of whether the economic requirements of foreign trade caused these conflicts or resulted from them, and to what extent the suppression of the slave trade after the middle of the century altered the socio-ecomomic structure of Yoruba communities. In so far as the primary products—palm oil and kernels, rubber, cocoa—exported from Yorubaland in the late nineteenth and early twentieth centuries did not involve economies of scale in production, the growth of these exports did create new income-earning opportunities for large numbers of small-scale producers. However, it is not clear that the shift in the composition of exports from slaves to agricultural and forest products similarly tipped the balance in favour of small-scale commercial enterprise. The financial advantages enjoyed by large-scale trading firms and the accompanying concentration of economic power in the hands of traders, which have been important features of the Western Nigerian cocoa economy since the early years of this century, seem likely to have characterized the nineteenth-century export sector as well.

The internal structure of the Yoruba economy around the turn of the century does not seem to have been greatly affected by the formal imposition of British rule. The end of the wars, however, followed by the gradual establishment of British colonial administration throughout Yorubaland, reduced the hazards of trade and travel and was followed by a general increase in movement among Yoruba communities. Also, demobilization left many men relatively unoccupied and free to devote a larger proportion of their time and energies to agriculture and/or commerce than they had done during the wars. These circumstances proved favourable to the widespread adoption of new productive activities—such as rubber tapping and, later, cocoa growing—which entailed considerable movement through the forest areas.

CHAPTER II

Early Experiments with Growing Cocoa

THE earliest cocoa farms in Western Nigeria were established in the vicinity of Lagos in the 1880s and 1890s,[1] mostly by African merchants based in Lagos whose businesses had suffered from the prolonged decline in the prices of palm produce during the late-nineteenth-century slump in world trade.[2] Information about the new crop spread fairly quickly into the interior, especially after the end of the Yoruba wars in 1893. By 1900 cocoa was probably known to at least a few people in most major Yoruba towns in the forest belt. However, farmers were much quicker to experiment with the new crop in some communities than in others and consequently cocoa growing developed into a major commercial crop at different times in different parts of the forest belt. In some Yoruba city-states most of the available uncultivated forest land was planted in cocoa before World War II; in others new farms are still being established today.

The Decision to Adopt a New Productive Activity

Theoretical discussion of the role of innovation in economic development, which began with Schumpeter's *Theory of Economic Development* (1911), has largely followed Schumpeter in treating innovative behaviour as an exogenous variable which stimulates changes in the volume and structure of a society's economic activities but is itself the product of socio-psychological forces which are beyond the economist's competence to explain.[3] At most, some

---

[1] The earliest cocoa farms in Nigeria were probably established near Bonny, but the area never became a major cocoa-producing area. Chief J. A. Ayorinde, 'Historical Notes on the Cocoa Industry in Western Nigeria', *Nigerian Agricultural Journal*, 3, 1 (Apr. 1966), p. 18.

[2] Hopkins, 'Economic Imperialism in West Africa: Lagos, 1880–1892', *Economic History Review*, 21, 3 (Dec. 1968), p. 592, and personal communication from the same author.

[3] Schumpeter himself regarded entrepreneurs—the men who successfully incorporated new techniques into economic processes of production or distribution—as individuals of unusual talent who, like artists, occur almost randomly in a given population. Since Schumpeter's time, several scholars have attempted to identify

economists have ventured to suggest that changes in entrepreneurial activity[4] may result from changes in economic opportunities for such activities—these opportunities being, in turn, determined by the structure and level of demand, the availability of other productive inputs, and the degree of market imperfections facing a particular group of potential entrepreneurs. According to this view, the amount of entrepreneurial activity occurring in a given situation is determined by the interaction between this 'demand' for entrepreneurial services and the 'supply' of such services, which reflect the strength of people's willingness or ability to exploit potentially profitable opportunities and which may be affected by social and cultural factors.[5]

For our purposes, this approach to explaining differences in observed patterns of economically innovative behaviour entails a couple of difficulties. One obvious one—present in any attempt to estimate supply and demand functions—is the identification problem. Since we cannot observe supply and demand schedules, but only single points on them, the question always arises whether a movement from one point to another represents a shift in the demand schedule, in the supply schedule, or in both. In our case, we would need to determine whether farmers in Ibadan and Ilesha adopted cocoa growing more quickly than did farmers in Ife and Ondo because the former were more highly motivated or better able to perceive and adopt new productive activities, or because economic conditions were more favourable in those communities—i.e. because cocoa growing was likely to have been more profitable in Ibadan and Ilesha than in Ife or Ondo around the turn of the century. As we shall see below, sufficient data do not exist to permit precise testing

psychological characteristics associated with innovative behaviour or social circumstances which favour the emergence of innovative personalities, but few of these theories have been satisfactorily tested against empirical data. For a recent collection of major contributions to this literature, see Peter Kilby, ed., *Entrepreneurship and Economic Development* (New York, 1971).

[4] In this discussion, I have used the terms 'innovation' and 'entrepreneurship' interchangeably. As Kilby points out in his introductory chapter, most entrepreneurial activity in developing economies today is directed towards adapting new techniques to local conditions so as to render them economically viable there, rather than the kind of pioneering effort depicted by Schumpeter. Cocoa is no exception: Nigerians were not the first people in history to grow cocoa commercially, but their success in developing the (to them) novel crop into a major commercial venture without external direction or assistance is nevertheless a remarkable example of entrepreneurial achievement.

[5] Kilby, pp. 23–6; John R. Harris, 'Industrial Entrepreneurship in Nigeria', Northwestern University Ph. D. thesis, 1967, ch. 2.

of these possibilities, although we may venture some comments on them.

More fundamentally, however, the concepts of 'supply' and 'demand' contain some implicit assumptions which are not appropriate to the present case. For one thing, they are generally construed to represent the potential responses of two distinct groups of people (usually buyers and sellers of something) to changes in a given external variable (usually market price), assuming other relevant variables unchanged. The decision-making process whereby these people arrive at their responses to changes in market values is one of the things assumed given—usually both buyers and sellers are presumed eager to maximise some utility function subject to various constraints. In other words, for any given set of demand and supply curves, individuals are assumed to respond automatically to changes in objective conditions according to the patterns depicted by the curves; their ability to perceive those conditions and willingness to react to them are taken as given. In seeking to explain entrepreneurial behaviour, however, part of our task is to identify and explain differences (or changes over time) in people's ability to perceive and willingness to respond to new ways of achieving economic returns, and it is not clear that supply and demand curves offer an appropriate conceptual apparatus for dealing with this problem.

Indeed, as I shall argue below, the strength of people's motives to adopt and develop new types of productive activity may be affected by *changes* in their economic circumstances, particularly when one considers innovative behaviour as a historical or dynamic process. In terms of the above model, this means that both the shape and the position of the entrepreneurial supply curve may be affected by shifts in the demand curve—a situation which would render the model completely untestable and therefore of little use in explaining actual behaviour.

In view of these considerations, I have not attempted to employ the concepts of supply and demand in analyzing the timing of farmers' early experiments with cocoa. Instead, I shall investigate the alternative possibilities that (1) cocoa was adopted more rapidly in some communities because there were individuals there whose personal backgrounds and experiences led them to be more willing to experiment with new productive activities than were the majority of their compatriots, and (2) cocoa was adopted sooner in some areas because local circumstances fostered greater incentives to

exploit new economic opportunities than did those in other areas.[6]
In investigating 'local circumstances' I shall attempt to consider
both economic conditions and non-economic factors which impinged
on economic behaviour.

The Introduction of Cocoa to Yoruba Communities

As I mentioned above, the earliest cocoa farms in Western
Nigeria were established by Lagos merchants and traders, who
took up farming in the late nineteenth century when returns to
commercial activities were low. Most of these men farmed near
Agege or Otta, although a few Ijeshas and Ondos planted farms
near their trading communities in Mahin territory or southern
Ondo.[7] Like other Yoruba farmers, they grew crops for their own
consumption and for sale; they also experimented with new crops,
especially for export. As members of the trading community of
Lagos, they were already familiar with the demands of European
markets and also likely to have heard of such ventures as the cocoa
and coffee plantations on Fernando Po and Sao Tome. J. P. L.
Davies had planted cocoa and coffee on his farm at Ijan before 1880,
using seeds which he obtained from Fernando Po.[8] Others—
J. K. Coker, F. E. Williams, A. A. Obadina, C. C. Cole, etc.[9]—
experimented with a variety of crops, including cocoa, coffee, cotton,
maize, and kola. After 1888 seeds for most of these crops were
available from the government Botanical Garden at Ebute Meta, as
well as from traders or labourers who had travelled to Fernando Po
or other parts of West Africa.[10]

J. B. Webster has suggested, and my own and others' findings
tend to confirm, that these early farms in Agege and southern

[6] In discussing the first possibility, I shall not attempt to show what might cause
relevant personality differences, since such a discussion would be beyond my competence and the scope of this study.
[7] Conversation with A. G. Hopkins. Cf. Webster, 'Agege: Plantations and the
African Church', *Nigerian Institute of Social and Economic Research Conference Proceedings*, Mar. 1962, p. 124, and 'The Bible and the Plough', *Journal of the Historical
Society of Nigeria*, 2, 4 (Dec. 1963), pp. 429 ff. See also p. 43, n. 23, below.
[8] Conversation with A. G. Hopkins; Webster, 'The Bible and the Plough', p. 428.
Cf. *Lagos Gazette*, 12 Aug. 1899, in which the Assistant Curator of the Ebute Meta
Botanical Garden reported: 'In 1895, we obtained some cocoa pods from Captain
Davies' plantation (this gentleman owns the best and largest cocoa plantation in this
Colony) for sowing.'
[9] Webster, *The African Churches Among the Yoruba: 1888–1922*, pp. 110, 182; 'The
Bible and the Plough', p. 431; 'Agege', pp. 126, 128.
[10] On the spread of cocoa from Fernando Po to the mainland see Ayorinde, p. 18;
K. M. Buchanan and J. C. Pugh, *Land and People in Nigeria* (London, 1955), p. 149;
A. McPhee, *The Economic Revolution in British West Africa*, pp. 40–4.

Egbaland served as an important source for the dissemination of knowledge about cocoa farming to the rest of Western Nigeria. Several groups of people were involved in this process. Merchants and clergymen from Lagos, many of whom had connections with the Agege planters, travelled inland carrying with them information about the new crops. At the same time, many men from the interior who took advantage of the peace to travel to the coast seeking opportunities for trade or employment also encountered these crops, on farms or in markets or both, and returned home with information and/or seeds.

Some of the most enthusiastic advocates of agricultural innovations in this period were Christian clergymen, and one of the best-known of these was the Revd. Charles Phillips.[11] Phillips's diaries and papers contain numerous references to his interest in agricultural innovation. In the 1880s he planted rice at Ondo and, in January 1895, urged Christian converts in an Ondo village 'to take up farm work and manufacture of palm oil and planting cocoa and coffee'.[12] The following year he 'planted some coffee' on his farm and, two years later, the elders of the Ondo church voted 'to secure . . . a coffee and cocoa plantation for the church's future support'.[13] In 1903 he met the elders of the Ife and Ilesha churches and 'advised [them] to encourage the congregation to make farms for the church, they should plant cocoa, coffee, etc.'[14]

The first cocoa in Ilesha was planted by Christians, led by James Gureje Thompson, who obtained seeds from Phillips and planted them in 1896.[15] Phillips also actively supported the founders of Ajebamidele—one of the trading and farming communities established near the lagoon by Lagos traders in the late nineteenth century.[16] He and his brother planted farms there, which Phillips visited each time he travelled to and from Lagos and in 1902 he helped the settlers negotiate long-term rights to the land. Judging both from

[11] The following account of Phillips's activities is based on his own diaries and papers in the National Archives, Ibadan, and on accounts in E. A. Ayandele, *The Missionary Impact on Modern Nigeria*, pp. 35–6; S. Johnson, *History of the Yorubas*, especially ch. XXIX; and Great Britain, House of Commons, Parliamentary Papers, 'Correspondence Respecting the War Between Native Tribes in the Interior . . . of Lagos', C. 4957, 1887.

[12] Phillips, Diary, 18 July 1888 and 2 Jan. 1895.

[13] E. M. Lijadu, Diary, 10 Apr. 1898.

[14] 'Papers relating to the Development of Churches and Schools in Ondo and Ilesha Districts, 1885–1907', CMS (Y) 2/2/4.

[15] Interviews with Chief S. O. Thompson and Mr. A. Apara of Ilesha, and Chief Ayorinde of Ibadan. Cf. Ayorinde, p. 19.

[16] See the sketch of Balogun Ipaiye in Appendix I.

his own activities and from the number of people I met in Ondo, Ilesha, and Okeigbo who associated his name with the beginnings of cocoa farming in their communities, it appears that Bishop Phillips played a major role in spreading knowledge of new crops to central and eastern Yorubaland.

Similarly, CMS agents in Ibadan sought to help their actual or potential converts improve their standard of living through agriculture. In two of the thirty-one Ibadan villages where I collected information about the history of local cocoa farming, people mentioned the Revd. Thomas Harding as the man from whom they had first learned about cocoa. In fourteen other villages the first man to have planted cocoa there was either a Christian himself or had learned about cocoa from Christian clergymen or their converts. Two of the villages I visited had originally been founded by groups of Christians, with the encouragement and assistance of their clergymen: Eripa, established some time before 1892 by four Christians from Aremo quarter in Ibadan,[17] and Onipe, where in 1892 a Yoruba pastor from Ibadan 'went . . . with the representative Christians of this place . . . to secure good lot of land in the bush for farming, being the chief occupation of our men'.[18] One of the founders of Onipe, Chief S. Orukotan, had already planted cocoa at two other villages, using seedlings brought from the Botanical Garden at Ebute Meta by his nephew, the Revd. D. R. Oyebode.[19] The elders of Onipe said that the first settlers planted cocoa almost as soon as they began to farm at Onipe.

Webster has shown that travelling African Church evangelists also encouraged farmers to develop their farms. In the words of one, they preached the gospel of 'coffee, cocoa, cotton and work'.[20] Many of these evangelists were supported by members of the Lagos business community or by Agege planters such as J. K. Coker. In return, the evangelists helped to recruit labour in the interior to work on the Agege farms. 'Between 1904 and 1920, over 2,000 labourers had fulfilled a year's contract with Coker.'[21] These

[17] The Christians obtained land at Eripa from an Ibadan hunter with the assistance of the CMS; Thomas Harding later testified on the Christians' behalf in a legal dispute over the land. Cocoa was first planted at Eripa in 1892, with seeds supplied by the CMS. According to Mr. A. A. Opasina, an Agricultural Officer with long experience in the south-eastern part of Ibadan, Eripa was the site of the first cocoa planted along the Akanran Road. These and most of the other villages referred to in this chapter are shown on Maps 2–4 in Chapter III.

[18] J. Okuseinde, Journal, 31 Aug. 1892, CMS (Y).   [19] Ayorinde, p. 19.

[20] Quoted in Webster, *African Churches*, p. 114.

[21] Webster, 'Bible and the Plough', p. 431; cf. 'Agege'.

labourers helped to spread both new crops and the African Church movement when they returned to their home towns. Some of the earliest cocoa farmers in Okeigbo were former labourers who had gained experience with cocoa while working at Agege. Okeigbo was also an early centre of African Church activity. Webster also mentions Ikirun and Oyan as places which became African Church strongholds under the influence of returned labourers from Agege.[22]

Clergymen were by no means the only source of information about cocoa and other new crops for farmers in the interior. Merchants and traders, resident in Lagos, who were interested in promoting the development of their home communities as well as of their own fortunes, also provided information. During the wars these people had supplied their home towns with arms, ammunition, and other imported goods, from both economic and political motives. Members of the Ijesha Association (later the Ekitiparapo Society) settled at various points along the routes from Lagos to the interior, such as Itebu, Aiyesan, Atijere, and, later, Ajebamidele, where they traded and farmed.[23] After the wars the strategic importance of these trading stations declined and some of the settlers either returned to Lagos or moved inland to their home towns.[24]

[22] Webster, *African Churches*, p. 105. African Church evangelists not only could recruit labour for their financial backers in Agege, but may have found it in their own interests to do so. Early in the nineteenth century, when abolition of the slave trade was the primary practical aim of British evangelical activity in West Africa, the missions sought to 'civilize' Africans through the combined influence of economic and religious development. In the words of a leader of the anti-slavery movement, 'Let missionaries and schoolmasters, the plough and the spade, go together and agriculture will flourish; the avenues to legitimate commerce will be opened; confidence between man and man will be inspired; whilst civilization will advance as the natural effect, and Christianity operate as the proximate cause, of this happy change.' (T. F. Buxton, quoted in Ajayi, *Christian Missions in Nigeria, 1841–1891*, pp. 10–11.) The missionaries regarded commerce as the major goal of economic development, but recognized the need to encourage production for exchange as well as market activity itself (ibid., pp. 16–17). In both economics and religion, they also sought to encourage Africans to become self-sufficient; in particular, they wanted their converts to develop autonomous and self-financing churches (ibid., pp. 174–8). Although this tradition was abandoned by some European missionaries in the latter part of the nineteenth century, it was carried on by others and particularly by the African churches, which emphasized independence and self-sufficiency to the point of breaking with the missions altogether (Webster, 'The Bible and the Plough', p. 425). In either case, clergymen often found it expedient to promote new crops or other income-earning activities among their converts and potential converts. By doing so they might both attract people to their religious teachings and augment their churches' often meagre finances.

[23] Akintoye, *Revolution and Power Politics in Yorubaland, 1840–1893*, pp. 126–7, 201–2; Ayandele, p. 35; Kopytoff, *Preface to Modern Nigeria*, p. 195; P. C. Lloyd, *Yoruba Land Law*, p. 132; Phillips, Diaries, 1896–1903, *passim*; interviews with A. B. B. Ipaiye of Ondo, and the Revd. S. C. Phillips of Oshogbo.

[24] Phillips reported, for example, that the Christian community at Itebu virtually

Also, many traders and migrant labourers from the interior encountered cocoa, coffee, and kola around Lagos, whether or not
they actually worked on cocoa farms. Some of these men went
home and planted the new crops for themselves, and their example
often had more influence on other farmers than did the advice of
clergymen who did not grow cocoa themselves. Bishop Phillips's
son, the Revd. S. C. Phillips, told me that many Ondos did not listen
to his father's advice about growing cocoa until labourers, returning from Agege, told them about cocoa or began to grow it.[25] In
most of the communities I visited, cocoa growing started when a
few farmers began to experiment with it on a small scale. When
their trees bore fruit and people saw that the cocoa beans could
be sold, others began to plant also. Within a decade after the earliest
experiments, many farmers had taken up the new crop.

However, not every community began to experiment with cocoa
immediately on hearing of it. Cocoa was known in most Yoruba
states before 1900, but farmers in some communities adopted it
much earlier than in others. Farmers began to experiment with
cocoa in Ibadan and Egba around 1890; in Ilesha by 1896. In Ibadan
many new farming hamlets were established in uncultivated forest
areas well suited to cocoa before 1900.[26] Similarly, a visitor to
Egbaland in 1901 found numerous cocoa farms between Asha
and Ilogbo (near Otta) and also around Okenla on the railway.[27]
Ilesha developed a little later but, by the early 1920s, was regarded
as one of the main cocoa-producing areas in Western Nigeria.[28]
From these major towns cocoa spread fairly quickly to smaller
ones such as Okeigbo and Gbongan. In Okeigbo, cocoa was first
planted before 1900 (probably with seeds supplied by Gureje
Thompson of Ilesha) and many people were growing it by 1910.

In Ife, Ondo, and the Ekiti states, however, farmers were slower
to experiment with and adopt cocoa. Available papers of British

---

disappeared when Haastrup was made Owa of Ilesha in 1896 and all the Ijeshas at
Itebu followed him home. 'Papers relating to . . . Churches and Schools', CMS (Y)
2/2/4.
    [25] See below, p. 53.
    [26] Lagos, *Annual Report*, 1900–1; file on land disputes, OYOPROF 3/1181, vol. i
(NAI).
    [27] Lagos, *Annual Report*, 1901–2; Ayorinde, p. 19. The spread of cocoa cultivation
to different parts of Egba Division is described in A. L. Mabogunje, 'Changing Pattern
of Rural Settlement and Rural Economy in Egba Division, South-West Nigeria',
University of London M.A. thesis, 1958.
    [28] Oyo Province, Annual Reports, 1921–5, CSO 26/06027, 09723, and 12723, vols.
i–iii (NAI).

officials and missionaries contain no reference to cocoa in Ife in the 1890s or early 1900s. The earliest planting date cited in any of the Ife villages I visited was 1910.[29] The prominent Ife chief, Lowa Omishore, who was one of the early cocoa farmers in the Ife area, first obtained cocoa from an Ijesha trader between 1910 and 1913.[30] In 1917 the District Officer wrote, 'The Ife people are entirely an agricultural people and possess a very rich country. Everything has been done to encourage their enthusiasm for cocoa-growing which is fast becoming their most important industry.'[31] However, the first noticeable growth in cocoa sales in Ife occurred only in the early 1920s, and the major expatriate trading firms did not bother to build stores there until after 1925.[32]

Similarly, in Ondo, although Bishop Phillips persuaded the church elders 'to secure . . . a coffee and cocoa plantation for the church's future support' in 1898,[33] and encouraged the settlers at Ajeba-midele to grow cocoa, almost no one in Ondo planted cocoa for himself until shortly before World War I. Widespread cocoa planting did not take place in Ondo until the 1920s; in Ekiti, not until the late 1930s.[34] In short, although information about cocoa and access to at least a few seeds were available in most Yoruba city-states in the 1890s, people acted upon this information much more quickly in some areas than in others.

Early Cocoa Planters

During my fieldwork I collected information on the personal backgrounds of the first men to plant cocoa in a number of villages in Ibadan and Ondo, and a few villages in Ife and Ilesha. As far as possible I tried to locate villages which had been among the earliest sites of cocoa growing in each city-state.[35] These data are

[29] With the exception of villages founded from Okeigbo on the Ife side of the border.
[30] Interview with Mr. E. J. F. Omishore of Ile-Ife.
[31] Ife Division, Annual Report, 1917, OYOPROF 4/6, 355/1917 (NAI).
[32] Oyo Province, Annual Reports, 1922–7, CSO 26/09723 and 12723, vols. i–v (NAI); Ife Customary Court Records, Case No. 74, 1968 (cited hereafter 74/68); interviews with Mr. Odutalayo and Chief O. Orafidiya of Ile-Ife.
[33] Lijadu, Diary, 10 Apr. 1898.
[34] Lloyd, p. 190; R. Galletti *et al.*, *Nigerian Cocoa Farmers*, p. 206.
[35] See above, pp. 12–13. In Ife, I collected information by a method somewhat different from the one employed in Ibadan and Ondo, since in Ife I was primarily interested in studying immigrant farmers who had come from the savannah areas of Yorubaland to grow cocoa in the Ife forests. This migration did not begin until the late 1920s and early 1930s—after cocoa growing had become established in Ife—and consequently many of the people I interviewed in Ife villages knew nothing about the earliest cocoa planters in Ife itself. However, I was also less successful in identifying early cocoa farmers from either documentary material or local historians in Ife than

summarized in Appendix I, in the form of short biographical sketches of twenty-two early cocoa planters: 7 in Ibadan, 5 in Ondo, 5 in Okeigbo, 3 in Ife, and 2 in Ilesha.

The majority of the early planters on whom I collected biographical data had travelled to Lagos or beyond present-day Western Nigeria before they planted cocoa; those who had not done so had all initially heard about cocoa from someone who had. Also, a majority of the early planters were Christian, at a time when Christianity was only beginning to attract many Yoruba converts.[36] Thirteen of the sixteen individuals whose religious affiliations I ascertained were Christians; of the remaining six, two had Christian names which suggests that they too had at least some connection with missionaries. Presumably, most of them were uneducated, although some of the Christians may have been able to read the Bible in Yoruba. Their occupational histories were not unlike what one would expect to find for their contemporaries—many had been farmers and/or warriors, few had engaged in any skilled craft. More than half of them had been traders or migrant labourers—experiences which were directly connected with their knowledge of cocoa and may also have enabled them to accumulate savings to help finance their first cocoa farms. (However, as I shall show in Chapter III, that was not a crucial condition for successful cocoa cultivation.) Only three had chieftancy titles, though several were leaders in the church and others—Gureje Thompson, Ipaiye, Kolajo, and F. E. Morakinyo—were fairly prominent men in their communities.

It is difficult to generalize about the characteristics of innovators from such limited and largely qualitative evidence. Clearly, formal education was not a prerequisite for experimentation with cocoa, but this does not mean that education is not important for innovation in other circumstances. My information on the occupational and social position of these early planters does not seem to indicate that they were 'marginal men' in the sense that they deviated from conventional occupational practices or were not fully accepted by their peers—on the contrary, several of them were respected and influen-

in any of the other towns I studied. Whether this was because the advent of cocoa attracted less attention and hence is less well remembered in Ife than in other towns, or because I never located the right people, or for some other reason, I cannot say. In any case, I do not have much information on early cocoa planters in Ife and thus cannot be sure that the following analysis is as valid for Ife as for the other communities discussed. See Maps 2–4 in Chapter III.

[36] Ayandele, pp. 155–7; Webster, *African Churches*, pp. 96–101; J. D. Y. Peel, *Aladura: A Religious Movement Among the Yoruba* (London, 1968), pp. 50–2.

tial members of their communities. On the other hand, the high proportion of them who had travelled extensively and/or converted to Christianity is distinctive and might be taken as evidence that these men had rejected or broken with established norms.

The fact that many of the early cocoa planters had travelled is, I think, open to a simpler and more direct interpretation. We have already seen that the end of the Yoruba wars was followed by a general increase in movement, as people took advantage of peaceful conditions to explore opportunities for trade and employment outside their own city-states. In this context, it is difficult to argue that men who left home to work were engaging in unusual or even especially innovative activity. On the other hand, travellers who later became cocoa farmers had in the course of their journeys seen cocoa being cultivated, and either witnessed it being sold or had a chance to observe that individuals who grew it for sale had prospered by doing so. Thus it seems more plausible to regard the early planters' travels as a source of first-hand knowledge of cocoa rather than an index of unusual or deviant behaviour.

The high proportion of Christians among the early planters can also be explained in part by the role which Christian clergymen played in spreading information about cocoa through Western Nigeria.[37] People who had already committed themselves to Christianity were no doubt more likely both to hear and to heed clergymen's advice than were non-Christians. But the number of Yoruba converts was so small in the late nineteenth century that conversion to Christianity was in itself an unusual decision. It is possible that the preponderance of Christians among these early planters indicates distinctive features of these men's personalities or social positions which my other information failed to reveal.

The available literature on Christianity in nineteenth-century Yoruba society does not suggest that Christians were treated as social outcasts. Certainly there are recorded instances of individual persecution, but there is even more evidence that educated Christians in particular often achieved positions of considerable influence in Yoruba communities.[38] In those cases where entire communities

[37] For returned slaves, travel and Christianity were closely related experiences. See Kopytoff, pp. 31–3.

[38] In addition to men such as Johnson and Phillips, whose role as negotiators in the Yoruba wars we have already noted, many Christians achieved considerable prominence within different Yoruba states. See Ayandele, chs. 2 and 5; G. D. Jenkins, 'Politics and Government in Ibadan', in P. C. Lloyd et al., The City of Ibadan, passim; and Johnson, pp. 361–3.

turned against the Christians living in their midst—as when the missionaries were expelled from Abeokuta in 1867, or the Christians were threatened by the Oni and chiefs of Ife in 1904—trouble occurred because the Christians were suspected of having co-operated with hostile forces. Thus, they were attacked for political rather than religious reasons.[39]

We do not have enough information about the personalities or social positions of early converts to test the alternative possibility— that most early converts turned to Christianity because they were already in some sense marginal members of the community. How-ever, individuals' accounts of their own (or their forebears') conver-sions do not support such an interpretation. At most, they suggest that conversion to Christianity, like the decision to try a new crop, often represented a willingness to experiment with new methods of solving practical problems.

Traditional Yoruba religion was largely concerned with problems of life in this world and much of its ritual aimed at improving one's earthly lot by placating the deities or spirits which might be causing misfortunes. Yorubas were accustomed to invoke divine aid in achieving such ends as health, fertility, and prosperity.[40] For example, one reason which people often give for having converted to Christi-anity is that they were able to have children after appealing to the Christian God. The Revd. E. A. Lijadu, the minister of an indepen-dent church in Ondo, told the following story of how his grandfather, the first Christian in the family, had become a minister. E. A. Lijadu's great-grandfather, an Egba also named Lijadu, was childless for many years. He tried appealing to many different deities, without success. Finally, someone told him about Christ, so he decided to try praying to him. He promised that, if a child were born, he would 'dash' it to Christ. Soon after that his wife gave birth to a son, so, in accordance with his promise, Lijadu sent the boy to the Christian missionaries to be raised and educated by them.

Yorubas also look to their deities for aid in achieving material well-being. The Revd. Charles Phillips, working in Ondo, wrote in his diary about a Bible society meeting at which a convert pointed out that the offerings they made in church were much cheaper than the cost of the ceremonies which he used to perform for Shango or

<hr>

[39] Ajayi, pp. 201–3; Ayandele, pp. 14–15, 161–6.
[40] E. B. Idowu, *Olodumare: God in Yoruba Belief* (London, 1962), ch. 8; Peel. pp. 114–18.

the Ifa oracle.[41] Other studies cite similar cases.[42] In general, then, Christianity and cocoa both seem to have offered opportunities for a better life through changes in two kinds of activities—religious worship and economic achievement—which were already associated with each other in Yoruba thought.

Moreover, Christians were prominent among early cocoa planters in nearly all the city-states I studied, whether or not Christianity was especially popular there. Thus, the earlier development of cocoa farming in, say, Ibadan or Ilesha cannot be explained by a greater predominance of Christianity in these communities. Nor are there systematic variations in other characteristics of the early cocoa planters in different city-states which would explain differences in the rate at which farmers took up cocoa growing. Thus, we must turn to differences in local conditions to understand the observed pattern of early cocoa development.

Demobilization and Incentives to Innovate

People's response to the opportunity to grow cocoa depended partly on the availability and attractiveness of alternative economic opportunities and partly on the strength of their incentives to exploit new means of earning income. There is little direct evidence on geographical variations in the opportunity cost of growing cocoa in the 1890s, so that we cannot adequately test the proposition that cocoa was adopted more quickly in some communities because it was relatively more profitable there than elsewhere. Certainly the fragmentary evidence available does not indicate any clear relationship between costs of production or returns to alternative activities and the speed with which farmers took up cocoa growing in different communities.[43] Of course there were other occupations in which people could earn more than they could from farming, but most of these required specialized training.

The advent of the railway to Abeokuta in 1897 and Ibadan in 1901 considerably reduced the cost of transporting produce from these towns to the coast, and the late development of cocoa farming in Ekiti has been associated with that area's 'remoteness' from the

[41] Phillips, Diary, 8 Oct. 1888.
[42] Cf. S. S. Berry, 'Christianity and the Rise of Cocoa Growing in Ibadan and Ondo', *Journal of the Historical Society of Nigeria*, 4, 3 (Dec. 1968), pp. 439–52.
[43] I discussed this question at length in my unpublished Ph.D. thesis, 'Cocoa in Western Nigeria, 1890–1940' (1967). I now feel that the data are probably even more inconclusive than I considered them then.

railway, navigable waterways, and even paved roads.[44] However, differences in transport facilities do not explain why cocoa farming developed fifteen to twenty years earlier in Ilesha and Okeigbo than it did in Ife or Ondo. Ife is no further from the railway at Ede than Ilesha is from Oshogbo; Ondo, on the main eastern trade route of the late nineteenth century, is considerably closer to the lagoon, and canoe transport to Lagos, than is either Ife or Ilesha.

Neither is there clear evidence of variations in costs of growing cocoa which would explain the observed pattern of development. As we have seen, the end of the Yoruba wars in 1893 increased the safety of trade and travel in Western Nigeria, and income-earning opportunities were further improved by reviving world market conditions in the early 1900s, and by the growth of employment in centres of commercial activity or on government projects. However, such opportunities were greater in Lagos and towns along the railway, such as Ibadan and Abeokuta, which were also early centres of cocoa growing. Thus it is difficult to argue that these opportunity costs significantly affected the rate at which farmers in different areas adopted cocoa. Similarly, although rubber was probably more attractive than cocoa in the 1890s, since it required no initial investment in planting and caring for young trees, there is no reason to think that it was relatively more attractive in some areas than in others.[45] The only exception to this pattern was the development of the timber trade in the early 1900s. This may have diverted local resources and entrepreneurship from cocoa, chiefly in southern Ondo, where there were both extensive hardwood forests and numerous streams and rivers on which logs could be floated to the lagoon.[46] Apart from timber, however, I have found no alternatives to cocoa which were more easily available or more attractive to people in Ife and Ondo than in Ibadan and Ilesha. Thus, it appears that differences in the level of opportunity costs of growing cocoa can offer at best only a partial explanation of the timing of cocoa development in different communities.

However, it does appear that some of the general economic and political developments discussed in Chapter I did affect incomes and employment differently in different Yoruba city-states, and that these differences were, in turn, systematically related to differences

[44] Lloyd, p. 190.   [45] See above, p. 29.
[46] 'Travelling Commissioner's Journal and Diary, 1897–1913', ONDODIV 8/1 (NAI).

in the timing of early experiments with cocoa. I have already mentioned one example—namely, the fact that the decline in world prices for palm produce in the late nineteenth century had a particularly severe impact on African merchants in Lagos, whose fortunes were by and large dependent on external trade, and that some of these merchants turned accordingly to farming and began to experiment with a variety of new crops. In this instance, it was not the 'opening up' of new external market opportunities which encouraged these men to experiment with new crops, so much as the deterioration of returns to their accustomed pursuits which apparently encouraged or forced them to search for alternative sources of income.

Similarly, although the end of the wars and the advent of British rule did not immediately affect the distribution of economic opportunities among different Yoruba communities, it did have rather different effects on people's incentives to search out new opportunities in different areas. I have already mentioned the impact of demobilization on the occupations of many Yoruba men. Warriors (both free and slave) who had relied largely on military activities to obtain wealth and social position found themselves with the coming of peace virtually unemployed. They had little choice but to look for new means of livelihood; moreover, since many of them had enjoyed considerable wealth and prestige before 1893, they would have to seek out the most lucrative pursuits now available if they wished to maintain their accustomed social and economic position. On the other hand, people who had been engaged primarily in farming or trade before 1893 could avail themselves of new means of earning income after the wars if they wished, but they were under no economic pressure to do so.

Presumably, the effect of demobilization on people's incentives to exploit new opportunities for earning income was greatest in those communities which had been most completely 'mobilized' during the wars. Certainly the state with the longest tradition of military specialization and success was Ibadan, where most of the adult freemen and many slaves spent most if not all of their time in military pursuits.[47] During the last quarter of the nineteenth century, however, the Ekitiparapo finally made a successful stand

[47] Johnson, esp. chs. XVII, XXI and pp. 643–4; B. Awe, 'The Ajele System: A Study of Ibadan Imperialism in the Nineteenth Century', *Journal of the Historical Society of Nigeria*, 3, 1 (Dec. 1964), pp. 47–60, and 'The End of an Experiment: The Collapse of the Ibadan Empire, 1877–1893', ibid. 3, 2 (Dec. 1965), pp. 221–30.

against Ibadan, partly by copying Ibadan's military techniques.[48] Although the Ekitiparapo was made up of a number of Yoruba sub-groups, including Ijeshas, Ekitis, Akokos, and Igbominas, the initial impetus for forming the Ekitiparapo came from Ilesha and, of the various member states, Ilesha probably maintained the largest number of full-time warriors.[49] Many men, especially in the smaller Ekiti, Akoko, and Igbomina communities, remained primarily farmers, coming to fight for a few weeks during the dry season when they could be spared from agricultural and other village duties. They usually brought their own provisions with them— a system which Akintoye suggests was partly responsible for the Ekitiparapo's success, since it ensured a steady supply of foodstuffs for the army.[50] However, it also meant that most of these part-time soldiers were easily reabsorbed into their traditional occupations after the wars. In Ilesha, on the other hand, demobilization left a large number of 'war boys' idle and restless; for two or three years after 1893 they engaged in sporadic raids against their neighbours, until finally suppressed by the British. Hence in Ilesha, as in Ibadan, there were a number of men left 'jobless' by the peace, who were more or less compelled to explore new economic activities.

By contrast, neither the Ifes nor the Ondos played a prominent military role in the Yoruba wars. Both were dislocated for a time during the wars: the Ifes by Oyos fleeing from Fulani attacks on their homes, and the Ondos by Ife soldiers who were called in to assist a group of rebellious slaves in Ondo and ended by sacking the town. The Ifes were apparently not strong enough to hold Ondo town, however, and retreated to Okeigbo. During the latter part of the nineteenth century the Ifes tended to sympathize with the Ekitiparapo, but were apparently too afraid of Ibadan to offer much concrete military or economic assistance to the Ekitis. Both Ife and Ondo towns remained open to traders for most of the Sixteen Years War; neither appears to have had a very large or

---

[48] Akintoye points out that a number of soldiers in the Ekitiparapo army had served in the Ibadan army as slaves and later escaped to their home communities, bringing with them first-hand knowledge of Ibadan's fighting methods. The Ekitiparapo was periodically aided by the Ijebus and Egbas, but one gets the impression from contemporary records that neither of these peoples specialized in warfare to the same degree as Ibadan and the Ekitiparapo during this period. Their contribution to the war effort often consisted in blocking Ibadan's supply routes to the coast. Johnson, pp. 439, 452, 610–13.

[49] Akintoye, 'Economic Background of the Ekitiparapo', *Odu*, 4, 2 (Jan. 1968), and *Revolution and Power Politics*, *passim*; cf. Johnson, pp. 645–6.

[50] Akintoye, *Revolution and Power Politics*, pp. 147–9.

well-organized army. Hence the effect of the peace in these states was to offer improved opportunities for trade and travel, but not necessarily to create a large group of unoccupied people seeking new means of earning income.[51]

Thus, apart from Egbaland, where the early development of cocoa farming was probably closely linked with the activities of Lagos merchants-turned-planters at Agege and Otta, cocoa farming was apparently adopted most readily in Ibadan and Ilesha—the two principal belligerents in the Sixteen Years War. In Ibadan the effects of demobilization combined, after 1900, with the exhaustion of wild rubber supplies and the advent of the railway to encourage early experimentation with new crops. Similarly, in Ilesha the presence of large numbers of former soldiers after the wars evidently helped bring about a more favourable response to Bishop Phillips's advocacy of cocoa growing than occurred in Ife, Ondo, or the other states of the Ekitiparapo. Just as the Agege planters turned to agriculture and began to experiment with new crops when their commercial ventures in Lagos suffered from depressed world market conditions, so many ex-soldiers in the interior 'fell back on' farming to escape the economic consequences of the peace.

[51] The most militarily oriented town in the Ife–Ondo area seems to have been Okeigbo where, as we have seen, cocoa farming caught on earlier than it did in either Ife or Ondo.

CHAPTER III

Migration, Capital Formation, and the Growth of Productive Capacity

ONCE cocoa 'caught on' in a given Yoruba city-state, many farmers took it up, moving gradually into the uncultivated (and largely uninhabited) forests surrounding the towns and food farming areas to establish new plots of cocoa trees. Amelonado cocoa—the variety planted by most Nigerian farmers until the 1950s—requires seven or more years to mature;[1] farmers who wished to establish new farms had, therefore, not only to find suitable land and supply the labour to clear and plant it and tend the young trees, but also to obtain some form of working capital, either to maintain themselves and their dependants while they worked on the farm or to hire labourers to do the work for them. Under these circumstances, we would expect the rate of new plantings to depend not only on the income which farmers expected to earn from their mature farms in the long run, but also on the costs of mobilizing and employing the necessary inputs to establish the farms in the first place.

Available studies of the economic determinants of cocoa supply in West Africa provide little direct evidence on the rate of investment in cocoa trees.[2] Since data on annual plantings are scarce,

---

[1] Before the 1950s there were two main varieties of cocoa planted in Western Nigeria. The primary one was Amelonado—a strain imported from the upper Amazon River basin in Latin America which is well adapted to heavily forested areas and therefore did very well in West Africa. The other was a rather heterogeneous strain from Trinidad which is highly domesticated and requires more careful cultivation than the Amelonado. They are easily distinguished by the colour of their pods: Amelonado is green, turning yellow when ripe, whereas the Trinidad variety is dark red. I am indebted to H. Toxopeus, formerly of the Cocoa Research Institute of Nigeria, for information on these early varieties of cocoa. Cf. D. H. Urquhart, *Cocoa* (London, 1955).

[2] The principal studies of long-run cocoa supply include: Peter Ady, 'Trends in Cocoa Production in British West Africa', *Bulletin of the Oxford University Institute of Statistics*, 2 (1940), pp 389–404; M. J. Bateman, 'Aggregate and Regional Supply Functions for Ghanaian Cocoa, 1946–1962', *Journal of Farm Economics*, 47, 2 (May 1965), pp. 384–401; Dean Sanders, 'The Price Responsiveness of Nigerian Cocoa Farmers', University of Michigan Ph.D. thesis, 1968; R. M Stern, 'The Determinants of Cocoa Supply in West Africa', in I. G. Stewart and H. W. Ord, eds., *African Primary Products and International Trade*. Ady's results were statistically significant, but her model is subject to question. Cf. Bateman, p. 384, and Stern, p. 72.

most studies have been forced to assume that output in any given year depends primarily on past plantings, which were, in turn, a function of expected future prices at the time the plantings occurred. Attempts to verify this hypothesis statistically have produced few significant results, except for the period since World War II—partly because current output depends not only on productive capacity, but also on current yields, which are in turn subject to a number of other short-run economic and ecological influences.[3] The only study which attempts to explain trends in planting directly found a very high positive correlation between five-year moving averages of acres planted and the 'real' price of cocoa in Nigeria during the period 1919/20 to 1944/5.[4] However, the data on acreage planted which were used in this study later proved to be defective. More complete figures now available show a much weaker relationship between plantings and the 'real' price of cocoa. In fact, during the period for which we have data on both plantings and price (1909/13–1940/4), the two series move together in only twelve of the thirty-one 'years' covered; the rest of the time they move in opposite directions. (See Figure 1.)

Not only have studies of long-run cocoa supply been hampered by lack of accurate data on acres planted, they have also made little effort to include costs of establishing and maintaining cocoa farms. Exceptions are Bateman's study of Ghana and Sanders's of Nigeria—both of which deal only with the post-World War II period. Bateman included the price of coffee as a measure of opportunity cost and found a significant relationship between output and lagged price in

[3] Such short-run variations may be very large; see Table 1 in Appendix III. Even with favourable weather conditions, a sudden drop in price may cause farmers to employ less labour to weed or harvest their cocoa and/or to devote more of their own time to other activities. For example, during World War I the price of cocoa was so low that, according to the Department of Agriculture, the farmers spent little time cultivating or harvesting their cocoa plots (Department of Agriculture, *Annual Report*, 1918). In 1919, however, cocoa was 'much more thoroughly picked than usual owing to the high prices that have ruled for this product' (ibid., 1919). After the collapse of the trade boom of 1920, and before the development of cheap motor transport facilities to Ondo, 'prices were so low that . . . much cocoa was allowed to rot on the trees' (ibid., 1921; cf. Ondo Province, Annual Report, 1924). Similarly, in 1936, 'the phenomenal rise' of the cocoa price 'diverted the activities of every farmer and trader in Ibadan and Ife to cocoa, to the exclusion of other crops' (Oyo Province, Annual Report, 1936). In general, the Department of Agriculture concluded that 'when the price of cocoa is high the Nigerian farmer harvests frequently . . .; when the price is low he is liable to be careless . . .' (*Annual Report*, 1930). Variations in weather can also cause substantial variations in yield—partly because heavy rainfall tends to increase the incidence of black pod disease. Cf. Western Nigeria Ministry of Agriculture and Natural Resources, *Tree Crop Planting Projects* (Ibadan, n.d.), pp. 12–13.

[4] Stern, pp. 66, 76–7.

six of seven cocoa-growing regions, but not for the country as a whole.[5] Presumably regional differences in investment and production behaviour may in part reflect local differences in costs, but Bateman did not explore the point. Similarly, Sanders found that cocoa output appeared 'responsive' to lagged prices in Oyo and Ondo Provinces where uncultivated land was still readily available

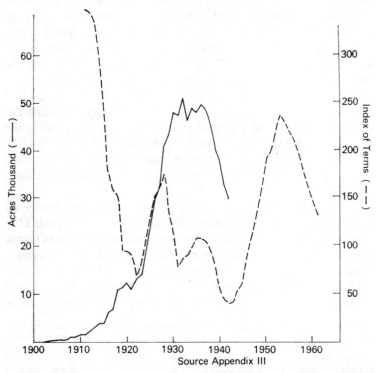

Fig. 1. Five-year moving averages of acres planted in cocoa and farmers' terms of trade

in the 1950s; he concluded that the high cost of land was a serious constraint on additional plantings in the older cocoa-growing areas.[6] His findings do not, however, shed much light on other costs of production, nor do they help to explain variations in rates of planting in the past, when uncultivated land was readily available in all parts of the forest belt.

In order to explain the rate at which new cocoa farms were

[5] Bateman, *passim.*   [6] Sanders, ch. 5.

established, once farmers in the area had accepted the crop, one must consider evidence on costs as well as on expected returns. The cost or availability of factors of production to farmers as a group depended, in turn, on the structure of alternative opportunities in other sectors of the economy, and on the institutional mechanisms available to farmers for mobilizing and employing productive services. Students of economic development have often pointed out that market imperfections may hinder producers' ability to develop potentially profitable lines of production by raising the actual cost of needed inputs above their opportunity costs. In particular, they argue that social or cultural institutions often restrict the flow of market information and/or the terms on which farmers can obtain productive services, causing rates of production or investment to fall below those one would expect from looking at the opportunity costs of inputs. On the whole, economists have paid little attention to the alternative possibility—namely, that apparently non-economic institutions or relationships may in some societies serve as *substitutes* for inadequate market mechanisms, providing farmers with access to information or services which are unavailable through market channels or which farmers could not afford to buy. In either case, it may not be possible to explain patterns of production or investment by relying solely on information about *market* costs and returns; it is also necessary to examine the institutional and structural context in which productive activity takes place.

In Western Nigeria land suitable for cocoa growing was readily available in most parts of the forest belt during the early decades of cocoa production; in some areas it is still available today.[7] Thus, in order to understand the rate at which cocoa growing spread in different areas, it is necessary to begin by examining patterns of migration into uncultivated forest areas, and the ways in which the migrants established themselves and organized their productive activities. This in turn will help us to assess the relative importance of market opportunities and non-market factors in determining the rate of investment in new cocoa farms.

Patterns of Cultivation and Migration

Almost from the beginning, the spread of cocoa farming in Western Nigeria entailed the opening-up of previously uncultivated forest areas. Initially this process amounted to an extension of

[7] Detailed evidence on this point is presented in Chapter IV.

the existing pattern of land-holding and land-use in each city-state. Yorubas had for a long time lived in towns, although many of them were farmers. Men travelled each day to their farms outside the town walls or, if the farms were too far from town, built small hamlets near their farms.[8] As more and more people took up cocoa, they planted new farms further and further from the towns, and built additional hamlets near their new farms. During the first few decades of cocoa cultivation in Nigeria, most farmers planted cocoa within the boundaries of their own city-states. However, some travelled farther afield and from the 1930s increasing numbers of farmers moved considerable distances to establish new farms. This movement involved not only farmers from communities in the forest belt who were unable to obtain land in their own city-states, but also men from the savannah where the climate was not favourable to cocoa cultivation.[9]

The Geographical Spread of Cocoa Growing within Yoruba City-states. In Ibadan, during the nineteenth century, most people farmed north of the town or within a few miles of it towards the south. This pattern reflected Ibadan's history as a refugee camp turned military state. The warriors and refugees who congregated at Ibadan after 1830 were nearly all strangers to the area, and simply took land where they could get it. According to the Bale of Ibadan, in 1913, 'Our fathers brought us here. We were fighting . . . and [we] drove away the people and took their land, and each man now holds his father's land. Each company or head man selected his own farms, lands and put his followers on the land.'[10]

[8] W. Bascom, 'Urbanization Among the Yoruba', *American Journal of Sociology*, 60, 5 (Mar. 1955), pp. 446–54; C. D. Forde and R. Scott, *The Native Economies of Nigeria*, vol. i of M. Perham, ed., *The Economics of a Tropical Dependency* (London, 1946) p. 80; R. Galletti, K. D. S. Baldwin, and I. O. Dina, *Nigerian Cocoa Farmers*, pp. 84 ff.; S. Goddard, 'Town–Farm Relationships in Yorubaland', *Africa*, 25, 1 (Jan. 1965), p. 23; P. C. Lloyd, *Yoruba Land Law, passim*; and A. L. Mabogunje, *Yoruba Towns*.

[9] Many Yorubas had, of course, travelled long distances within Nigeria and elsewhere in West Africa for trade and other economic purposes before the twentieth century. However, both the volume and the directions of migration changed significantly during the colonial period, and the particular patterns of migration described here are clearly associated with the spread of cocoa farming. Cf. A. L. Mabogunje, *Regional Mobility and Resource Development in West Africa*, published for the Centre for Developing Area Studies, McGill University (Montreal, 1972), pp. 42–3, 76–7, and Mabogunje and M. B. Gleave, 'The Changing Agricultural Landscape of Southern Nigeria—The Example of Egba Division, 1890–1950', *Nigerian Geographical Journal*, 7, 1 (June 1964).

[10] WALC, *Papers and Correspondence*, printed for the use of the Colonial Office (1916), p. 201. Cf. E. N. C. Dickenson, 'Intelligence Report on Ibadan Town, 1937', IBAPROF 3/4 (NAI); S. Johnson, *History of the Yorubas*, pp. 244–6; Lloyd, pp. 51–3.

Later, as the Ibadan warriors organized themselves into an effective army, they began to conquer neighbouring towns, establishing officials there to collect regular tribute. Most of these towns also lay north and east of Ibadan itself. The forests south of Ibadan, on the other hand, offered little to conquer and were difficult to cultivate. Accordingly they were left to the hunters who pursued their profession there and occasionally held off Egba or Ijebu raiding parties, or served as guides to Ibadan warriors who set out to raid Egba or Ijebu farms.[11]

When Ibadans began to seek additional farmland after the peace of 1893, those who turned southwards often sought the advice of hunters concerning good sites for settlement and cultivation. The hunters, in turn, welcomed the opportunity to bring more people to their area and show them land for cocoa farming. When asked how their forebears originally acquired land in this area, many of the farmers I interviewed said they were invited by the 'landlord' who would be glad of their company in the village and could promise them good farming land. Later, as people discovered that much of the land which the hunters controlled was good for growing cocoa, they began to ask for plots there. In 1904 the British Resident at Ibadan informed the chiefs that one land-holding family had thirty-two settlements on their land.[12] 'During the next twelve years the forest south of the Alagutan stream was cleared by cutting and burning until a large portion of it became farmland.'[13] In 1917 a British official found 'hundreds of farmers' in the area. Later, when another District Officer asked a number of 'tenant' farmers their reason for moving to this area, 'they invariably replied that they had sought for and obtained land here *not* because they were unable to obtain land elsewhere but because they *could not grow cocoa elsewhere*'.[14]

Farmers came to the forests south of Ibadan, not only from Ibadan itself but also from farming villages north of Ibadan and from other towns, such as Ede and Ofa, which had been under Ibadan's sphere of influence during the wars. I did no extensive fieldwork in the cocoa areas north of the town, but informants now living in villages south of the town frequently mentioned that their forebears had originally planted cocoa farther north, on land

[11] I. B. Akinyele, *Outlines of Ibadan History*, p. 95; Johnson.
[12] Resident's statement to the Ibadan Town Council, 23 Nov. 1904, in file on land disputes (untitled), OYOPROF 3/1181, vol. i (NAI).
[13] Ibid. [14] His underlining. Ibid.

which had been in the family for a couple of generations, and later moved south to seek more or better cocoa land. Similarly, disputes brought before the Ibadan Lands Court in the 1930s and 40s sometimes involved people who had come from the dry northern parts

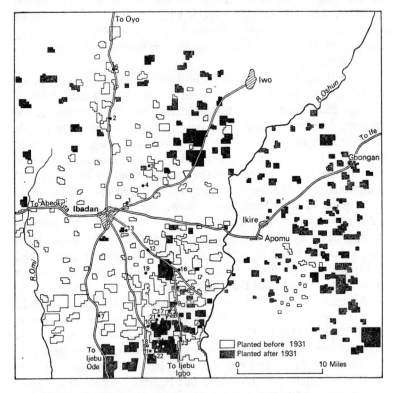

Map 2. Distribution and age of cocoa trees in the Ibadan area

Sources: Western Nigeria Ministry of Agriculture and Natural Resources and my own fieldwork.

of Ibadan Division to plant cocoa.[15] Map 2, based on the Swollen Shoot Virus Disease Survey, shows that before 1931 most of the cocoa in Ibadan was planted south and east of the town, within a radius of twenty miles or so, although there were also a number of plantations on the north-eastern edge of the town and strung out

[15] Ibadan Lands Court Records, cases 156/49, 139/52, 84/37; interviews in Iroko village.

KEY TO MAP 2
DATES ON WHICH COCOA WAS FIRST PLANTED IN SEVERAL IBADAN VILLAGES

Date	Village	Number on Map
	North of town:	
Before 1892	Agbakin	1
1890s	Otun-Agbakin	2
c. 1900	Arun	3
Before 1907	Kute	4
1907–10	Iroko	5
	South of town:	
1892	Eripa	6
1890s	Onipe	7
1890s (after Eripa)	Isokun	8
1890s (after Isokun)	Gbedun	9
1901–2	Olojuoro	10
1901–2	Ayorinde	11
c. 1904	Idi-osi	12
c. 1905	Ogbere	13
c. 1905	Alabidun	14
1904–7	Alagutan	15
1907–10	Olorunda	16
1907–10	Onimo	17
1907–10	Akinboade	18
1907–10	Laogun	19
1910–12	Aladun	20
1910–12	Abulega	21
1911	Ajugbono	22
1914	Araromi-Aperin	23
1915	Amodu Afunsho	24

along the Oyo road to the north for ten or fifteen miles. During the 1930s most new cocoa farms were established east and north of the older cocoa areas—many by farmers from independent towns such as Ikire, Apomu, Iwo, or Gbongan.

In Ife the earliest cocoa farms were probably also established fairly near the town or existing villages. As Ife farmers expanded their cocoa plantings, they too moved south and, especially after the break-up of Modakeke in 1909, south-west. In the course of my fieldwork, I found evidence suggesting that some cocoa was planted before World War I at Ladin, Ishoya, and further south towards Oyere, and also west of Ife towards Ashipa and Gbongan. (See Map 3 and Table III. 1.) Cocoa was planted at Okeigbo before the turn of the century, and Okeigbo farmers had begun to plant cocoa in the eastern parts of Ife Division before 1914. Towards the end of

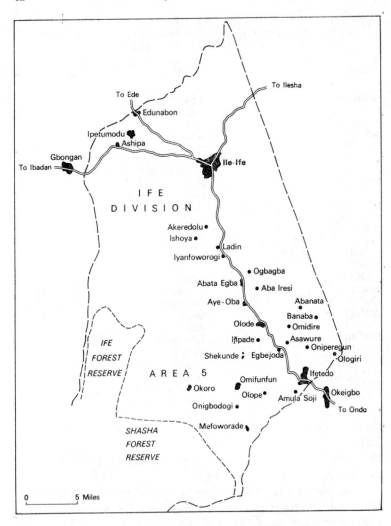

Map 3. Some villages in Ife Division

World War I cocoa planting began to spread in Ife and continued to do so during the 1920s.[16] By the end of this decade, local British officials spoke of the 'sudden wealth' brought to Ife by cocoa and

[16] Ife Division, Annual Report, 1917, OYOPROF 4/6/355/1917 (NAI); Oyo Province, Annual Reports, 1920s, CSO 26/06027, 09723, 12723, vols. i–vii (NAI); Ife Customary Court Records, 74/68.

TABLE III.1

Dates of Establishment and Arrival of Strangers in some Ife Villages

Village	Founded	First strangers arrived	Last strangers arrived
Aba Iresi	1929	1929	late 1940s
Abanata	1928	1945	—
Akeredolu	19th century	mid-1950s	—
Amula Soji	19th century	*c.* 1960	still coming
Asawure	1936	late 1940s	*c.* 1960
Aye-Oba	—	late 1930s	*c.* 1960
Banaba	19th century	1959	still coming
Egbejoda	1924	*c.* 1950	—
Ijipade[a]	19th century	—	—
Ishoya[b]	before 19th century	*c.* 1936	—
Okoro	—	1947	—
Ologiri	1960[c]	1960	1968
Olope	1920s	1947	1960
Omidire	—	1947	late 1950s
Omifunfun	1934[c]	*c.* 1939	late 1950s
Onigbodogi	1947[c]	1947	early 1960s
Oniperegun	19th century	*c.* 1950	still coming
Shekunde	long ago	1931	—
Womonle	—	*c.* 1945	—

[a] There are no strangers in Ijipade.

[b] During the wars the population of Ife was dispersed for a time and many Ifes settled at Ishoya. One of the trade routes to Lagos passed through Ishoya and during the Sixteen Years War, an Ijebu army camped there. (Johnson, p. 472.)

[c] The area was considered the farmland of an Ife family before this date, but there was no settlement there.

even felt that cocoa development was proceeding faster in Ife than in Ilesha, which the British had always considered a more progressive community. 'Cultivation has spread very rapidly in Ife District and this in a short time (especially when railway facilities are provided) will probably rank as one of the most important Cocoa Centres in the country. Extension in the Ilesha District is not quite so apparent, and there may be a tendency for the Ilesha producer at present to "rest on his oars".'[17]

Most of the cocoa planted during this period was located south and south-west of Ife, towards Oyere and the Oshun River, and much of the forest south-east of Ile-Ife was still uncultivated and unoccupied in the late 1930s and 1940s.[18] One informant, describing

[17] Oyo Province, Annual Reports, 1926–7.

[18] 'Ishakole: Collection of', IFEDIV 1/1/113 (NAI). In a survey of 136 Ife villages, J. O. Adejuwon discovered that the founders of 126 of them came from Ile-Ife or the Origbo towns. He concluded that 'the countryside was colonized mainly by the move-

the arrival of stranger farmers at Omifunfun *c.* 1940, said that at
that time Ife farms extended no further than Iyanfoworogi; until
the strangers came, Omifunfun itself was only a hunter's camp.
Others in Omifunfun and nearby villages said that when they
arrived the whole area was 'forest' or 'thick bush'. In 1953 the Ife

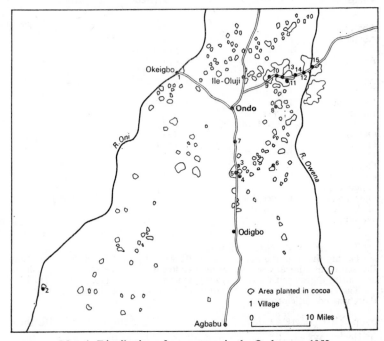

Map 4. Distribution of cocoa trees in the Ondo area, 1952

Sources: Ministry of Agriculture and Natural Resources and my own fieldwork.

District Officer reported that many cocoa farms in Ife were growing
old and unproductive, but that new, high-yielding farms 'are
scattered about in villages with net work roads connecting the new
Ife–Ondo road'.[19] And a few years later an official report on the
availability of uncultivated land in 'area 5' (see Map 3) described

ment of people from the existing towns to the countryside' rather than by immigrants
from other parts of Yorubaland. This is true of many villages south and south-west of
Ife town, but in the south-eastern part of the Division most of the farmers are not from
Ife, although they usually name the local land-holding families (or their representatives)
as the founders of the villages. Adejuwon, 'Agricultural Colonization in the Forest
Areas of Western Nigeria: The Movement of Yoruba People to the Countryside',
1970, mimeographed, p. 10.

[19] Ife Division, Annual Report, 1917.

this as land which 'has only been opened to farming to any great extent since 1950 . . .'[20]

In Ondo, cocoa farming began, as we have seen, at the edges of Ondo territory, around Okeigbo and Ajebamidele; later, as people in Ondo town took it up, they planted north and east of the town towards the Owena River, although there was some cocoa to the

KEY TO MAP 4

DATES ON WHICH COCOA WAS FIRST PLANTED
IN SEVERAL ONDO VILLAGES

Date	Village	Number on Map
	West of town:	
1898	Okeigbo	1
	South of town:	
1909	Ajebamidele	2
1905–6	Bagbe	3
1912	Igunshin	4
c. 1914	Ogun	5
1901–17*	Lemosho	6
1901–17*	Igbado	7
	East of town:	
1901–17*	Fagbo	8
1918	Oboto	9
c. 1920	Bolorunduro	10
1922	Wasimi	11
1922	Ago-Ileshi	12
1926	Adegbulu's Camp	13
1926	Obun-Ondo	14
1926	Owena	15

* In these villages farmers said the first cocoa was planted there during the reign of Oshemawe Tewogboye I, which lasted from 1901 to 1917. I am inclined to think that in most cases the actual date falls towards the end of this period, although in Fagbo it may have been earlier.

south as well. Map 4 shows the distribution of cocoa trees in different parts of the Ondo area as of 1952. For information on the time pattern of plantings, it was necessary to rely entirely on interviews and occasional documentary sources. As far as I could tell, after the early developments around Okeigbo and Ajebamidele, Ondo farmers first planted cocoa south and east of the town (e.g. at Bagbe, Igunshin, Lemosho, and Fagbo), and after 1920 farmers began to move north-east towards the heavily forested areas near the Owena

[20] 'Ishakole: Collection of'.

River to establish cocoa farms. During the 1920s villages were founded every couple of years along the Ondo-Akure road. Nowadays farmers cannot easily obtain land in this area, but there is still uncultivated forest land south of Ondo towards Odigbo and also around Okeigbo and Ile Oluji, and new farms are being planted there today.

Similar patterns of development have been documented in other city-states. In Egba Division the earliest cocoa farms were established around Otta, near Agege. Towards the end of the nineteenth century farmers began to move north-east from Abeokuta into a forest area which, because of Ibadan raids, had been uncultivated for fifty years and had 'thus become thickly forested and ideal for cocoa growing'.[21] As cocoa became popular, more and more people moved into this area. As early as 1901, a British Forestry Officer found numerous cocoa farms between Asha, in the eastern part of the Division, and Ilogbo, and also around Okenla on the railway.[22] The development of the north-eastern part of the Division continued into the 1920s.[23] In other areas as well, farmers moved into the forests to plant cocoa. In Ijebu there was 'a rush to acquire land in the forested north of the kingdom which is ideal for cocoa',[24] and further east, farmers from Ilesha, Okeigbo, and Ile Oluji established many farms in the Ilesha and Ondo forests along the Omi River.

Migration Between City-states. To some extent the period of long-distance migration by farmers seeking land to plant cocoa overlapped with the period of expansion within the forest states, but most of the movement from the savannah to the cocoa belt occurred after World War II. Migration from the northern to the southern parts of Yorubaland seems to have begun towards the end of the nineteenth century, as part of the general increase in movement which followed the peace of 1893 and the subsequent improvement of trade and employment opportunities, especially in large towns and on the railway.[25] In 1912 J. Mackay—a missionary who

[21] Lloyd, p. 230.
[22] Lagos, *Annual Report*, 1901–2.
[23] A. L. Mabogunje, 'Changing Pattern of Rural Settlement and Rural Economy in Egba Division, South-West Nigeria', University of London M.A. thesis, 1958.
[24] Lloyd, p. 142.
[25] B. A. Agiri, 'Kola in Western Nigeria', University of Wisconsin Ph.D. thesis, 1972, pp. 168 ff.

had lived in Oshogbo since the turn of the century—told the West
African Lands Committee:

Perhaps the greatest factor in the breaking down of 'tribal customs' has
been the Lagos Government Railway and the opening up of the hinter-
land to trade which the railway has effected. Within the last few years tens
of thousands of young farmers have left the land to take up work as
labourers on the railway and on road construction, to say nothing of the
hundreds in the employ of trading firms.[26]

Like early emigrants from Ondo or Okeigbo, some of the northerners
became traders or managed to acquire training and skilled jobs,
but most worked as labourers—for trading firms, on the railway
or at the docks in Lagos, or on farms where they encountered cocoa
and other tree crops.[27]

Like earlier migrants from towns in the cocoa belt who had
worked as labourers at, for example, Agege, the northern Yoruba
migrants were impressed by the evident prosperity of people engaged in growing or selling cocoa and, by engaging themselves as
labourers on cocoa farms, soon learned how to cultivate the crop.
By the 1920s some individuals had acquired the use of uncultivated land around Otta and begun to plant cocoa for themselves.
(See Appendix II and Map 5.) Other northern Yorubas who wished
to follow their example found it difficult to obtain land in Egba
Division or Colony Province, however, and began to move eastwards in search of land. They were aided in their search by other
migrants, especially men such as Bajepade of Isanlu or the Oladiran
brothers of Iresi who had previously found work around Ife, where
uncultivated forest land was still relatively abundant. During the
1930s, the migrants' first settlements in Ife—for example, Aba
Iresi, Aye-Oba, and Imokore—grew and by the 1940s had become
centres of local dispersal, where migrants coming directly from
the north to plant cocoa in Ife found shelter, contacts with local
landowners, and an opportunity to accumulate savings and acquire
experience with cocoa growing in preparation for establishing
their own farms.

At first the number of migrant farmers was fairly small but, from
the late 1940s on, more and more people joined the movement

[26] WALC, *Minutes of Evidence*, question 8847. Cf. J. O. Oyemakinde, 'A History of
Indigenous Labour on the Nigerian Railway, 1895–1945', University of Ibadan Ph.D.
thesis, 1970.
[27] Interviews with the Olusin and Chiefs of Isanlu, and with migrant farmers in Ife
and Ondo villages. M. Hündsalz and B. A. Agiri report similar findings.

into the cocoa belt. Also, farmers from older cocoa-growing areas, such as Ibadan and Egba, began to move beyond the borders of their own states in search of more land. In several of the Ibadan villages I visited, farmers told of friends or relatives who had gone

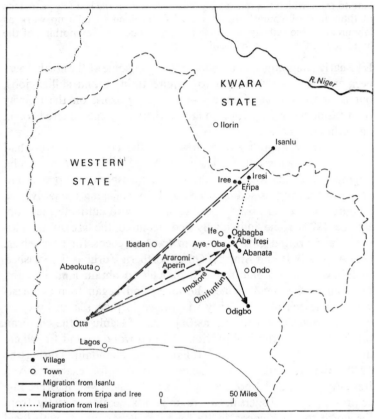

Map. 5. Sample migratory patterns

to such places as Ago-owu, Ife, Ijebu, Ile Oluji, Ondo, and Ore to obtain additional land for planting cocoa. I also met farmers from Ibadan and Egba in seven of the twenty villages I visited in the Ife area: Aye-Oba, Asawure, Ishoya, Akeredolu, Onigbodogi, Shekunde, and Womonle.[28] In most of these villages migrants from

[28] Chief Ayorinde says that Ibadan and Egbado cocoa farmers have gone to Araromi Ago-owu and Omifunfun areas especially. I also encountered Ibadans farming in a couple of Ondo villages. In 1935 a village of migrant cocoa farmers, some from Ibadan and Ijebu-Ode, was reported as far east as Owo. 'Intelligence Report on Ifon and Owo Districts', CSO 26/29956 (NAI).

the old cocoa-farming areas arrived during the 1940s and 1950s, although in some cases they began coming even earlier. In two communities there were enough people from Egba or Ibadan to have their own head or *bale*, who represented their interests in village meetings. In Aye-Oba the head of the Egbas said that his people had come to Ife from Oluke village (Egba Division) in 1940 because their cocoa farms at Oluke were growing old and they could not get more uncultivated bush at home. Some of them now have farms at a village in Ondo Division (Kajola on the Ondo–Akure Road) as well as at Aye-Oba; they first went to Ondo about 1960. hekunde—another Ife village—is divided into two sections: one comprised of farmers from Ife and Ibadan, the other of Igbomina farmers. The head of the Ibadans came to Shekunde in 1931 from Edun (near Lalupon), together with three relatives, because they could not get as much land for planting cocoa in Ibadan as they wanted. Other Ibadan farmers later joined them at Shekunde; the last arrived in the early 1960s. In other villages the Ibadans had no separate leader of their own but were represented in village affairs by the head of all the non-Ife strangers, of whom the Ibadans usually constituted a minority.[29]

The great majority of immigrant cocoa farmers whom I met in Ife villages came from the northern parts of Yorubaland. I encountered farmers from northern Oshun Division and/or Kwara State in all but one of the twenty Ife villages I visited and in each of the five Ondo villages where I specifically asked about strangers. In each case, farmers from savannah areas appeared to constitute a majority of the stranger population of the village; in Ife the strangers often outnumbered the local people as well, especially in the south-eastern part of the Division.

Most of the northern Yorubas I interviewed had come to Ife in the 1940s and 1950s. In the early 1940s the first migrants to settle at such places as Omifunfun, Asawure, Onigbodogi, etc. found almost no one living there except a few relatives or followers of the Ife landowners, who were engaged primarily in hunting and growing food crops. By the late 1940s, however, the stream of settlers had become a flood. People 'rushed' to obtain land and plant cocoa, as several of my informants put it. In Ifetedo 1948 is thought of as the

[29] Ife Customary Court Records, 49/58, 63–65/69. R. C. Clark, I. A. Akinbode, and Y. O. K. Odebunmi, 'Case Studies of Four Nigerian Villages', University of Ife, Department of Extension Education Research Monograph 2, 1967, reports that Ibadan farmers were found in Alapata village in 1965.

year of the 'influx of strangers'.[30] In 1957 a British forestry officer
remarked that the south-eastern part of Ife Division 'has only been
opened to farming to any great extent since 1950. From casual
knowledge through passing through the roads leading to the [Shasha
forest] reserve I would say that the majority of the persons there
making farm and cocoa plantations are non-Ife natives. Many are
from Ilorin and Oshun.'[31] In 1963 an observer reported that since
1947 immigrants from Ilorin and Kabba Provinces had been coming
to grow cocoa around Ifetedo; in one village, he found that the
majority of the population came from Ilorin and Oyo Provinces.[32]
These observations were corroborated by several agricultural
extension officers and prominent Ife citizens whom I interviewed
in 1970-1,[33] and are consistent with evidence collected in savannah
areas.[34]

This rapid flow of immigration into the Ife forests continued
well into the 1950s, until settlers began to find it difficult to obtain
additional uncultivated land. Table III.1 shows the approximate
dates of establishment and of the first arrival of strangers in nineteen Ife villages. In most of them, my informants said people had
stopped coming there because there was no more uncultivated land
available for planting cocoa. In Asawure, for example, the population doubled between 1952 and 1962,[35] but, according to the
present inhabitants, there has not been any uncultivated land
available there since the early 1960s. Although in some parts of the
Ife Division immigrants can still obtain uncultivated land today,

[30] J. F. A. Ajayi and A. A. Igun, *Population Census of Nigeria: Lists of Historical
Events for Determination of Individual Ages*, 1963, mimeographed.
[31] 'Ishakole: Collection of'.
[32] R. Fashola, 'Changing Landscape of Ifetedo Area', Original Essay, Geography
Department, University of Ibadan, 1963.
[33] Interviews with Principal Agricultural Officer, Akure; B. A. Elujobade and
members of the Ifetedo branch of the Western State Farmers Union; Odutalayo, Ife;
Olaniran, Agricultural Officer, Ondo; A. Awe, Abewela family, Ife; Adeyeba, Timi
family, Ife; J. Adeyeye, Otutu family, Ife; Chief Y. O. Orafidiya, Chief Magistrate,
Abeokuta; Chief B. O. Ogunniya, Ondo; Abe, Agricultural Officer, Ondo; E. T.
Ademiluyi, Ibadan. Cf. above, p. 62, n. 16.
[34] In a survey of 25 towns in north-eastern Oshun Division M. Hündsalz found that
from 15 per cent to 60 per cent of the population of each town were farming elsewhere in
1969. Most of these people were growing cocoa in Ife and other parts of the forest belt.
Hündsalz interviewed 10 per cent of the households in each town concerning the location and occupations of all household members. Similar observations have been made
in studies of individual villages in the Igbomina area of Kwara State, by J. Olukosi
and others from Ahmadu Bello University. Cf. M. Upton and D. A. Petu, 'An Economic Study of Farming in Two Villages in Ilorin Emirate', *Bulletin of Rural Economics
and Sociology*, 1, 1, 1964.
[35] Fashola, op. cit.

since the late 1950s newcomers or earlier settlers wishing to expand their cocoa farms have usually had to go to Ilesha or Ondo to find land. As I indicated earlier, migrants are still arriving in Ondo.

Migration and Capital Formation

In order to establish a cocoa plot, a farmer needed not only land and labour, but also some means of providing for himself and his dependents for seven years or more until the cocoa farm began to yield significant returns. It has been suggested that this problem was solved automatically for most West African cocoa farmers since they could usually grow food crops in addition to cocoa trees and thus meet their subsistence requirements while waiting for the trees to mature.[36] Undoubtedly many farmers did grow much of the food they consumed, especially while they were establishing their first cocoa plots,[37] but it takes more than foodstuffs to support a family for the better part of a decade. In particular, many farmers were likely to require resources to cover extraordinary expenses during such a period of time—expenses connected, for example, with illness, births, deaths, housing, and transportation, to mention only a few obvious examples. Also there was always a certain amount of risk that a particular plot of cocoa trees would never yield well, because of poor location, disease, pests, etc. Finally, for a great many farmers, the risks of undertaking a new type of agricultural investment with a long gestation period were enhanced by the fact that they were establishing themselves in uninhabited forest areas, and, in the case of migrants from older cocoa-growing areas or savannah communities, in 'foreign' territory.

In principle, most of the inputs and other resources a farmer might need to establish his first cocoa farm could be purchased. Internal trade in all kinds of consumer goods was, of course, well established in Yorubaland before the introduction of cocoa, and there is also evidence that some Yoruba farmers used hired labour from the earliest days of cocoa cultivation.[38] Some of my informants

[36] See, for example, W. A. Faulkner and J. T. Mackie, *West African Agriculture* (London, 1940), p. 106; Forde and Scott, p. 81.

[37] Even today, most cocoa farmers grow some food crops, but most of my informants said that they did not normally produce enough foodstuffs to meet their families' needs, but purchased at least part of the food they consumed. The cocoa belt as a whole has been a food-importing area since before World War II. Galletti, *et al.*, p. 61; Forde and Scott, p. 87; R. Güsten, *Studies in the Staple Food Economy of Western Nigeria*, Afrika-Studien Nr. 30 (Munich, 1968), p. 62.

[38] See Chapter V for details.

specifically stated that the earliest planters in their families or villages had used money earned from trade or other cash employment in establishing their first cocoa farms. This was more common among farmers who had taken up cocoa growing in the 1920s or later. Often, such men had worked as traders, craftsmen, or labourers around Lagos or other centres of commercial activity for some years before they turned to farming, and many of them used savings from their previous occupations in establishing their first cocoa farms. As Table III. 2 shows, early planters in Ibadan and Ife, where cocoa growing began well before the 1920s, were less likely to have had previous 'commercial' employment than farmers in Ondo or strangers from savannah communities, who took up cocoa farming later on.

For many farmers it was not possible to establish their farms entirely with purchased inputs, either because the necessary goods and services were not available in newly settled areas, or more often, because they simply did not have enough money. Many farmers relied therefore on their participation in various non-economic institutions or networks of communication and mutual responsibilities for the services and support they needed to establish themselves as cocoa farmers. I shall discuss their use of 'traditional' methods of land acquisition and labour employment in Chapters IV and V; for the present I wish to concentrate on traditional or non-economic institutions—particularly kinship and ethnic ties— as sources of savings and security for cocoa farmers.

In describing how they or their forebears had begun growing cocoa in the forest surrounding their home towns, my informants frequently stated that they had moved into the forests to plant cocoa together with several friends or kinsmen. My informants used no particular term to describe these groups of farmer-settlers and ascribed no distinctive form of organization to them. When asked to explain the purpose or significance of the group, they simply stated that, as one farmer put it, 'You cannot stay alone in the bush.' Since these informal groups of friends or relatives seemed to have little in common with the land-buying 'companies' which played such an important role in the early development of cocoa growing in Ghana,[39] I paid little attention to them while collecting material on the early spread of cocoa cultivation within Yoruba city-states. Their significance became clear to me only when I began to inter-

[39] P. Hill, *Migrant Cocoa Farmers of Southern Ghana*, especially ch. II.

TABLE III.2

Previous Occupations of Early Planters[a]

Occupation	Ibadan[b]		Ondo[b]		Ife[c]			
					Ifes		Strangers	
	No.	%	No.	%	No.	%	No.	%
Farmer	50	74	32	57	2	14	6	40
Warrior	12	18	2	4	—	—	—	—
Hunter	12	18	2	4	4	28	—	—
Trader[d]	4	6	18	32	3	21	3	20
Craftsman	4	6	14	25	—	—	4	27
Labourer: Farm	—	—	—	—	—	—	3	20
Commercial[e]	—	—	5	9	3	21	5	33
Other	8	12	6	11	2	14	—	—
Total number of early planters	68		56		14		15	

[a] For some early planters more than one occupation was given, so percentages do not add to 100. Most informants probably mentioned only those occupations which early planters were following at the time they took up cocoa growing; hence the prevalence of some occupations may be understated. This may well account for the low proportion of warriors in Ibadan and of farmers in Ife.

[b] Based on interviews conducted in 1966. Informants were asked about the first individual(s) to have planted cocoa in their village. Interviews covered 31 villages in Ibadan, 19 in Ondo.

[c] Based on interviews conducted in 20 Ife villages in 1970/1. Informants were asked about (1) the first person to plant cocoa in their village and (2) the first stranger (non-Ife) to plant cocoa there.

[d] Includes contractors.

[e] 'Commercial' labourers include dock, road, and railway labourers, porters, and men employed by various 'contractors'. Most of these people had worked in Lagos or some other large town.

view migrant farmers, especially those from savannah towns, who live and farm away from their home communities.

Despite the fact that most of the migrant farmers one encounters in rural areas of Ife and Ondo are Yorubas, who share a common language, culture, and historical tradition with Yorubas resident in the forest belt, they are regarded (and consider themselves) as 'strangers' in the forest states, even if they have lived there for a couple of generations.[40] Their sense of ethnic distinctiveness is

[40] The Yoruba term *alejo* (usually translated 'stranger') has a wide variety of meanings, depending on the context in which it is used. Briefly, it may be applied to anyone from a visiting kinsman to a person from another tribe, nationality, or race. In this chapter I use the term to refer to anyone not claiming descent from a given Yoruba city-state but, as we shall see in Chapter IV, for some purposes people from the same city-state consider each other as 'strangers'. Cf. O. Esan, 'Xenos: Alejo—Some Aspects of Greek and Yoruba Hospitality', *Odu*, 3, 1 (July 1966), pp. 29–39.

reinforced by a strong sense of attachment to their home towns, and a well-organized network of communications with fellow towns-men in other parts of the cocoa belt. Moreover, in Ife at least, they are also considered—both by the Ifes and by themselves—to be exceptionally dedicated and successful cocoa farmers.

As the case studies presented in Appendix II suggest, cocoa farmers from savannah communities relied heavily on each other in organizing their movements to the cocoa belt and the establishment of their first cocoa farms. Despite the fact that many of the earliest migrant farmers had probably saved some money from trade or wage employment which they used in establishing their first farms (see Table III. 2), this was not true of the majority of stranger farmers

TABLE III.3

Previous Occupations of Cocoa Farmers in Three Villages

Occupation	Abanata		Orotedo		Omifon	
	Ifes	Strangers	Ondos	Strangers	Odigbos	Strangers
Farmer	4	21	1	10	1	8
Hunter	—	—	—	—	—	—
Trader	—	4	—	3	—	—
Craftsman	1	3	1	4	—	5
Labourer: Farm	—	3	—	—	—	2
Commercial	—	3	1	1	1	—
Other	—	2	1	5	—	1
Number of Informants	4	26	3	12	2	13

Source: based on detailed interviews with a sample of adult men in each village. The Ibadan village was excluded from the table because most of the cocoa farmers I interviewed there were second or third generation.

I interviewed in the detailed village studies. Most of these men had been farmers all their lives, growing food crops at home before they decided to migrate to the cocoa belt. (See Table III. 3.) Although many of them had undoubtedly grown food crops for sale, and could therefore have accumulated some cash savings to invest in cocoa farming, it is clear from their accounts of their early farming activities that most of them relied primarily on non-market sources of credit and assistance.

I have already mentioned the fact that the villages in which the earliest immigrants from savannah communities settled became reception centres for later immigrants, who lived with their kinsmen or fellow townsmen while they acquired experience and information about local farming conditions and established contact with a local landowner. They also often worked on the farms of established immigrants—*not* in this case for a cash wage, but for 'assistance' in starting farms of their own. In other words, they accumulated a kind of credit which they could later draw on for maintenance or help while planting and tending their own farms. Since this 'credit' had to operate over long periods of time and often considerable distances (since successive waves of immigrants obtained land further and further from the earliest migrants' farms), it functioned best among people known to each other as members of the same kin group or community.

The fact that, in low-income and/or largely non-literate societies, institutions such as the lineage or ethnic community may facilitate the flow of information or mobilization of capital necessary for many commercial activities has been observed in other contexts. In his study of Hausa cattle and kola traders in Ibadan, Abner Cohen argues that in 'pre-industrial' societies, political, cultural, and even religious institutions or associations can play an important part in the successful organization of commercial activity. In long-distance trade involving perishable commodities, he says, 'the technical problems can be efficiently, and hence economically, overcome when men from one tribe control all or most of the stages of the trade.... Hausa northern dealers will entrust their goods and money only into the hands of Hausa "brothers abroad" who live within a highly stable and organized Hausa community.'[41] In effect, cultural, religious, and political ties perform some of the same functions for Hausa traders that banks and electronic communications facilities do for businessmen in industrial societies. In cocoa farming, where the abundance of land relative to labour has placed a premium on making good use of available human resources rather than seeking to increase yield per acre, social and cultural institutions or relationships have provided particularly appropriate mechanisms for organizing and expanding cocoa production.

The ability to turn to friends and neighbours or, in some cases,

[41] Abner Cohen, *Custom and Politics in Urban Africa* (Berkeley, Calif., 1969), pp. 20, 22. Another interesting study of alternatives to conventional Western credit institutions in 'underdeveloped economies' is D. Caplovitz, *The Poor Pay More* (New York, 1967).

to draw on kinsmen or friends in one's home town for assistance and support was undoubtedly important to the farmers who first opened up the forests within their own city-states for cocoa growing, as well as to migrant farmers later on. The former did not stress the point in conversation because, I think, they took it for granted; they were farming within the borders of their own commumities among their fellow townsmen, and had no particular need to emphasize their membership in those communities. On the other hand, the migrant farmers had moved further from their homes and hence incurred greater risks in establishing their farms; their contacts with each other and with their home towns tended to be more explicit and more formally organized. As more and more people came to the forest belt from savannah towns to grow cocoa, the network of communications and mutual assistance organized by the early immigrants tended to expand and be strengthened. New immigrant villages were established and the first inhabitants provided later arrivals with food, shelter, and a start in cocoa farming in return for labour on their farms. Immigrant farmers have organized their own branches of the Western Nigeria Cooperative Produce Marketing Union and the Cooperative Thrift and Credit Society; Igbomina Cooperatives are, for example, to be found in a number of the larger Ife villages. Migrant farmers are also expected to contribute regularly to funds for building or other improvement projects in their home towns, and the authorities at home keep close track of the emigrants to see that they do. Many of the migrants return home annually during the dry season for festivals and ceremonies. They also often send their children home to attend school, and invest part of their earnings in building houses in their home towns to which they intend to retire in their old age.[42]

In other words, northern Yoruba farmers growing cocoa in Western Nigeria have generally stuck together and provided one another with economic services without which many of them probably could not have established cocoa farms. Like the Hausa traders whom Cohen studied in Ibadan, the northern Yoruba cocoa farmers have, over time, maintained and even strengthened their sense of ethnic distinctiveness—in large part because it has served their economic ends. Indeed, the fact that as strangers in the cocoa belt, the migrant farmers have had to depend more explicitly on their

---

[42] Cf. Hill, *Migrant Cocoa Farmers*, pp. 190–1, and D. Brokensha, *Social Change in Larteh, Ghana* (Oxford, 1966), pp. 57–8.

fellow townsmen for assistance in their farming activities than have farmers growing cocoa within their home states may actually have contributed to their success as cocoa farmers, by facilitating the organization of their farming activities and fostering a sense of pride in and dedication to their agricultural achievements. In Ife, where the migrants have been established for some time, the largest farms and most attractive, well-built houses in many villages belong to immigrant rather than to Ife farmers, and the strangers are regarded, both by themselves and by the Ifes, as cocoa farmers *par excellence*.

The economic advantages which northern Yoruba farmers have derived from emphasizing their common ethnic background stand out clearly when their experiences are contrasted with those of non-Yoruba cocoa farmers in Western Nigeria. There are very few non-Yorubas growing cocoa for themselves in the areas where I worked; most of the non-Yorubas I met in rural communities either worked as farm labourers or were engaged in non-agricultural pursuits. In fact, in conversations with several hundred farmers over a period of nearly two years, I met at most half a dozen non-Yorubas who owned cocoa farms. Although it is asserted that non-Yoruba strangers do not become cocoa farmers because they cannot acquire land for that purpose,[43] the following cases suggest a somewhat different reason.

The only non-Yoruba cocoa farmer I encountered anywhere in Ife was an Ibo who had come to the West from Awka around 1950 and bought two cocoa farms at a village called Egbejoda. He was an established member of the village, who spoke Yoruba well. He had remained there throughout the civil war and planned to leave his farms to his children when he died. Egbejoda is an unusual community: it was founded in 1924 by a group of people from Okeigbo who had been working on the Ife–Okeigbo road and had selected an area in the forest for farming. The Bale of the village said proudly that there were no tenants there and no strangers' associations; people who wished to join the community were accepted as equals and they all 'did things together'. I interviewed several farmers there, including the Ibo, who all confirmed this story. Thus, the Ibo farmer had acquired cocoa farms, but had done so in a somewhat exceptional context.

[43] Such opinions were, for example, voiced by officials and university staff members in Nigeria with whom I discussed matters of land tenure.

In Ondo I met two non-Yoruba cocoa farmers in Omifon. One was an Igara who had come to Omifon, after working in Akure as a labourer, and bought a cocoa farm in 1962. He was having financial difficulties and complained that he could not get loans from anyone in Omifon; he attributed this state of affairs to the fact that there were none of his own people living there permanently. (One other Igara had owned a cocoa farm there in the past but sold it when the civil war broke out. The other Igaras in Omifon were all migrant labourers, who looked to this man for leadership and assistance but apparently provided little for him in return.) The other non-Yoruba cocoa farmer was an Igbirra from Okele. He had worked as a tailor in Ife until 1969, when he moved to Omifon and acquired land for planting cocoa in exchange for an initial payment and a promise to pay *ishakole*.[44] Although there were no non-Yoruba cocoa farmers in Orotedo, some of the non-Yoruba labourers there expressed the hope of obtaining land for cocoa growing. Most of the other non-Yoruba labourers I met, especially in Araromi-Aperin, expressed no desire to obtain land and become farmers in the cocoa belt.

The experiences of the three non-Yoruba cocoa farmers I interviewed (and of their friends and relations) suggest that, at least in Ondo, non-Yorubas can obtain cocoa farms (or land for planting cocoa) if they can pay for them, but that they are at a definite disadvantage, compared to local or other Yoruba farmers, in their ability to obtain credit or other non-monetary forms of assistance while getting their farms established. For instance, the Igara farmer in Omifon was struggling to maintain two wives, a small son, and a daughter in secondary school without access to local credit facilities; the Igbirra, on the other hand, who seemed to be managing more successfully, had fewer dependents and several junior brothers to help him on his farm—much like many of the northern Yoruba migrants I interviewed in both Ife and Ondo. Perhaps if large groups of non-Yorubas deliberately joined forces to help establish one another as cocoa farmers, they might be able to overcome the difficulties facing them in an alien community. As it is, without nearby relatives or compatriots to turn to, their lives are so insecure that the possibility of obtaining land for cocoa farming is not sufficiently attractive to offset the risks of economic failure or other misfortune.[45]

44 See below, pp. 94 ff.
45 Conceivably there have been non-Yoruba cocoa farmers in Ife who have had to abandon their farms for such reasons; those in Ondo may eventually do so. There are

In general, I have argued in this chapter that the spread of cocoa growing in Western Nigeria can best be understood as a process of agricultural capital formation in a land surplus economy. By examining the patterns of migration associated with the spread of new plantings and the ways in which migrant farmers organized the establishment of new farms, we can see how this investment process was implemented, both technically and financially. In particular it appears that Yoruba farmers have, from the earliest days of cocoa production in Western Nigeria, used both market and non-market mechanisms to mobilize the working capital needed to establish their farms and also to ensure themselves against economic failure and/or personal misfortune during the long gestation period of their investment projects. In the remainder of this chapter I shall use these findings to help elucidate the historical pattern of new cocoa plantings in Western Nigeria.

The Rate of Investment in New Cocoa Farms

Figure 1, which charts a five-year moving average of acres planted in the whole of Western Nigeria up to the early 1940s, illustrates

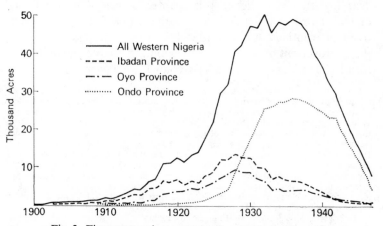

Fig. 2. Five-year moving averages of acres planted in cocoa

reported to be a number of Igbirras growing foodstuffs around Ife and it is sometimes claimed that they would grow cocoa if they were allowed to. However, I have not seen any systematic investigation of the circumstances under which the Igbirras came to Ife; such an investigation might indicate whether they sought and were refused land for growing cocoa at times and in places where it was available or whether, like the Yoruba strangers in Araromi-Aperin, they have settled in areas where the expansion of cocoa planting had already stopped, and specialized in producing foodstuffs for which there was a ready local market.

the general historical trend of investment in new farms. Actually, the rate of planting did not always move in the same direction in all parts of the cocoa belt; in the 1930s, for example, new plantings declined in Ibadan and Oyo Provinces, whereas in Ondo they rose sharply from the mid-twenties till the early thirties, and remained at a high level for the rest of that decade (see Fig. 2). There are no reliable data on plantings after World War II, but the trebling of annual output which occurred during the 1960s seems likely to have been associated primarily with new plantings in the late 1940s and 1950s—especially in Ife and, later, Ondo, which received a large influx of migrant farmers during these years.[46]

When one takes into account the divergences in the rate at which cocoa growing first caught on in different parts of Western Nigeria. and also the likelihood that migrant farmers planted new farms extensively for at least ten to fifteen years after World War II, it appears that in periods of high or rising 'real' cocoa prices, the rate of planting usually increased—at least in areas where uncultivated land was readily available. For example, the rapid expansion of cocoa cultivation in Ibadan during the decade preceding World War I, described earlier in this chapter, coincided with a period of high terms of trade for cocoa farmers (see Fig. 1). The rising trend of plantings in Ondo after 1926 was partly associated with the improvement of transportation facilities,[47] but the main impetus for new plantings appears to have come from higher prices.

[46] The present state of knowledge concerning the effects of chemical sprays is not adequate to enable us to estimate their quantitative effect on output. The West African Cocoa Research Institute estimated that spraying against capsid attack would increase yield by 'approximately 100 lbs. of dry beans per acre' (*Annual Report*, 1957/8). Using this figure and MANR's estimates of the number of acres sprayed with capsidicides, we can estimate roughly the resulting increase in average annual output by the late 1960s at between 22,000 and 27,000 tons—or less than 15 per cent of the over-all increase after 1956 (*Tree Crop Planting Projects*, pp. 12–13). However, regular spraying against capsid attack tends to increase a cocoa farm's susceptibility to black pod disease, and the effectiveness of chemical control measures against black pod is subject to considerable uncertainty. (See, e.g., G. Weststeijn and A. M. Gorenz, 'Studies on the Chemical Control of *Phytophthora Palmivora* (Butl.) Butl. on *Theobroma Cacao* L. in Nigeria, VII. Returns of Fungicide Spraying', CRIN typescript, n.d.) These considerations, plus my evidence that large numbers of farmers migrated to Ife and Ondo after 1945 to plant cocoa, suggest that MANR's estimate of 15,000 acres planted between 1947 and 1963 is too low. Cf. FAO, *Agricultual Development in Nigeria, 1964–80*, p. 54.

[47] In most of the areas I studied, motorized transport facilities were not a necessary precondition for the development of cocoa production. In many areas, feeder roads to the railway were constructed after cocoa had been planted extensively and at the instigation of local farmers and traders, who put pressure on the government to build more roads. See S. S. Berry, 'Cocoa in Western Nigeria, 1890–1940: A Study of an Innovation in a Developing Economy', 1967.

In the early 1920s, according to the District Officer, the price which Ondo farmers obtained for cocoa averaged around £8 per ton.[48] (See Table III.4.) The Director of Agriculture in Southern

TABLE III.4

Cocoa Prices in Ondo, 1920/1–1932/3

Crop Year	(£ per ton) Fair Average Quality[a]	Good Fermented[a]
1920–1	—	—
1921–2	c. 8[b]	—
1922–3	—	—
1923–4	3·7[c]	—
1924–5	16·5[d]	22·0[t]
1925–6	17·7[e]	—
1926–7	42·0[e]	—
1927–8	43·4—47·9[f]	—
1928–9	28·6[g]	30·6[j]
1929–30	—	—
1930–1	16·7[h]	19·3[k]
1931–2	—	—
1932–3	—	19·9[l]

Notes and Sources: [a] Good Fermented cocoa was any cocoa which, in the judgement of European buyers or officials or, after 1929, government produce inspectors, has been 'properly' fermented and dried; Fair Average Quality referred to all other cocoa. Buyers would generally pay a premium for cocoa judged to be 'good fermented'. [b] Ondo Province, Annual Report, 1926. [c] Lagos price, £16·2, minus transport cost from Ondo, £12·5. *Trade Supplement to the Nigeria Gazette,* 1924; G. Walker, *Traffic and Transport in Nigeria,* Colonial Research Studies No. 27 (London, 1959); 'Correspondence Concerning Railway Freight on Cocoa', CSO 26/16570 (NAI). [d] Lagos price minus average of transport costs from Okeigbo, Igunshin, and Bolorunduro to Lagos. Transport costs from Okeigbo and Bolorunduro equal lorry fares to Ilesha plus price differential between Ilesha and Lagos. Transport cost from Igunshin equals cost of headloading to Okitipupa plus price differential between Okitipupa and Lagos. Data from *Trade Supplement to the Nigeria Gazette,* and 'File on Grading and Inspection of Produce', CSO 26/50480 (NAI). [e] Lagos price minus transport cost from Ondo, *Trade Supplement to the Nigeria Gazette,* and Ondo Province, Annual Report, 1926. [f] Lagos price minus transport cost from Ondo. Walker; 'Correspondence Concerning Railway Freight on Cocoa'; Ondo Province, Annual Report, 1927. [g] Department of Agriculture, Annual Report, 1929. [h] *Trade Supplement to the Nigeria Gazette.* [i] FAQ plus average premium at Ilesha of £5·5. 'File on Grading and Inspection of Produce'. [j] FAQ plus average premium at Ondo of £2. Ondo Province, Annual Report, 1931. [k] Ondo Province, Annual Report, 1931. [l] Ondo Province, Annual Report, 1933.

Nigeria had stressed the need for better transport facilities to develop the industry: 'To our knowledge there are areas of cocoa in this region [i.e. Ondo Province] which are harvested in some years and not in others, according to the price, or according to whether any travelling middleman goes round them.'[49] In 1925 and 1926 the

[48] Ondo Province, Annual Report, 1927.
[49] Comments by the Director of Agriculture on a Memorandum by the General

price in Lagos rose to about £16 or £18 for cocoa of fair average quality (FAQ), and more people could afford the lorry fare to Oshogbo. In 1927 the price increased again, and in December the road was opened to Agbabu, cutting transport costs by anything from £4 to £8 per ton and raising the price in Ondo to almost £50.

The effect of these developments on the economy of Ondo was dramatic. Farmers who had left their cocoa pods to rot a few years earlier now rushed to plant more trees. European merchant firms set up branches in Ondo itself to purchase cocoa and palm kernels and dispense imported goods to the *nouveaux riches*.[50] The Department of Agriculture complained that farmers paid less attention to proper fermentation of their cocoa because of 'the simple fact that when a man who had been used to getting £20 a ton for his cocoa is suddenly offered £50 a ton, he begins to regard a premium of £5 . . . as much less important than he did before'.[51]

Finally, the soaring prices of the late 1940s and early 1950s undoubtedly helped to bring about the massive influx of northern Yorubas to Ife, Ilesha, and Ondo. There is also evidence that high prices encouraged many local people to expand their farms or even to invest in cocoa growing for the first time.[52] In Ibadan, on the other hand, uncultivated land was already scarce by this time, and there is no evidence that plantings increased substantially during this period. In general, then, it appears that the rate of planting did increase when prices rose, both because higher prices led to optimistic expectations about future returns to cocoa and because increased receipts from established farms provided a greater supply of funds for new investment. To this extent, the historical evidence on Nigeria does conform to others' findings about the 'price responsiveness' of West African cocoa farmers in the post-World War II period.

On the other hand, in some areas of Western Nigeria farmers also embarked on new investment in cocoa farms during periods of falling cocoa prices. The most dramatic instances of such apparently 'perverse' economic behaviour occurred in the 1930s. At that time the rate of plantings rose substantially in Ondo Province (and,

---

Manager of the Railway, 13 Feb. 1926 in 'Correspondence Concerning Railway Freight on Cocoa', CSO 26/16570 (NAI). Cf. above, p. 55, n. 3.

[50] Ondo Province, Annual Report, 1927.

[51] Department of Agriculture, *Annual Report*, 1926.

[52] See below, p. 123.

to a lesser extent in Abeokuta and Ijebu Provinces) despite the fact that farmers' terms of trade fell sharply from 1927–8 to 1931, and remained relatively depressed until after World War II, except for a short recovery in 1936–7. (See Fig. 1 and Appendix III.) Moreover, as we have seen, towards the end of the 1930s, the first migrant farmers began moving towards Ife and opening the way for the rapid expansion of plantings there after the war.

At first it may seem paradoxical that the depression—which in the wealthy, industrialized economies of Europe and North America involved drastic declines in investment and massive increases in unemployment—should have been associated with agricultural expansion in Western Nigeria. However, this result is not so surprising when viewed in the context of changing economic opportunities outside cocoa farming and of Nigeria's colonial economic structure at that time. The principal economic activities in Nigeria in the 1930s were agriculture and commerce; industry was virtually non-existent and the public sector fairly small.[53] The international depression of the 1930s affected the Nigerian economy primarily through its external trade. World prices of all Nigerian export commodities fell sharply, with corresponding reductions in Nigeria's foreign exchange earnings and capacity to purchase imports. 'Between 1929 and 1931, the value of Nigerian exports plummeted from £17·8 million to £8·8 million, the purchasing power of exports dropped by 38 percent, and the value of imports fell from £13·2 million in 1929 to £6·5 million.'[54] Incomes of Nigerian traders and export producers declined, and their demand for domestic as well as imported commodities fell accordingly, leading to declining incomes for people who produced for domestic markets as well. At the same time, the colonial administration in Nigeria was forced to cut its expenditures, both because the depression hurt its major source of revenue—customs duties—and because the British government was less disposed than ever to subsidize the colonies. As a result, many government employees were laid off.[55]

Although incomes and spending declined throughout the Nigerian economy, there is little evidence that this led to large-scale unemployment. Instead, ex-government workers and traders whose businesses failed because of the depression tended to move into

[53] See, e.g., G. K. Helleiner, *Peasant Agriculture, Government and Economic Growth in Nigeria*, ch. 1.
[54] Ibid., p. 18.   [55] Oyemakinde, op. cit.

E C R W N—D

agriculture, where they could provide themselves with at least a subsistence income. One official report of this period refers to a ' "Back to the land" drift of unemployed clerks, artisans, etc., who are now growing their own foodstuffs',[56] and others noted that the supplies of, for example, palm kernels offered to European trading firms increased in the early 1930s, despite declining prices. In Ondo an official attributed the increased supply of palm produce to labourers released by timber concerns which were forced to close because of the depression.[57]

The tendency to move into farming was not confined to unskilled labourers and petty traders who lost their jobs or sales because of the depression. In Ibadan, for example, J. A. Obisesan, who had worked as a railway clerk and then as an agent for different European trading firms, was forced to close his shop with the United Africa Company in 1930 because of financial difficulties. He began to spend increasing amounts of time on his farms where he discovered that closer supervision improved the efficiency of his labourers. He became quite proud of his accomplishments as a farmer, remarking once in his diary that 'God loves me much. A man without any means . . . [does] farm work like a man possessing 100 souls.'[58] During this time, he also became increasingly concerned with cocoa marketing from the farmers' point of view and began to organize what eventually became the Cooperative Produce Marketing Society of Western Nigeria.

I heard a similar story about a produce buyer in Ife, named Jones Adeyeye, whose business suffered during the depression. In 1934, when 'there was no other work for him', he settled down to farm on his family's land near what is now Omifunfun in south-eastern Ife Division. He soon recognized the advantages to be derived from giving out land to the strangers who were beginning to come to Ife in order to plant cocoa. In fact, he did not wait for prospective tenants to seek him out, but went to Bajepade at Aye-Oba to recruit them. When his tenants began to prosper from the cocoa they planted on his land, Adeyeye also planted cocoa for himself. His efforts were eminently successful. When he died in 1969, he had six cocoa farms of his own and his family are now the principal land-holders at Omifunfun, where they have hundreds of tenants. The careers of men such as Obisesan and Adeyeye suggest, in other words, that

---

[56] Ilorin Province, Annual Report, 1932.
[57] Ondo Province, Annual Report, 1931.   [58] J. A. Obisesan, Diary, 1 Sept. 1934.

during the depression not only unskilled labour but also a certain amount of entrepreneurial talent may have moved into agriculture from trade and government employment.

Moreover, for farmers in the forest belt of Western Nigeria, cocoa remained a relatively attractive economic crop.[59] For one thing, cocoa farms planted in the late 1920s came into bearing during the early 30s, so that farmers' incomes did not decline so much as the price of cocoa. Moreover, prices of alternative crops fell too: from 1927 to 1934, the unit export value of cocoa fell 67 per cent, while those of palm kernels, rubber, and cotton fell 69 per cent, 78 per cent, and 53 per cent respectively.[60] Since cotton is grown mainly in the drier parts of Western Nigeria and yields considerably lower absolute returns than cocoa even today, when cocoa yields are lower than in the past, it seems unlikely that farmers had much incentive to switch from cocoa to cotton during this period. In other words, the opportunity cost of growing cocoa probably declined as much if not more than the real price, so that the crop remained relatively attractive to farmers.

It also appears from contemporary records that the depression may have enhanced the relative advantages of farming in the forest belt as opposed to the savannah areas of Yorubaland. Official reports of the 1920s indicate that northern Yorubaland produced mainly foodstuffs and handicrafts which were sold in the urban markets of southern and, to some extent, northern Nigeria.[61] Foreign trading firms in Ilorin purchased shea nuts and some groundnuts and cotton, but, in general, farmers found yam and guinea corn more remunerative than these export crops and hence preferred to grow them.[62] During the depression, however, southern demand for foodstuffs 'imported' from savannah areas appears to have declined—both because income fell and because more people took up farming and grew their own food crops. As a result, prices fell and, by 1933, the export of foodstuffs from Ilorin Province had practically ceased.[63] Expatriate firms' purchases of exportable crops had also dwindled to almost nothing by 1932 and 1933. (See Tables III. 5 and III. 6.) In short, the possibilities for earning cash income were so poor north of the forest belt in the 1930s that growing cocoa

[59] See Appendix I.
[60] Helleiner, p. 19.
[61] Ilorin and Oyo Provinces, Annual Report, 1920s.
[62] Ilorin Province, Annual Report, 1929 and 1939.
[63] Ilorin Province, Annual Report, 1933.

TABLE III.5

Price Indices of some Staple Foodstuffs

	Lagos			Ilorin	
Year	Yam	Maize	Plantain	Yam	Guinea corn
1927–9	100	100	100	100	100
1930	94	86	151	67–71	80
1931	94	86	151	33–56	18–26
1932	31	86	142	12–26	8–17
1933	31	75	57		
1934	31	75	57		
1935–8	31	69	57		

Sources: Southern Nigeria, *Bluebooks*; Ilorin Province, Annual Reports.

TABLE III.6

Goods Purchased by Foreign Firms In Ilorin Province (tons)

Year	Palm kernels	Cotton	Groundnuts	Shea nuts
1924	502	354	—	290
1925	565	175	—	1,882
1926	693	257	256	2,065
1927	824	230	434	374
1928	563	181	806	1,890
1927/8		281	657	1,795
1928/9		405	430 (638)	1,538
1929/30		—	—	—
1930/1		—	122	1,279
1931/2		99	36	931
1932/3		29	188	619
1933/4		60	182	400

Source: Compiled from Ilorin Province, Annual Reports.

in the south may have appeared more attractive than ever to northern Yorubas, despite the steep decline in cocoa prices.

Finally, the fact that farmers did not have to depend on the market and on accumulated cash savings in order to establish or maintain cocoa farms meant that they could undertake new planting even at a time when the absolute returns to cocoa growing were very low and there were few opportunities to accumulate savings in other occupations. In commenting on returns to established cocoa farms in the 1930s, C. D. Forde noted that

For the cocoa grower who works his own farm with only supplementary hired labour, the reward, even at low prices, has probably been somewhat greater than he would have received if he had devoted his labour to a corresponding production of food crops or oil-palm products for sale. But for the farmer . . . who has depended on hired labour and has made payment for land, these prices have involved a loss.[64]

Similarly, even the establishment of new farms seems to have remained a relatively attractive undertaking for farmers who relied largely on non-market resources throughout the great depression.

Such considerations could conceivably help to explain the steady increase in plantings in Ibadan and Oyo Provinces during and after World War I, when farmers' terms of trade also underwent a prolonged decline. Evidence on this period is too scanty to warrant firm conclusions; the data on plantings may themselves be less accurate than those for later periods, since they are based on farmers' estimates of the age of their trees in the 1940s, and memories of planting dates may have been less precise for older farms. Information on opportunity costs in this period is also limited, but what we have does not indicate corresponding declines in the prices of other crops or in income-earning opportunities in other sectors which would have maintained the relative attractiveness of cocoa.[65] However, in so far as farmers relied on non-market resources to cover the costs of planting and operating their cocoa farms, even complete data on market costs and returns to cocoa growing and alternative activities would not necessarily account for observed trends in planting or output.

Conclusion

The widely accepted notion that the growth of export crop production in West Africa since the late nineteenth century was due to

[64] Forde and Scott, p. 98. Forde assumes that only farmers with large cocoa holdings would use mainly hired labour or 'make payments for land', and concludes that the effect of low prices during the depression was 'to discourage the development of . . . large units and to restrict cocoa growing to small-scale production auxiliary to subsistence farming' (ibid.). There is, however, no necessary association between farm size and method of financial operation. In my experience, farmers with large holdings may have even greater access to non-market sources of labour and credit than small-scale farmers. (See, e.g., Obisesan's diaries.) Also, there is no reason to assume that cocoa growing is an 'auxiliary' activity for men with small farms. Thus, in absence of direct evidence, Forde's conclusion seems unwarranted.

[65] Between 1912 and 1916 the price of rubber fell relative to that of cocoa, but prices of other exportable crops did not and, in the next two years, the price of cocoa declined while all others were rising. The cocoa price increased sharply in the post-war boom, but collapsed again in 1921; only the price of cotton was affected more severely by the recession of that year. Data on prices of domestic foodstuffs are scanty; there is no reason to think they increased relative to the price of cocoa since, by 1917, British officials in Ibadan were complaining of 'a growing tendency to neglect foodstuffs in favour of cocoa' in the south-eastern part of the Division (Ibadan Division, Annual Report, 1917). But there is no evidence that food farming became less attractive relative to cocoa in this period either.

the employment of previously idle land and labour in response to increased external market opportunities does not fully explain the development of cocoa growing in Western Nigeria. Clearly, the spread of cocoa production did involve bringing unused land under cultivation and may have entailed some sacrifice of leisure. However, the cost of labour employed in establishing cocoa farms was not zero; would-be cocoa growers had to mobilize working capital in some form, to maintain themselves and/or remunerate others whose labour services they employed during the lengthy gestation period of a young cocoa farm. Thus, the growth of cocoa output in Western Nigeria required more than two factors of production and probably entailed some reallocation of resources from alternative productive activities.

Furthermore, in the case of cocoa, it is not clear that exports grew solely in response to expanding market opportunities. Available data indicate a rather weak relationship between trends in acres planted and farmers' terms of trade. In particular, there were periods in recent Western Nigerian history when investment in new cocoa farms proceeded at a high or rising rate despite a steady downward trend in the 'real' price of cocoa.

Such periods do not, however, necessarily reflect perverse or irrational economic behaviour on the part of Nigerian farmers. The rate of investment in new cocoa farms must be examined in the context of alternative economic opportunities and institutional mechanisms for resource mobilization available to Western Nigerian farmers at various times. Since most farmers had to move into areas where there was suitable land in order to grow cocoa, the process of investment in new farms was closely associated with migration. And, in establishing themselves in new surroundings, migrant farmers often relied on their participation in such 'non-economic' institutions as the lineage or ethnic community for economic support and assistance—especially with providing working capital, insurance, and, as I shall show in Chapter V, labour services.

Since the mobilization of potential savings and investment of these resources in agricultural ventures took place partly through non-market channels, information on market costs and returns will not necessarily suffice to explain patterns of investment or output. Indeed, in so far as farmers relied more heavily on non-market resources in some periods or geographical areas than in others, the relationship between market prices and production or investment decisions would also tend to vary from one situation to another. Since it seems likely that farmers would turn to non-market institutions in just those circumstances where market opportunities were limited, there is no reason to expect that agricultural output or investment would decline in periods of falling market prices. And the available evidence suggests that, in the 1930s anyway, new investment occurred in the Western Nigerian cocoa economy precisely because other income-earning opportunities were curtailed and because farmers did not need substantial monetary resources to maintain or expand their cocoa farms.

CHAPTER IV

Cocoa and the Commercialization
of Rural Land Tenure

THE spread of cocoa cultivation in Western Nigeria has affected not
only migration and the character of Yoruba villages, but also patterns
of rural land tenure in the cocoa belt. Although the spread of cocoa
growing involved the extension of the 'traditional' Yoruba farming
system into the forests surrounding the towns, it also brought about
substantial changes in established methods of exchanging rights to
land and in the distribution of rural land-holdings. Broadly speaking,
these changes involved relationships between different groups of
people who exerted or claimed to exert various rights to rural land
in the cocoa belt. The rising demand for good cocoa land has tended
to commercialize relations between land-holders and land-users, but
this process is still far from complete. It cannot yet be said that there
is a landowning class in rural Western Nigeria whose economic power
and interests are markedly different from those of the rest of the
population, nor does there appear to be a clear-cut pattern of stratification along ethnic lines with respect to the terms on which land
may be obtained for cocoa growing. In the areas I studied, most
farmers have been able to acquire the right to plant cocoa on similar
terms, regardless of their ethnic background.[1] However, in some areas
the presence of large numbers of 'stranger' farmers from other city-
states has apparently accentuated the commercialization of relations
between land-holders and land-users.

The Development of Tenancy[2]

Before the introduction of cocoa, the ownership of farmland in
most Yoruba city-states was vested in patrilineages (*idile*). Any male

[1] As was pointed out in Chapter III, few non-Yorubas have obtained land for
planting cocoa, but this appears to be the result of their inability to finance cocoa
farms rather than any outright prohibition against granting land to non-Yoruba
strangers.
[2] Some of the effects of cocoa on rural land tenure are briefly discussed in P. C.
Lloyd, 'Some Problems of Tenancy in Yoruba Land Tenure', *African Studies*, 12, 3
(Sept. 1953), pp. 93–103.

member of the lineage had the right to farm on a piece of the lineage's land, but could not dispose of the land without the consent of the rest of its members. If a lineage grew too big for its farmland, individual members would have to seek land from other lineages. Permission was usually granted to outsiders (*alejo* or 'strangers' to the lineage in question) on condition that the latter acknowledge the grantor lineage's superior claim to the land by annual gifts or contributions of produce (*ishakole*), and obey the authority of the lineage head. If the stranger decided to settle permanently with the new lineage, he was gradually absorbed into it, often through marriage. In that case, he could pass his farmland on to his children, but could not alienate it. (Neither could any individual member of the lineage, without the consent of the others.) These rules were 'not so much concerned with rights in land as with immigration; a grant of land to a stranger suggests that he is planning to settle permanently in the community and it is for the leaders of the community to accede to this proposal; they may deny the right of permanent settlement to any person suspected of hostile intentions or of bad character.'[3]

Although these generalizations were broadly applicable to most Yoruba communities, the actual pattern of landownership and rules for acquiring rights to use land varied considerably from one city-state to another.[4] In Ibadan the importance of lineage rights to and control of rural land was, if anything, strengthened by the manner in which the town was founded. The warriors and their followers who gathered there in the 1830s joined forces to ward off common enemies, but each maintained a jealous watch over his own family's position and prerogatives within Ibadan society, including their exclusive right to the land they had seized when they settled there. The importance which lineages attached to these rights is manifested in their insistence—right up to the present day—on collecting *isha-kole* from strangers farming on their lands. Many of the cases heard

---

[3] P. C. Lloyd, *Yoruba Land Law*, pp. 64–5. My brief discussion of the ownership and transfer of rights to rural land in Yoruba communities before the advent of cocoa hardly does justice to the extensive research which has been done on the subject. For more detailed discussions, see Lloyd, *Yoruba Land Law* and 'Some Problems of Tenancy'; W. Bascom, 'Urbanization Among the Yoruba', *American Journal of Sociology*, 60, 5 (Mar. 1955), pp. 446–54; C. W. Rowling, *Report on Land Tenure in Ondo Province* (1952), and *Land Tenure in Ijebu Province* (Ibadan, 1956); H. L. Ward Price, *Land Tenure in the Yoruba Provinces* (Lagos, 1939). All future references to Lloyd in this chapter are to his *Yoruba Land Law*, unless otherwise specified.

[4] I mention here local peculiarities of land tenure in only three city-states—Ibadan, Ife, and Ondo—which I have studied myself. On other areas of Yorubaland, see especially Lloyd and Ward Price.

by the Ibadan Lands Court since its establishment in 1936 have concerned either farmers' failure to pay *ishakole* to the 'owners' of their
land or disputes between different families over the right to receive
ishakole from people farming in a particular area. Ife and Ondo, on
the other hand, are older communities in which there is no history
of recent settlement by conquest. In both communities the *oba* holds
all land in trust for the whole community. In Ife, the Oni may allocate unoccupied portions of land to individuals or lineages who
thereby become the owners of the land, with the exclusive right to
allot portions of it to others and to receive *ishakole* from them.
However, he may not interfere with land already held by a lineage
nor may he reclaim land once he has allotted it, unless it had been
abandoned for a long period. It strengthens a lineage's claim to title
over a piece of land if it can show that the land was originally allocated to its ancestors by an Oni, but this is not necessary to establish
ownership.[5]

In Ondo, families have also settled in particular areas, with the
permission of the Oshemawe, and farmed there for generations, but
the land is not considered lineage property. According to P. C.
Lloyd, many Ondos deny that family land exists in rural areas:
'By this they do not mean to deny the right of a man to continue to
farm where his father farmed, but they wish to emphasize that a man
is not *confined* to farming where his father and grandfathers farmed,
and that past cultivation of a piece of land gives no permanent
rights in the land.'[6] A family may continue to use a piece of land as
long as it likes and may divide it among its members in any way it
wishes. However, 'the descent group has theoretically, no power to
alienate its land to non-members . . .'[7] In an interview with the
District Commissioner in 1913, the Oshemawe stated that there was
'individual ownership' of land, but then apparently contradicted
himself by asserting that all land belonged to the Oshemawe, even
when individuals were using it. He went on to explain that an Ondo
man could only obtain unoccupied rural land by permission of the
Oshemawe but, once he began to use a piece of land, no one could
deprive him of it. In general, 'As the head is to a man's body, so is
the Oshemawe to the Ondos, what belongs to a man's hand or foot
belongs to the head—what belongs to the head belongs to the foot

[5] In six of the twenty villages I visited in the Ife area, informants said that the founder of the village did not obtain the Oni's permission to settle there.
[6] Lloyd, p. 111.   [7] Ibid., p. 130.

or hand—but the head is the most honourable portion and directs the remainder of the body.'[8]

Under such circumstances, one would not expect to find one Ondo paying *ishakole* to another so long as uncultivated rural land was readily available, since an Ondo who wanted additional farmland could presumably always obtain it without seeking permission from another lineage.[9] Many of the farmers I interviewed, especially in the major cocoa-growing area along the Akure Road, betwen Ondo town and the Owena River, in fact declared that the 'system of *ishakole* does not exist in Ondo' and that, apart from a small gift to the Oshemawe's representative when he first showed them land for farming, they paid nothing to anyone for the right to farm there. In some areas the Oshemawe appointed a chief to oversee the allocation of rural land to new settlers,[10] but his function seems to have been mainly one of ensuring that the process of settlement was reasonably orderly. He received no money from the settlers and exerted no authority over their lands once they began to farm them. All of the farmers I interviewed about the early development of cocoa farming in their own villages said that they or their fathers had acquired land for growing cocoa without paying anything for it. About one-fourth of them had planted cocoa on land inherited from relatives or granted them by close friends; most of the others had been given land by the Oshemawe or someone representing him; a few simply stated that they had planted on 'Ondo land', referring to their right as Ondos to farm anywhere they liked in Ondo territory.[11]

In other areas, however, where Ondo families have farmed for a long time, some Ondo farmers apparently do consider themselves 'tenants' of the first family to have settled there. In one recent case the customary court rejected the claim of such a 'tenant' to ownership of the land on which his cocoa farm was planted;[12] in another, the customary court ordered the eviction of an Ondo tenant for

[8] WALC, *Papers and Correspondence*, p. 209.
[9] Lloyd, pp. 110–11, 133.
[10] For example, Chief Lodasha of Oboto served as the Oshemawe's representative in the area from Oboto to the Owena River when that area was opened up for cocoa cultivation in the late 1920's and early 1930s. In all of the villages I visited in that area, people said that the first settlers there got permission to settle from Chief Lodasha; later arrivals usually obtained permission from the *bale* of the village where they decided to stay. Cf. Lloyd, p. 132.
[11] In subordinate towns, such as Igunshin, Odigbo, Oro, or Ile-Oluji, the *oloja* showed newcomers from Ondo town where to farm as part of admitting them to the community, and usually received a gift of drinks, kola nuts, or a little cash in return. Cf. Lloyd, p. 127.
[12] Ondo Grade B Customary Court Records, 209/65. Cf. cases 78/59, 155/59.

falsely claiming ownership of land at Adepa, near Igbindo.[13] In such cases the tenant does give something annually to the family who gave him permission to farm, but the amount is nominal—usually five shillings or a few yams.

The advent of cocoa farming tended to modify methods and costs of acquiring rights to farmland, but it did not completely disrupt the old system. In Ibadan the hunters who initially acted as guides to farmers seeking land in the forest areas subsequently began to claim rights of ownership over the lands they showed to others, receiving initial presents (*ishagi*) and often *ishakole* from settlers in their respective areas. In exchange for these 'gifts', the settlers acquired the right to plant permanent crops or, in some cases, permanent crops already planted, rather than the land itself. Even after the advent of cocoa, the land-holding family retained the right to dispose of the land and could reclaim it if the tenant abandoned it, although they could not evict a tenant or the tenant's children except for antisocial behaviour.[14] As before, the annual payment of *ishakole* served primarily as a token or acknowledgement of the land-holder's ultimate claim to the property, rather than as a form of rent, in the economic sense of that word.

By the time of World War I, the Ibadan hunters had shown land to hundreds of farmers, who could not be readily absorbed into the hunters' lineages in the 'traditional' manner. As Lloyd points out, customary rules concerning relations between a community head and a stranger treated the latter primarily as an immigrant and only incidentally as a user of land. But in the early twentieth century Ibadans moved into the southern forests, not to join or to conquer new communities, but to acquire a particular type of land for economic exploitation. Thus, although relations between these farmers and the families asserting prior claim to the forest areas retained some of the characteristics of the traditional dependent relationship between a Yoruba lineage head and strangers on the lineage's land, in some respects they came to resemble the predominantly economic relationship between landowner and tenant generally found in societies where cultivable land has long been a relatively scarce factor of production.

[13] Ondo Grade B Customary Court Records, 18/59.
[14] WALC, *Minutes of Evidence*, question 14,861; Lloyd, p. 91. This practice still holds and tends to render a tenant's position fairly secure. The Ibadan Lands Court, for example, has consistently upheld tenants' rights to cultivate farms they planted as long as they committed no crimes and continued to pay *ishakole*. See below, p. 101, n. 39.

The transitional nature of the relationships between land-holders and land-users in the cocoa-farming areas of Ibadan (and other parts of Western Nigeria) is reflected both in the terms people use to talk about them and in the nature of the land-holder's and land-user's obligations to one another. Yorubas often refer to tenants as *alejo* (strangers), but this term may also refer to strangers who have no rights to land at all. Moreover, the term *alejo* does not distinguish between someone who is not a member of the lineage (*omo idile*) and someone who comes from another city-state (i.e. who is not *omo Ibadan*), although in some cases this distinction affects the terms on which a stranger may obtain land.[15] Alternatively, a tenant farmer may be denominated *olori oko* (head or owner of the farm), because he owns the crops he has planted, but this term may also be used to refer to the landowner! In this study I shall follow the practice of English-speaking Yorubas and use the terms 'landowner' and 'tenant', but must ask the reader to bear in mind that they do not mean quite the same thing in Western Nigeria as they do in other societies.

The form and amount of *ishakole* which tenants pay to their land-owners also illustrate the changing relationships between them, and these also may be associated with the spread of cocoa. In Ibadan *ishakole* consisted originally of a small annual gift of produce—a few yams or a tin of palm oil—or of occasional labour service on the landowner's own farms. In his evidence to the West African Lands Committee, F. E. Morakinyo stated that his father did not require any specific payment from farmers to whom he gave land, but the 'tenants willingly rendered him any help they thought right'. For example, 'they helped us when we put up our father's house'.[16] Another hunter's son, Chief J. Akinpelu Obisesan, referred frequently in his diary to services rendered him by his family's tenants. These ranged from hospitality offered him when he visited their villages to contributions to his family's festivities or labour on his cocoa farms.[17] In judging land disputes involving landowners and their tenants, the Ibadan Lands Court often referred to the tenants' obligation to 'serve' the landowner every year, either with gifts of palm oil or by actually working for him.[18] Similarly, a number of the farmers

---

[15] See Chapter V, below.
[16] WALC, *Papers*, p. 203.
[17] Obisesan, Diary, 1 Jan. 1921, 19 Apr. 1930, 7 Sept. 1932.
[18] Ibadan Lands Court Records 72/37, 74/37, 88/37, 84/37, 42/37, 134/52; Ibadan Native Court Records 1048/11.

whom I interviewed stated that they gave annual presents of food-stuffs to the owner of their farmlands.

Often, however, tenants paid *ishakole* in cash. This practice appears to be an old one in the Ibadan cocoa-farming areas. Informants whose fathers had begun planting cocoa around the turn of the century stated that they had always paid *ishakole* in cash, and cash payments of *ishakole* were stipulated in judgements by the Ibadan Native Court as early as 1914.[19] Farmers who acquired land south of Ibadan for planting cocoa after World War I almost invariably paid *ishakole* in cash rather than in kind. Nevertheless, *ishakole* has not evolved into an economic rent in Ibadan. Usually the amount is nominal—five or ten shillings per farmer—and remains fixed over time.[20] In some cases, *ishakole* is paid by a village as a whole rather than by individual farmers, but the amount rarely exceeds five shillings and bears no necessary relation to the economic resources of the village. Similarly, variations in the amounts paid by individual farmers are not usually associated with differences in the size or productivity of their farms.

Before cocoa growing became widespread in Ife, an outsider or an Ife farmer seeking land from another lineage could obtain it with little difficulty. When asked what strangers had to pay in order to use land in Ife, the Osho Eremese told the West African Lands Committee: 'It is not that they pay anything. Whenever they wish to give anything they give it, but they are not made to pay for the use of land.'[21] Even in the 1920s, when many Ife farmers took up cocoa and began to move further into the forests to plant it, they rarely paid either an initial amount or regular *ishakole* to the family from whom they obtained permission to farm. Sometimes they simply settled in an uncultivated area, without obtaining permission from anyone or after 'informing' the Oni of their intention.[22] Uncultivated forest land was sufficiently abundant for even jurisdictional disputes to have little sense of urgency about them. In settling one such dispute in 1929 the Oni's chief concern was not to husband or share equitably a scarce resource but to keep the peace: 'I do not

---

[19] Ibadan Native Court Records 163/14. Today farmers in the Ibadan area distinguish between land acquired for planting tree crops (*ra*) and land acquired with the right to plant food crops only (*toro*). In the latter case, *ishakole* is still often a small gift of produce rather than a cash payment.

[20] A. Obisesan to District Officer, Ibadan, 31 May 1918, in OYOPROF 4/5/12, and interviews in a number of Ibadan villages.   [21] WALC, *Minutes*, question 13,460.

[22] Among the villages I visited, such was the case in Olope, Egbejoda, Ijipade, Omifunfun, Oniperegun, Ifetedo, Abanata, and Amula Soji.

want quarrel among these people, if anyone does not get land I should give him.'[23]

However, in the next decade the continued spread of cocoa cultivation in Ife, which was accelerated by the arrival of would-be cocoa farmers from other Yoruba communities, began to influence the terms on which farmers could obtain land for planting cocoa. Within the next twenty or so years a system of tenancy developed in Ife which was more exclusively economic in character and retained fewer of the social and personal aspects of the traditional relationship between lineage head and stranger than the system of tenancy we have observed in Ibadan.

The early immigrants to Ife usually obtained land for planting cocoa in exchange for a small present to the head of the landowning family (e.g. a cutlass or two, salt, drinks, and/or a small sum of money—usually less than £1 per acre) and a promise to pay *ishakole* annually. In Ife, as in Ibadan, the payment of *ishakole* signified that the payer did not own the land in question, but used it only by permission of the individual or family to whom he paid *ishakole*. Also, especially in the early days of cocoa growing in Ife, the amount of *ishakole* bore little relation to the amount of land allotted to a stranger. Usually a landowning family asked the same amount of *ishakole* from each tenant regardless of how much land he cultivated (often the land was not even measured or boundaries clearly marked), but if a tenant acquired additional plots of land he was usually expected to pay additional *ishakole*.

However, the collection of *ishakole* in Ife differed from that in Ibadan in one important respect. In Ibadan the amount of *ishakole* was nominal—a small gift of produce or, later, a little cash—rarely more than five shillings per tenant. In Ife strangers paid a nominal amount at first, but *once their cocoa trees began to bear marketable amounts of fruit*, the amount increased significantly. Thus, a tenant might give a few yams each year to the owner(s) of his land until his cocoa began to yield. Thereafter, he paid a certain amount of dried cocoa—one hundredweight (112 lbs.) is the amount one most frequently encounters, although two quarters (56 lbs.) is not uncommon—or its equivalent value in cash every year for as long as he continued to use the farm.[24] If a tenant transferred his farm to

[23] Ife Customary Court Records, 420/29; cf. the Oshemawe's statement to the West African Lands Committee, quoted pp. 92–3, above.

[24] Sometimes the amount of *ishakole* is stipulated in cash—e.g. £2. 10s. or £5 per tenant per annum. However, it is usually stated in kind, so that the value fluctuates from year to year with changes in the price of cocoa.

someone else, through inheritance, pawning, or sale, the new owner would continue to pay *ishakole* to the landowner.

I do not know the origin of the system of fixing the amount of *ishakole* in terms of a certain weight of dried cocoa, but it does seem to have been associated with the arrival of the first immigrant cocoa farmers from northern Yorubaland in the 1930s. All of the immigrants I interviewed who had planted cocoa or purchased established cocoa farms paid *ishakole* in this manner and said that they (or their fathers) had done so since they first came to Ife.[25] In the period of high cocoa prices following World War II, a hundredweight of cocoa came to be worth quite a bit of money and Ife families with many tenants grew wealthy in a short time. However, when the system of paying two quarters or one hundredweight of cocoa as *ishakole* began in the 1930s, the price of cocoa was so low that the value of these quantities was usually less than £1. Thus, tenant farmers in Ife paid little more than their counterparts in Ibadan, whose *ishakole* was usually fixed at five or ten shillings in cash. Since the immigrant farmers came to Ife explicitly to grow cocoa, it may have been felt that their *ishakole* should be directly related to their cocoa farming; in any case, it is difficult to argue from the available evidence that the Ife system of *ishakole* was initially designed to extract a sizeable rent from non-Ife farmers. Indeed, it was soon applied to all tenant cocoa farmers, Ifes and non-Ifes alike.

In recent years the practice of collecting a substantial amount of *ishakole* on bearing cocoa farms has also begun to spread to Ondo, as migrant cocoa farmers have pushed eastward from Ife in search of more uncultivated forest land. As in Ife, the *ishakole* is usually fixed in terms of dried cocoa and tends to be one hundredweight or less per annum. In some areas this is beginning to create lineage rights in rural land similar to those which obtain in Ibadan and Ife.[26] Strangers are shown land by an Ondo family farming in the area and they then pay an initial amount plus *ishakole* to that family.[27]

[25] There are also men, both strangers and Ifes, who 'lease' cocoa farms temporarily and maintain and harvest them in exchange for a cash payment or a share of the crop, but these men are considered labourers, not tree-owning farmers. See Chapter VI below.

[26] On occasion, the courts have recognized uncultivated rural land as family property in Ondo (Ondo Grade B Customary Court Records 258/62, 209/65, 201/64, 18/59). The recent development of 'family land' in Ondo should be distinguished from family ownership of cocoa trees which has existed in Ondo, as elsewhere, since cocoa farmers first began bequeathing tree crops to their heirs. See below, pp. 101–2.

[27] Interviews in Idi Iroko, Okeigbo, and Omifon; also Ondo Grade B Customary Court Records 038/61, 96/59, 284/62, 201/64, 192/62, 45/67.

In other cases they have obtained land from the chief (*oloja*) of a subordinate town and sometimes pay *ishakole* to him or his representative.[28] Often, however, this *ishakole* is voluntary; in Orotedo, for example, most farmers refused to pay. The Oshemawe has sometimes attempted to assert that it is his customary right to collect *ishakole* from all strangers farming on Ondo land, but individual families have resisted such attempts.[29]

As the economic value of *ishakole* has increased with the spread of cocoa cultivation, its non-economic implications have declined in importance. Historically, the payment of *ishakole* carried with it overtones of the tenant's social subordination to or dependence on the landowner. In Ibadan, as we have seen, tenants were often expected to perform labour service for the landowner and to join in his family's celebrations of marriages, funerals, chieftancy titles, etc. The landowner, in turn, was responsible for representing his tenants in community decisions, for settling disputes among them, and for seeing to their general welfare, in much the same way as a lineage head is responsible for the members of his compound. Obisesan's diary contains several references to his family's authority over its tenants: for example, 'Some of the Aperins believe stupidly that they are to govern and are not prepared to respect the dignity and personality of the men under their feudal authority. . . .'[30] The Ibadan Lands Court not only usually upheld landowners' claims to receive service or *ishakole* from their tenants but sometimes even specified that a tenant must not show hostility or arrogance or 'seem to make himself a man of high [*sic*] value than the grantor' of his land.[31] In some cases, the court refused to adjudicate at all, preferring to turn the matter over to the landowner to 'settle amicably at home'.[32] Many of these mutual obligations still exist between landowners and tenants in Ibadan villages. In most of the villages I visited in the Ibadan area, the head man (*bale*) was either a member of the principal landowning family in the area or an old and trusted tenant who could be relied upon to collect *ishakole* and to represent the landowners' interest in the village.

To some extent, the same conditions obtain in Ife and Ondo. In

[28] Interviews in Bamikemo, under Ile-Oluji, and Orotedo.
[29] Interviews with the Oshemawe, with Ipaiye's descendants, and with farmers in Oboto.
[30] Obisesan, Diary, 28 June 1935.
[31] Ibadan Lands Court Records 42/37; also 77/37 and Ibadan Native Court Records 1003/11, 342/14.
[32] Ibadan Native Court Records 12/14; Ibadan Lands Court Records 44/37.

Abanata, for example, the principal landowner in the area lived in the village and presided over its affairs as *bale*. During one of my visits to Omifon in Ondo, the tenants all went to Odigbo one morning to help their landowner launch the roofing of a new house. On the other hand, it is very unusual now for tenants to work on the landowner's farms without pay, although anyone who is short of cash may hire out his services temporarily to a neighbour—who may be the landowner or another tenant. Many Ife and Ondo landowners do not live in their villages and visit them only occasionally. Often the tenants govern themselves, with one of them serving as *bale*. In Ondo some tenants prefer to pay cash rather than participate directly in the landowner's family projects or ceremonies and others refuse to contribute anything at all. In settling disputes, the customary courts in Ife and Ondo rarely concern themselves with non-economic issues, such as the tenant's social behaviour or his attitude towards his landowner.

In general, the spread of cocoa cultivation in Western Nigeria has tended to distinguish the relationship between landowner and tenant from that between a lineage or village head and a stranger who wishes to settle in the community. The economic obligations of a tenant to his landowner have been regularized—the amount being explicitly agreed upon in advance—and related directly to the type of farming the tenant is engaged in. The mutual social obligations between landowner and tenant still exist, but appear to have declined in importance. These trends are most noticeable in areas where much of the recent increase in cocoa planting is attributable to immigrants from other parts of Yorubaland, but the terms of tenancy apply equally to local and immigrant farmers.

The Right to Transfer Landed Property: Inheritance, Pawning, and Sale

The spread of cocoa farming has also led to the development of a market in certain forms of landed property. In the case of cocoa and other economic tree crops, this development was a logical extension of existing practices. In all Yoruba communities, customary law distinguishes between land and man-made improvements on the land; the latter are considered to be the personal property of the individual(s) who made them.[33] Thus, a man who plants tree crops is considered the owner of the trees, whether or not he owns the land

---

[33] Lloyd, pp. 13, 82, 310, and discussions of particular communities.

on which they are planted. If an individual plants cocoa on land belonging to his lineage, the trees are his personal property.[34] Similarly, tenants own the trees they have planted. The customary courts have consistently upheld this principle, awarding the right to harvest tree crops to the individual who planted them or to those who could prove themselves the rightful heirs of the original planter.[35] In one Ibadan case (45/37), a cocoa farm was awarded to the owner of the land rather than to the man who planted the trees because the latter had never obtained the landowner's consent to plant cocoa in the first place. On another occasion a tenant in Ife was evicted for refusing to pay *ishakole* to the landowner, but the court ordered the landowner to compensate the tenant for his permanent crops.[36] In some instances the courts have explicitly stated that ownership of a piece of land did not imply ownership of tree crops planted on the land.[37]

The courts have also generally prevented landowners from evicting tenants unless the tenants either refused persistently to pay *ishakole* or committed a serious crime.[38] In one case the Ibadan Lands Court declared that a man could not be driven away from his cocoa farm for stealing or any other offence except that of trying to poison the *bale*.[39] Another time, the court pointed out the social value of upholding tenants' rights: 'In strict conformity with the Yoruba custom, once a piece of land or farmland is granted to a person, it, in the absence of any heinous crime, belongs to him forever. Violation of this hoary tradition renders everyone unsafe as every land was held of and granted by somebody.'[40]

If tree crops are the individual property of the man who planted them, then according to customary law the planter should be free to dispose of them as he wishes. In all of the areas I have studied, tenants are allowed to pass their cocoa farms on to their heirs according to customary law, whereby, unless a man specifies differently before he dies, his personal property is inherited jointly by his

[34] Ife Customary Court Records 74/68.
[35] Ibadan Lands Court Records 25/37, 33/37, 74/37, 64/37, 8/42, 75/45, 26/47, 74/48, 43/48, 104/48, 47/48, 142/49, 156/49, 36/59, L1/64, 134/52, 139/52, 44/55, 48/60; Ife Customary Court Records 15/48, 74/68, 86/69, 104/69; Ondo Grade B Customary Court Records 75/60, 103/59, 270/61, 270/59, 385/60, 172/64, 202/69.
[36] Ife Customary Court Records 1/51.
[37] Ibadan Lands Court Records 40/48, 88/49.
[38] Ibadan Lands Court Records 5/42, 47/39, 96/52, 139/52, 28/53, 141/50; Ife Customary Court Records 9/38.
[39] Ibadan Lands Court Records 68/37. Cf. 42/37, 104/48, 141/50.
[40] Ibadan Lands Court Records 104/48.

children. In this way, many cocoa farms have become family property over time.

Also, tenants may use their cocoa farms as security for loans. The practice of 'pawning' tree crops in exchange for a cash loan appears to be a development of the twentieth century, although the idea of pawning is much older in Yorubaland. Originally, individuals rather than farms were used as pawns (*iwofa*). When a man borrowed money he, or a junior relative, agreed to work for the creditor until the loan was repaid. The *iwofa*'s presence constituted security, his labour interest on the loan.[41] In 1913 a witness told the West African Lands Committee that a man could offer his farm as security for a debt but that this did not give the creditor the right to collect produce from the farm. Instead, if the borrower defaulted, the creditor had to get the local authorities to put pressure on the borrower by, for example, placing an aged man or woman in the debtor's compound. The debtor immediately became responsible for maintaining the old person; if the latter died in his house, the debtor and his relatives could be held responsible. In such circumstances, the debtor's relatives usually paid promptly.[42] It is not clear, in this case, whether the witness was referring to cocoa or to food farms. Usually, however, when a farm was pawned, the creditor had the right to reap the cocoa and keep the proceeds for himself until the loan was repaid. The proceeds were considered interest on the loan, as were the services of a human *iwofa*. In some cases, part of the proceeds from the farm could be counted towards repayment of the principal, although in Ibadan this may have been a fairly recent development.[43] In either case, however, the use of a farm as a pawn did not threaten the landowner's rights, since the creditor could not claim ownership of the farm; if the original borrower failed to repay the debt, his descendants could do so whenever they wished.

However, if a tenant wishes to sell his cocoa (or other) tree crops outright, the possibility arises that the buyer will some day claim title to the land as well as to the trees.[44] In Ondo, where lineages did not have strongly vested rights to particular rural areas until recently, this

[41] See Chapter VII, below.

[42] WALC, *Minutes*, questions 7,538–63. Cf. 'A Report on the Yoruba, 1910', ed. A. G. Hopkins, *Journal of the Historical Society of Nigeria*, 5, 1 (Dec. 1969), p. 91.

[43] The Ibadan Lands Court recognized the existence of such contracts in 1948, but stated that at the time the disputed farm had changed hands—1926—the proceeds of a pawned farm were only counted as interest on the loan, not as partial repayment of the principal. Case 43/48.

[44] Many disputes over title to cocoa farms have revolved around the issue of

has never been considered much of a problem. Sales of cocoa farms occur frequently, and have done so since the early days of cocoa cultivation. In fact, it is more common for a farmer to sell a plot of cocoa in Ondo than to pawn it, if he wishes to raise cash. A number of the farmers I interviewed had either bought or sold cocoa farms themselves, and the others acknowledged the practice as usual and accepted.[45]

In other areas, where lineage rights in rural land have been more clearly established and more closely guarded than in Ondo, landowners may be reluctant to permit tenants (or even lineage members) to sell cocoa farms. This is particularly true in Ibadan, where many people still deny that cocoa farms may be sold at all and where the courts have, on occasion, prevented tenants from selling the trees they had planted.[46] Others admit that it is done but do not approve of the practice. In both Ibadan and Ife a tenant who wishes to sell his farm must inform the landowner, who will continue to collect *isha-kole* from the purchaser.[47] In some cases, landowning families may try to impose additional restrictions on tenants' rights to sell, such as a requirement that the purchaser must be a member of the landowning family or one of its tenants. Nowhere in Yorubaland may family property be sold without the consent of the entire family (often difficult to define)—a condition which renders the sale of family-owned tree crops somewhat difficult.

Landowners seem to have raised fewer objections to the sale of tenants' cocoa farms in Ife than in Ibadan.[48] All of my informants in Abanata, and several in other villages, said that tenants could sell their cocoa farms, though not many had actually done so. Sales have been recognized by the customary courts in Ife since the 1930s,[49]

whether the farms had been pawned—in which case title remained with the original owner or his heirs—or sold in the past. Ife Customary Court Records 49/37, 88/37, 74/48, 43/48, 142/49, 98/52, 33/61, 187/51, 18/60, 58/61.

[45] Lloyd, pp. 128–9, 311; C. W. Rowling, *Land Tenure in Ondo Province*; Ondo Grade B Customary Court Records, *passim*.

[46] Ibadan Lands Court Records 74/47, 105/47.

[47] Ife Customary Court Records 104/69; Ibadan Lands Court Records 88/37. Similarly, the court usually stated that tenants must pay *ishakole* to whomever could legitimately claim title to the land. Thus, if in a dispute over landownership between A and B, the court awarded the land to B, all tenants farming on the land were henceforth expected to pay *ishakole* to B, even if A had originally given them permission to farm there. Ibadan Lands Court Records 74/37, 47/39, 139/52, 28/53, 56/55. In Araromi-Aperin, most farmers who had acquired cocoa farms since 1940 had purchased them rather than obtaining uncultivated land and planting cocoa for themselves; in all but one case, the purchaser pays *ishakole*.

[48] This point is more fully discussed in Chapter V, below.

[49] Ife Customary Court Records 66/36, 7/49, 10/53, 49/58, 72/58, 55/59, 104/69 Cf. 'Ife–Modakeke Dispute Court Cases', IFEDIV 1/1/113B (NAI).

although they are said to have been uncommon before the late 1940s.[50] And even in Ibadan, tenants' farms have sometimes come to be regarded as sold, either because witnesses cannot be found to corroborate the original landowner's claims or because the 'purchaser' has used and expanded the farm for many years without interference from either the 'seller' or the landowning family. Several of my informants in Araromi-Aperin and other villages stated that they had bought cocoa farms.[51]

Moreover, one occasionally encounters cases in which rural *land* has been sold outright or come to be considered as sold.[52] In a couple of recent decisions, the Ibadan Lands Court has argued that 'land on which a person has been allowed to plant permanent crops becomes his own in perpetuity and can never be taken back', and has accordingly allowed the grantee to sell the land itself.[53] Similar cases may be found in the Ife customary court records;[54] in Ondo the practice has been recognized for some time.[55] In a case heard in 1965, the Ondo court stated that 'it is generally known in Ondo farming tradition that a farmer who cultivates a bush and plants it is the one who virtually owns the land around and adjacent to it reaching to the points where he shares boundaries with other farmers', and concluded that the plaintiff in this case had the right to sell uncultivated portions of land adjacent to his own farm.[56] Even strangers have often bought land or cocoa farms in Ondo, with no obligation to pay *ishakole* and the right to sell the farm again if they wish.

The Rising Cost of Rights to Land

Not only have methods of transferring rights to land become increasingly commercialized with the spread of cocoa growing in Western Nigeria but also the cost of acquiring them has tended to

[50] Interview with Mr. Odutalayo, a former customary court judge in Ile-Ife.

[51] On 3 Mar. 1926 J. A. Obisesan noted in his diary that he was considering purchasing a farm; a decade later (13 Feb. 1937), he criticized his cousin, Motosho, for selling cocoa farms and uncultivated land.

[52] As in the case of tenancy, Yoruba terminology is confusing on this issue. Thus, cocoa farmers in Araromi-Aperin often speak of having 'bought' (*ra*) their land even though they continue to pay *ishakole* and have no right to alienate the land itself. Apparently the term *ra* is often used to refer to a large initial payment for the right to cultivate permanent crops, rather than the transfer of outright ownership implied by the English word 'buy'. Cf. above, p. 96, n. 20.

[53] Ibadan Lands Court Records 40/60; also 25/61.

[54] Ife Customary Court Records 74/68, 99/68.

[55] Ondo Grade B Customary Court Records 214/59 (dealing with land sold in 1946), 88/68 (land sold in 1954), 258/62 (land sold in 1955).

[56] Ondo Grade B Customary Court Records 209/65.

rise over time. It is difficult to depict this process precisely, because data are scanty, but in general the cost of acquiring either the right to plant cocoa on uncultivated land or landed property—cocoa farms or even rural land itself—has risen in different areas when demand began to press on a fixed supply of uncultivated forest land. I have found no evidence in any of the three city-states to suggest that such costs were higher at any given time for immigrants than for sons of the soil. The system of collecting a quantity of cocoa as *ishakole* was associated, in Ife and Ondo, with the advent of a large number of migrant farmers from outside these city-states, but the amount collected from individual tenants has not increased over time and *ishakole* is usually asked of anyone from outside the landowner's lineage, regardless of his birthplace.

In Ibadan, when a farmer sought forest land for planting cocoa, he usually gave a present to the family or family representative who showed it to him. At first this initial present generally consisted of drinks or kola nuts, although sometimes it took the form of a small cash payment. In interviews with fifty-four descendants of early cocoa planters in different Ibadan villages, I found that in forty-two cases the informant's ancestors gave drinks or nothing at all to the man who showed them land for planting cocoa. Before World War I cash presents were rarely more than £2.[57] During the war and in the 1920s, however, as the demand for good cocoa land brought farmers flocking to the hunters' domains, the initial present began to increase in value. In a review of several land disputes in the area, written in 1930, a District Officer reported that the landowners involved had given out plots of land for amounts ranging from £5 to £50 each.[58] In Araromi-Aperin, which was first settled during the reign of Bale Shittu in Ibadan (1914–25), some farmers reported that they or their fathers acquired the right to plant cocoa for nothing; others had paid as much as £6 per acre.

In Ife also the early immigrant farmers gave only token presents to the family or individual who showed them land. Even during the early years of the post-war price boom, landowners made little attempt to raise the price charged to each tenant for the right to

[57] Cash payments for the right to cultivate land around the turn of the century are also mentioned in Resident's Letter Book, 1901–3 (Mapo Hall); *Lagos Gazette*, 7 Feb. 1903; Ibadan District Council Church Farm at Eripa, 'Judgement re Ownership of Land, etc.' from Lagos Supreme Court, 19 Mar. 1906.

[58] 'Memorandum by Assistant District Officer', 14 Oct. 1930, File on land disputes (untitled), OYOPROF 3/1181, vol. i (NAI). Cf. Obisesan, Diary, 5 May 1930.

plant and cultivate cocoa, relying instead on the steady inflow of tenants and the rising cash value of a given weight of cocoa to increase their incomes. Towards the end of the 1950s, however, as good cocoa land became scarce in Ife, initial payments started to rise. Figure 3 gives the initial payment per acre for all the farms on which I could get such information in Abanata.[59] In general, *ishagi* was less than £2 per acre for plots acquired before 1957; after that, as good cocoa land became harder to find, farmers sometimes paid

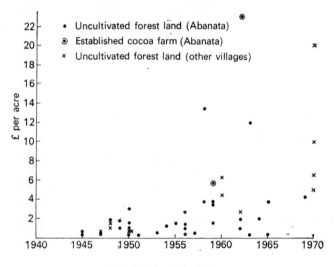

Fig. 3. *Ishagi*, Ife Area

considerably more than £2 per acre for additional plots. Similarly in several other villages, I was told that when strangers first came there (in the late 1940s or early 1950s) they gave a cutlass or a small amount of money (estimates ranged from 10*s.* to £1. 10*s.*) for being shown land on which to farm. Often the land was not measured; the tenant was simply shown a spot in the forest and told to cultivate as much land as he liked. Nowadays, however, plots are usually measured and initial payments may run from £5 to £20 per acre.[60]

---

[59] Based on interviews with 24 tenant farmers. Data were collected for each plot of land, since some farmers had more than one. In a few cases, farmers paid no *ishagi* or were not sure of the dates on which they acquired their plots; their answers were not used in constructing the chart.

[60] Plots are measured by laying a rope of a certain length along the ground. In some cases only the width of the plot is measured—the farmer may then plant cocoa

In Ondo initial payments for the right to use land can hardly be said to have existed before the advent of stranger farmers, since any Ondo could farm on any uncultivated portion of Ondo land without permission from anyone.[61] Strangers have, however, been asked to pay cash initially for the right to plant cocoa, as well as annual *ishakole*. In the two villages where I interviewed a number of recent immigrants, this initial payment has clearly risen in the last ten years. (See Figs. 4, 5.)

As I have already pointed out, once uncultivated forest land became relatively scarce in a given area, people who wished to invest

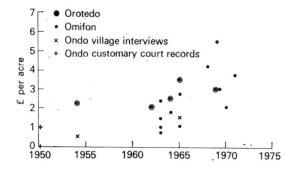

Fig. 4. Initial payments for uncultivated land in Ondo

in cocoa farms there had to buy farms which were already planted. I do not have enough data on the prices paid for cocoa farms at different times in Ife or Ibadan to give any indication of their trend. In Ondo, where cocoa farms have been bought and sold freely ever since cocoa growing became popular there, it was possible to collect more information. Prices vary widely according to the age and condition of the trees and it is difficult to discern a trend, but the transactions plotted in Fig. 5 do not contradict farmers' assertions that the cost of bearing cocoa farms has risen, especially in the last ten years.

on a strip of indefinite length (cf. Polly Hill, *Migrant Cocoa Farmers*, pp. 43–9); in others the length of the plot is also measured. The length of the rope used for measurement varies from one village to another, but 50 to 60 feet seemed to be common. Thus, the size of a plot on which a tenant would pay 1 cwt. of cocoa as *ishakole* might vary from 50 × 100 feet to 120 × 200 feet or more, in the case of strips of unspecified length.

[61] Farmers who were shown land by a representative of the Oshemawe usually presented him with gin, kola, or other small gifts, in return for his assistance, but such gifts did not imply that the *oba*'s representative 'owned' the land.

Unlike payments for established cocoa farms or the right to plant cocoa on uncultivated land, *ishakole* has not been deliberately increased as cocoa land has become scarce. The traditional conception of *ishakole*, as a token payment acknowledging the limitations of a stranger's rights to land rather than as an economic rent, implied that *ishakole* should not be onerous—a stranger should not be expected to pay more than he was able.[62] Before the advent of cocoa farming, the amount of *ishakole* was often undetermined; a stranger

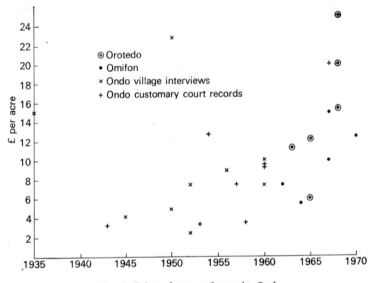

Fig. 5. Sales of cocoa farms in Ondo

gave 'what he liked', as my informants frequently put it. As cocoa growing spread in Ibadan, the amount of *ishakole* came to be fixed in terms of cash, but remained nominal and could be reduced or waived altogether in times of poor harvests or personal misfortune.

Similarly, the system of collecting a certain amount of cocoa as *ishakole* in Ife may have originated primarily as a method of relating *ishakole* to a tenant's ability to pay. In Abanata, for example, farmers with less than three acres of cocoa are more likely to pay two quarters (or £2. 10s.) than one hundredweight (or £5) annually, although there are several exceptions. (See Fig. 6.) In some of the

[62] Cf. Lloyd's discussion of *ishakole* in Ado Ekiti, pp. 213–22.

early *ishakole* cases brought before the Oni's Appeal Court in the
1940s, the Oni stated that *ishakole* should depend on a tenant's
ability to pay: '*Ishakole* shall vary from time to time according to
the year's yield and market price'[63] or, henceforth, the amount of
ishakole 'will depend entirely on the quantity planted and harvested
by the tenants'.[64] In one case the court raised the *ishakole* paid by a
group of tenants from one to five hundredweight per annum when it
was discovered that the tenants had planted 19,000 cocoa trees
instead of 4,000 as they originally claimed. Later, however, the courts
largely abandoned their attempts to relate the amount of *ishakole* to

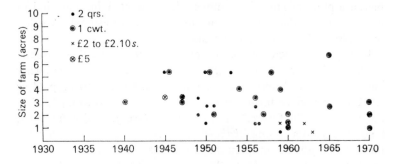

Fig. 6. *Ishakole*, Ife area

the extent of a tenant's bearing cocoa farm. In subsequent cases, the
judges usually awarded landowners *ishakole* of two quarters or one
hundredweight of cocoa without reference to the size of the farm in
question; once, a tenant was ordered to pay one hundredweight
ishakole on each of his two farms, though one farm was twice as
large as the other.[65] During a land tenure dispute between the Ifes
and the Modakekes, the Ife District Officer reported a 'verbal agreement' between the two factions which provided among other things
that *ishakole* should henceforth be calculated according to the number of trees owned by each tenant. The District Officer termed this
provision 'revolutionary' and the farmers evidently agreed, for two
weeks later representatives of the Modakeke tenants in thirteen
villages wrote to the District Officer repudiating the whole agreement

[63] Ife Customary Court Records 35/45.
[64] Ife Customary Court Records 95/45.
[65] Ife Customary Court Records 65/69.

in the strongest terms. There is no evidence that it was ever put into effect.[66]

The growing tendency to measure plots of land may have increased the effective rate of *ishakole*, although this was not apparent in Abanata. (See Fig. 6.) One landowner whom I interviewed said that the rate of *ishakole* had risen since the late 1940s: whereas formerly tenants paid one hundredweight of cocoa for a farm of about three acres, now they would have to pay that amount for two acres. He added, however, that no individual would be expected to pay more than two hundredweight annually, even if his farm(s) were larger than four acres. In other cases, where landowners did not formerly measure plots of land, it is impossible, without doing the kind of detailed survey that I carried out in Abanata, to estimate whether or not *ishakole* per acre has increased.

In any case, increases in the effective rate of *ishakole* usually applied only to recently acquired plots of land. Once a landowner and tenant agreed upon the amount of dried cocoa to be paid as *ishakole* for a given farm, neither party was expected to try to alter the amount in the future.[67] The Ife courts have generally prevented landowners from raising *ishakole*[68] and have tended to give tenants the benefit of the doubt when they have fallen into arrears. In several cases, the court recognized a landowner's right to collect *ishakole*, but reduced the amount claimed by one-half or more.[69]

On the whole, then, there is little evidence that the cost of *ishakole* has risen over time in Ife and Ibadan, as have payments for cocoa farms or the right to plant them. (In Ondo the institution of *ishakole* is too recent to warrant any generalizations about trend.) This in turn suggests that the cost of acquiring land (or cocoa farms) has risen primarily because of the spread of cocoa cultivation and the resulting scarcity of good land, rather than in response to the advent of large numbers of migrant farmers from other states (except in so far as the latter contributed to the growing demand for land). In both Ife and Ibadan the cost of acquiring rights to land has increased

[66] Correspondence in 'Ishakole: Collection of', IFEDIV 1/1/113 (NAI).

[67] Since the value of the *ishakole* fluctuates with the price of cocoa, the landowner benefits from upward movements in the price and the tenant is protected against an increase in the relative burden of his obligation in depressed years. *Ishakole* which is fixed in terms of cash rather than cocoa may be renegotiated from time to time.

[68] Ife Customary Court Records 94/45, 37/45.

[69] Ife Customary Court Records 24/47, 95/45, 35/45, 73/52. The question of evicting tenants rarely arose; in the two cases I encountered, the court protected the tenant in one (9/38) and supported the landowner's request for eviction in the other (1/51).

for strangers and local farmers alike. In Ife the great increases in the value of *ishakole* after World War II were largely the result of world market trends. These trends also brought increased numbers of migrant farmers to Ife, but they paid *ishakole* on the same basis as their predecessors and Ife farmers who sought land outside their own lineages were subject to similar conditions. Measurement of newly allocated plots of land does not seem to have become common until the late 1950s, when uncultivated forest land was growing scarce in Ife; it is not yet widely practised in Ondo. Thus, in so far as measurement and the assessment of *ishakole* per plot rather than per tenant have increased the effective rate of *ishakole*, this also appears to be primarily an economic rather than an ethnic phenomenon.

Strangers and Land Tenure in the Cocoa Belt

In so far as migrant cocoa farmers from the savannah or old cocoa-growing areas simply added to the over-all demand for cocoa land in Ife and Ondo, the effects of their advent on the local system of land tenure are indistinguishable from the effects of the spread of cocoa cultivation in general. I found no real evidence that local land-holders discriminated systematically against outsiders (i.e. non-Ifes or non-Ondos) in the terms on which they accorded them the right to use land for growing cocoa. In Araromi-Aperin most of the non-Ibadans were not cocoa farmers, although many of them had obtained the use of land for food crops. However, it turned out that most of these people had only come to the Ibadan area after uncultivated forest land became scarce there. They had come to Ibadan primarily to trade or to produce non-agricultural goods for the local market, and had never attempted to obtain land for cocoa growing. Indeed, many were from other parts of the forest belt and could have obtained land for planting cocoa at home if they wished. Thus, there is no reason to argue that they had been denied access to good cocoa land because of ethnic origin.[70]

The influx of immigrant farmers to Ife did, however, influence the relationship between landowners and tenants there. The fact that many of the people who sought land for cocoa growing in Ife and, more recently, in Ondo, were strangers may have helped to push the general process of commercialization even further than it would have otherwise have gone. In particular, I think it may be argued that in areas where many of the cocoa farmers are strangers, relations

[70] See Chapter VI, below.

between landowner and tenant are more strictly economic in character and the development of a market in landed property has proceeded more easily and explicitly than is the case in areas where most of the cocoa was planted by citizens of the local city-state. These points emerge most clearly when one compares the rural land tenure systems in Ibadan and Ife; in Ondo the situation is complicated by the peculiarities of traditional land law and the fact that most migrant farmers have arrived within the last decade.

All the evidence I was able to collect on transactions in established cocoa farms and in rural land itself indicates that although sales of cocoa farms and even of land itself occur in all three areas, they occur more frequently and are more readily accepted in Ife and Ondo than in Ibadan.[71] In Ondo this was true long before the advent of immigrant farmers and may be attributed to the historical absence of lineage rights to uncultivated rural land. Here, the advent of stranger farmers appears likely to promote the establishment of lineage lands, as families seek to capitalize on the rising demand for cocoa farms and land in a situation in which sales of tree crops and uncultivated land are readily accepted. In Ife, on the other hand, as in Ibadan, lineage ownership of rural land antedates cocoa. However, lineage resistance to the sale even of established tree crops has been much stronger in Ibadan than in Ife.

The reason usually given by Ibadan landowners to explain why they are reluctant to permit tenants to sell their cocoa farms is that they are afraid the buyer will claim ownership of the land, as well as of the trees growing on it. In Ife this problem is dealt with quite simply: if a tenant sells his farm, he is expected to inform the landowner, who will then collect *ishakole* from the purchaser. The *ishakole* not only provides the landowner with income, but serves as continuing evidence of his ultimate title over the land. In court disputes one of the most convincing pieces of evidence a man (or family) can present in support of a claim to title over land is testimony that he has received *ishakole* from persons actually farming on the land. Since the system of *ishakole* is also well established in Ibadan, one would think landowners there could also permit tenants to sell cocoa farms, as long as the buyers agreed to continue payments of *ishakole*. In fact, they have not, or have done so only reluctantly.

The chief difference between Ife and Ibadan which might explain this difference in landowners' attitudes towards sales of cocoa farms

[71] See above, pp. 129–30.

is the fact that most tenant farmers in Ibadan are from Ibadan, whereas in many parts of Ife they are strangers. Because Ibadan tenants belong to Ibadan lineages, who presumably have some rural land of their own in Ibadan, the distinction between landowner and tenant may easily become blurred unless great care is taken to maintain it. If both landowner and tenant come from the same town, the only way of establishing their positions with respect to a piece of land is to ascertain their economic rights to it, which will be indicated primarily by the transactions they have engaged in. In the absence of written agreements between owner and tenant, landowners must rely chiefly on witnesses to substantiate their claims to receive *isha-kole* on a farm which has been sold. This can be a risky business, especially if the original grant of land occurred a long time ago. A tenant from another city-state, on the other hand, is easily identifiable as a stranger, with no possible lineage rights to local land. Thus, in Ife, where in many areas the majority of tenants are strangers, there is no question of a tenant claiming ownership of rural land—his ancestry is sufficient to rule out that possibility, without reference to his past land transactions. Thus, the presence of large numbers of stranger farmers in Ife may have facilitated the development of a market in rural landed property there, by providing an independent criterion by which to distinguish landowner from tenant and thus relieving landowners' fears of having their titles challenged by tree-owning tenants.

Indeed, the arrival of many immigrant farmers in Ife may, in itself, have helped to clarify the distinction between landowners and tenants there. There are, after all, Ife tenants in Ife, some of whom were tenants to other Ife families before the immigration began, but their existence does not appear to constitute the same kind of threat to Ife landowners as Ibadan landowners feel from their predominantly Ibadan tenants. We have seen that the line between landowner and tenant appears to be more sharply drawn in Ife than in Ibadan: *ishakole* is closer to a form of economic rent in Ife, and there exist fewer mutual social obligations between landowners and land-users than is often the case in Ibadan. That this distinction may be partly due to the predominance of strangers among the tenant cocoa farmers in much of Ife is suggested by the history of a land dispute (or, more accurately, series of land disputes) which escalated into a major political crisis in Ife before it was settled. This was the Ife–Modakeke dispute of the late 1940s and early 1950s.

The Modakekes were originally refugees who had fled from Oyo during the upheavals of the early nineteenth century and settled at Ife.[72] Their relations with the Ifes were not very cordial; there were open clashes after the death of Oni Abeweila c. 1850 and again during the Sixteen Years War, when the Oyos sided with Ibadan whereas the Ifes were inclined to sympathize with the Ekitiparapo. An uneasy truce prevailed from 1886 until 1909, when the Modakekes left Ife town altogether, moving to their farms south and west of Ile-Ife or across the Shasha River to Gbongan, Odeomu, and other towns in what is now southern Oshun Division. In the early 1920s they were allowed to return to Ife town and settled in their own quarter there. Many Modakeke farmers planted cocoa, especially south of Ife town. In 1921 the District Officer (H. L. Ward Price) commented, 'There must be about 5000 of them in different farms in the Ife district alone.'[73] In 1949 Modakeke farmers were reported to be living in a large number of Ife villages.[74]

In the late 1940s a dispute broke out between the Ifes and the Modakekes over whether or not the Modakekes owned the land they were farming on in Ife Division. It began when an Ife man success-fully prosecuted several Modakeke farmers for non-payment of *ishakole*. The customary court upheld the Ife's claim and ordered the Modakekes to pay one hundredweight of cocoa apiece as *ishakole*; in effect, the decision declared the Modakekes to be tenants.[75] The case set a precedent for several similar ones pending before the court and the Modakeke community became alarmed. They petitioned the government repeatedly, with complaints ranging from individual instances of harassment or assault to charges that the Ife Native Court was biased against them and hence incompetent to adjudicate any case involving Ife claims for *ishakole* from Modakeke farmers. They were particularly incensed because a number of Ife families began to hire Urhobo labourers to cut the palm fruit on Modakeke farms.[76]

---

[72] On the history of the Modakekes' settlement at Ife and their relations with the indigenous inhabitants, see S. Johnson, *History of the Yorubas*, esp. pp. 230–3, 525 ff., 646–8; J. A. Mackenzie, 'Report on the Native Organization of Ife District—Oyo Province', 1934, CSO 26/29829 (NAI); and 'Intelligence Report, Ikire District, Ibadan Division', 1934.

[73] Oyo Province, Annual Report, 1921, CSO 26/06027 (NAI).

[74] District Officer, Ife, to Resident, Oyo, 2 May 1949 in 'Ishakole: Collection of'.

[75] Acting District Officer, Ife, to Oni of Ife, 20 Dec. 1948 in 'Ishakole: Collection of'.

[76] This was an effort on the Ifes' part to strengthen their claims to title over the land since, according to customary law, only the owner of a piece of land may cut the palm fruit there, whoever may be using the land for other purposes. 'Ishakole: Collection of'; Lloyd, p. 274.

As individual court cases between Ifes and Modakekes proliferated, feelings in the community ran high. Efforts by the Bale and chiefs of Modakeke quarter to urge their people to compromise led to dis-affection—at one point, a group of Modakekes petitioned the government to depose the Modakeke chiefs.[77] Various political organizations became involved. An Ife organization, known as the Egbe Omo Ibile (Society of Native Sons), tried to organize a cam-paign against the Oni and chiefs of Ife on behalf of Ife tenants, and the Egbe Omo Oduduwa attempted to mediate between Ifes and Modakekes.[78] In May 1949 there was a small riot in Ile-Ife when police tried to arrest some Modakeke farmers accused of cutting palm fruit unlawfully. Eventually attempts at a negotiated settlement failed and the issue was resolved only in 1953, when the Native Courts were legally empowered to attach immovable property in order to enforce compliance with their decisions. Faced with the prospect of having their cocoa farms sold by court order, the Modakekes gave up and began to pay *ishakole*.[79]

From the official correspondence concerning this dispute, it ap-pears that up until the 1940s Modakekes had grown both food crops and cocoa on Ife rural land but had paid little or no *ishakole*. Ac-cording to some of their own spokesmen, 'the Modakekes have for years recognized the Oni of Ife as their suzerain, but since 1938 they have been subjected en bloc to arbitrary and unwarrantable demands of Ishakole . . . by individual Ife people.'[80] It is not clear how many of the Ife demands were for more *ishakole* from admitted tenants, how many were attempts to collect *ishakole* from farmers who had never previously paid it, but the fact that many Ife 'landowners' had not previously bothered to try cutting palm fruit on Modakeke farms suggests that they had not been assiduous in collecting *ishakole* either.

With the sudden increase in cocoa prices in the late 1940s and early 1950s the Ifes apparently used the precedent set by their relations with the early immigrant farmers to claim *ishakole* from another group of 'strangers' in their midst. While the dispute was still in progress, a District Officer noted its wider implications: 'The whole

---

[77] Ife-Ilesha Division, Annual Report, 1950, IFEDIV 3/9 (NAI).
[78] District Officer, Ife, to Resident, Oyo, 14 Feb. and 8 Apr. 1949, in 'Ishakole: Collection of'.
[79] Ife-Ilesha Division, Annual Report, 1953.
[80] Petition to the Governor of the Western Region, from B. Olowofoyeku for Six Modakeke Farmers, 8 Oct. 1954, in 'Ife–Modakeke Dispute Court Cases'.

ECRWN—E

relationship between landlords and tenants, of whatever tribe, in the Ife district is being affected by the Modakekes' apparently successful stand against the Ife landowners.'[81] On another occasion he commented that although traditionally *ishakole* consisted merely of a gift of yams in acknowledgement of the landowner's title, the Ifes had 'made the most of cocoa . . . to extract an economic rent not only from Modakeke but from Ife and other tenants as well.'[82] Whether these developments would have occurred as a result of the rising market price, had there not been a growing influx of immigrant farmers, is of course impossible to say. However, the outcome of the Ife–Modakeke dispute probably cemented the claims of Ife lineages to rural landownership and helped to define relations between Ife landowners and all their tenants in largely economic terms.

Landowners and Chiefs

The spread of cocoa cultivation and the resultant 'commercialization' of exchanges of various rights to land opened up new economic and social opportunities to families (or individuals) who had or could establish control over uncultivated forest land in the cocoa belt. In most city-states uncultivated rural land was abundant and often unoccupied because of the upheavals and hazards of the nineteenth-century wars, so that when cocoa was introduced to Western Nigeria, many families could and did claim rights of 'ownership' over land suitable for the crop. By doing so, they acquired the power to allocate rights of usufruct to other farmers who, in turn, acknowledged them as 'owners' of the land who were entitled to certain expressions of loyalty and subordination from their 'tenants'. Since cultivable land was not scarce, however, families claiming jurisdiction over rural land did not thereby acquire the power to demand a substantial portion of their tenants' produce in payment for the right to farm. Some families acquired very large holdings and subsequently amassed considerable wealth and influence in their respective communities, as we shall see, but they did so by accumulating tenants rather than rents,[83] and did not develop into a distinct class of rural landowners.[84]

---

[81] District Officer, Ife, to Resident, Oyo, 14 Feb. 1949, in 'Ishakole: Collection of'.

[82] The same to the same, 2 May 1949, ibid.

[83] Or by investing in cocoa farms. I have encountered cases in which some individual members of landowning families were clearly wealthier than others—often because they were more successful as farmers or traders. Galletti *et al.* discuss variations in farm sizes, but do not relate this clearly to the question of land ownership.

[84] Potentially, every resident of a city-state is a landowner, every stranger a tenant,

Most of the families I encountered who have held extensive lands for some time are descendants of chiefs and/or hunters, who obtained their lands through the achievements of their forebears.[85] Such families have often used the wealth and influence (e.g. over large numbers of tenants) derived from their land-holdings to advance their social and political power in their respective states. More recently, men who have gained wealth and influence in other ways have begun to invest part of their earnings in cocoa farms and even in land itself. This is particularly noticeable in Ondo, where landed property is readily saleable, but has occurred in Ife and Ibadan as well. Thus, over time, landownership has served both as a means to wealth and prestige and as an end for which wealth and prestige have been employed. These points may be illustrated by the histories of two major land disputes—one in Ibadan, the other in Ife—in which hunters claiming jurisdiction over large forest areas came into conflict with the traditional authorities.

As we have already seen, most of the best cocoa land in Ibadan was unoccupied during the wars and hence unclaimed by Ibadan lineages at the end of the century. It therefore fell to the hunters to help the first cocoa farmers find good places to settle and, as the demand for uncultivated forest land increased, to receive gifts and even *ishakole* from the settlers. As more and more settlers moved into the forest (especially the area south of Ibadan town between the Oshun and Omi rivers), rivalry among the hunter-landowners gave rise to frequent jurisdictional disputes. Many of these disputes involved members of the Aperin family which by the 1920s had established itself as the largest land-holding family in the area, a position it has retained ever since. The Aperins are descended from a hunter-warrior named Obisesan who helped defend Ibadan's southern territory against Ijebu raiders during the wars.[86] In 1893 he escorted

but in fact many local men are tenants to other local families. There is probably more of a potential class distinction between cocoa farmers and cocoa buyers, from whom most farmers obtain credit, than between landowners and land-users, although this distinction also tends to become blurred as cocoa buyers invest their profits in land and cocoa farms. See S. M. Essang, 'The Distribution of Earnings in the Cocoa Economy of Western Nigeria', Michigan State University Ph.D. thesis, 1970.

[85] Since men are often chosen to take chieftancy titles because of their wealth or other accomplishments, it is not always possible to tell whether a chief acquired large land-holdings through the powers of his office, or whether he became a chief because he was already wealthy and influential. Certainly, not all chiefs have large land-holdings. In the case of the hunters, their familiarity with the forests led would-be cocoa farmers to seek them out as guides. Later, the hunters often claimed ownership of the land they had shown to farmers.

[86] Obisesan, Diary, 12 Nov. 1921.

Captain Bower (on his peace-making tour of Yorubaland) through the Ibadan forests and was given a chieftancy title (Agbakin) in recognition of his contributions to the defence of Ibadan.[87] He died in 1901 and was succeeded as Agbakin and as head of the family by his son Akinoso, who is said to have been the first Aperin to plant cocoa.[88] During the 1890s and early 1900s Obisesan and his sons began to give out land to farmers around the family's villages of Idi-Osi, Odi-Aperin, and Akanran.[89] By 1905, when Akinoso had a dispute with another man (usually referred to as Areago, although it is not clear whether this was a name or a title) who also claimed ownership of an extensive forest area south of the town, the Aperins were reported to have thirty-two settlements under their jurisdiction.[90] This dispute was settled by the Ibadan District Officer, who demarcated a boundary between Areago and the sons of Obisesan, but others soon followed.[91] During World War I the Aperins 'completely over-ran the whole area' south of the Alagutan Stream.[92] The Aperins' holdings were so extensive that they tended to become divided into several domains, each presided over by a different member or branch of the family. At times this led to disputes within the family over the degree of autonomy individual members might enjoy in the administration of their domains and the disposition of the proceeds thereof.[93] Eventually the Aperins clashed with the descendants of Sanni Oke Offa. In the late 1920s and the 1930s rivalry between the Aperins and the Sannis grew into one of the bitterest and most prolonged land disputes in recent Ibadan history. The families harassed each other's tenants and sometimes resorted to outright battle.

By 1928 the increasing friction between the Aperins and Sannis

[87] Johnson, p. 637; Obisesan, Diary, loc. cit.; Akinyele, *Outlines of Ibadan History*, p. 46; Eripa Farm, 'Judgement'.

[88] He reportedly planted cocoa first at Odi-Aperin, using seeds purchased from 'Christians on the Lagos Road'—i.e. from Onipe? Aperin means elephant killer and refers to the original Obisesan's prowess as a hunter.

[89] Eripa Farm, 'Judgement'.

[90] Resident's statement to the Ibadan Town Council, 23 Nov. 1904 in OYOPROF 3/1181, vol. i.

[91] In 1903 the Lagos Supreme Court heard another dispute over the ownership of the land at Eripa between Akinoso and Bakare, the son of Shodun—another hunter turned landowner in the area (Eripa Farm, 'Judgement'). The families were reconciled in 1923, according to J. A. Obisesan, Diary, 5 Sept. 1923. Others claiming ownership rights in this area by 1916 were Olubode, Laogun, Ogundipe, Amosun, and Sanni Oke Offa. OYOPROF 3/1181, vol. i. Cf. Appendix II, below.

[92] I.e. roughly the area south of Alabidun (No. 14) on Map 2. OYOPROF 3/1181, vol. i.

[93] Obisesan, Diary, *passim*.

came to the notice of the British officials in Ibadan. They began to investigate the bases for each family's claims to title over the land and were told by the Bale and chiefs that, as Ibadan had been settled 'by conquest', all Ibadan land belonged to the entire community, and the disputed area should therefore be administered by the Ibadan Native Authority on behalf of the whole community. On these grounds, the chiefs claimed the right to receive all rents and other tributes payable on the lands. At first, the British were inclined to take the chiefs' part,[94] but their enthusiasm cooled late in 1931 after a number of the chiefs went to one of the Aperins' villages, asserted their ownership over the land, and began taking bribes from the farmers in exchange for 'permission' to remain on their farms.[95]

In 1933 the Resident of Ibadan Province, H. L. Ward Price, attempted a compromise solution. He reaffirmed the existence of family land in Ibadan rural areas, but attempted to reduce the Aperins' and Sannis' powers by partitioning the land between the two families, and declaring that tenants 'cannot be evicted except by order of a court; no rent is payable; no Ishakole is due to the "landlords". Yearly presents are not forbidden but they are voluntary.'[96] This attempt to turn the clock back to the days before cocoa and *ishakole* apparently satisfied no one. J. A. Obisesan complained that the decision not only deprived both families of 'ownership right as known in the native way but gives them no authority in the usual way over the farmers'.[97] The chiefs continued to protest the hunters' 'usurpation' of their rights;[98] the Aperins and Sannis continued their feud; and the Ibadan Lands Court, after some initial confusion, continued to order tenants to pay *ishakole* to landowners.[99] Eventually,

[94] In March 1930 the District Officer in Ibadan wrote to Ross, the Resident in Oyo, that the Aperins and Sannis had 'assumed the title or roll (*sic*) of Landlords' and should be told that they held their farms only 'at the pleasure of the Bale and Chiefs'. Ross was inclined to agree. 'Land Tenure in Ibadan', IBAPROF 3/0718 (NAI). Cf. reports by the District Officer (3 Sept. 1929) and Assistant District Officer (14 Oct. 1930), OYOPROF 3/1181, vol. i.

[95] District Officer, Ibadan, to Resident, Oyo, 5 Nov. 1931, OYOPROF 3/1181, vol. i.

[96] Judgement in Provincial Court, 26 June 1933, quoted in OYOPROF 3/1181, vol. i.

[97] Obisesan, Diary, 25 July 1933.

[98] 'Worst of all hundreds of the descendants of these warriors are now tenants to Aperin Family horrible, who would dare attempt such awful and cruel usurpation when we were not under the British Protection, the family would be blown off in an hour.' Ibadan Judicial Council to Senior Resident of Oyo Province, 26 Oct. 1936, in 'Land Tenure in Ibadan', IBAPROF 3/0718 (NAI). Cf. Akinyele, pp. 91–5.

[99] Ibadan Lands Court Records 88/37, and subsequent cases.

the issue died away, leaving the Aperins and Sannis in possession of large territories and many tenants.

In one respect, the chiefs' unsuccessful efforts to deprive the Aperins, Sannis, and other families of their large land-holdings may be said to illustrate the disruptive effect of cocoa cultivation on established patterns of social and political power in Yoruba communities. Before the advent of cocoa, farmland in Ibadan was plentiful relative to the community's demand for it and large areas of rural land were unoccupied and unclaimed by anyone. As late as 1913, the Bale of Ibadan disclaimed any 'ownership' of Ibadan territory: 'I, as Bale, have no lands; I have my family lands only. I have no control over lands except to settle disputes.'[100] Two years later Bale Shittu wrote to the Resident that there was no reason for landowners to consult the Bale and chiefs before giving out portions of their land to others: 'As this had not been so in the past we beg you would kindly not press it.'[101] And F. E. Morakinyo, the son of a hunter (Shodun) who had staked out a large claim in the southern forests, told the West African Lands Committee that his father had given land to many people, including a couple of chiefs, who in turn recognized him as their 'head' and, after his death, continued to render service to the 'sons of their benefactors'.[102]

When cocoa growing was introduced into Ibadan, the hunters were among the first people to realize its implications for 'owners' of uncultivated forest land and to capitalize on the situation. As Sir Isaac Akinyele put it, 'Hunters at Ibadan simply took this advantage because the chiefs and people of Ibadan were warlike and did not care for agriculture until the advent of cocoa and other valuable trees . . .'[103] By the 1920s the chiefs' attempts to assert their 'traditional prerogative' to administer all Ibadan lands on behalf of the people were largely anachronistic.[104] The farmers growing cocoa on Aperin or Sanni land considered themselves tenants to these land-

[100] WALC, *Papers*, p. 202. Also in 1913 a group of Lagosians, alarmed by rumours that the government planned to apply Northern Nigeria's land laws to all of British West Africa, toured several Yoruba towns to awaken public sentiment against such a move. At a public meeting with these men in Ibadan, the Osin Bale stated 'No King or chief has the right to interfere with any man's property in land . . . He could only exercise control over his own land which he has inherited as others have inherited theirs.' *The Land Tenure Question in West Africa*, reprinted from *Lagos Weekly Record*, 1913, p. 9.

[101] Bale's Letter Book, 1915–17 (Mapo Hall).

[102] WALC, *Papers*, p. 203, and *Minutes*, questions 7,607, 10,980, 12,152.

[103] Akinyele, p. 91.

[104] Indeed, some observers felt they were simply making a belated attempt to share in the proceeds of Ibadan's cocoa economy. On one occasion, when the Bale suggested

owners, and the families' influence over their tenants and in Ibadan
was strong enough to thwart the efforts both of the chiefs and of the
British administration to reduce it. Eventually, their position became
part of the precedent or tradition according to which other land disputes were settled. In 1960, for example, the Ibadan Customary
Court rejected an attempt by the Aleshinloye family to block several
sales of rural land by persons who resided and paid taxes in the
Aleshinloye compound in Ibadan. The family, said the court, were
'misconstruing political leadership for land ownership' and accordingly their claims were dismissed.[105]

However, self-made landowners were not always so successful in
withstanding the claims of traditional political authority. The spread
of cocoa cultivation was only one factor affecting the distribution of
control over the means of production in Yoruba communities; in
Ibadan, the Bale and chiefs were not very successful in employing
political power to gain control of a major economic asset, but in Ife
the balance tended to swing the other way. There, some of the
largest land-holders are royal or chieftancy families. Moreover, in
1950 the Oni successfully challenged the claims of a group of hunters
and hunters' descendants to ownership of large areas of Ife rural
land, and actually redistributed parts of the hunters' lands to other
families.

Ife is an ancient kingdom, unlike Ibadan which was founded only
c. 1830, and it might seem therefore, that the Oni and chiefs derive
their land-holdings and authority over other families' land-holdings
from the age and stability of the traditional political system in Ife.
Evidence, however, does not wholly support such a hypothesis. Life
in Ife was thoroughly disrupted during the nineteenth-century wars,
largely by groups of Oyo refugees who settled at Ife but did not get
along very well with the local inhabitants. Repeated civil strife
kept the Ifes scattered in different villages much of the time. As late
as 1886 the Oni-elect refused to leave the comparative safety of
Okeigbo and come to be properly installed as Oni in Ile-Ife—a policy
which was no doubt the better part of valour, considering the violent
ends of some of his predecessors.[106] In such circumstances it seems
unlikely that the Oni exerted much authority over any but his

to the Resident that he partition the Aperins' lands among several other families,
J. A. Obisesan complained that the Bale had 'opened another avenue of opportunity
for himself and his Chiefs to chop' (Diary, 7 Mar. 1928).

[105] Ibadan Customary Court Records 48/60.

[106] Johnson, p. 560; Correspondence of J. B. Wood, 1880–93, CMS (Y) 1/7/5.

immediate followers, or that he effectively controlled the use or disposition of Ife land.

Under the colonial administration, however, the Oni's position
improved. In their efforts to apply the methods of Indirect Rule to
the Yoruba city-states, British officials sometimes sought to govern
not through those indigenous leaders who actually held power in the
late nineteenth century, but through those who, according to Yoruba
legend or custom, were supposed to hold it. For example, the
colonial administration treated Ibadan, the state which had come
closest to ruling all of Yorubaland for much of the nineteenth century, as subordinate to Oyo, whose power had disintegrated at the
beginning of the century. This policy led to decades of confusion,
ill-feeling, and a general undermining of the authority of the Bale and
chiefs.[107] In Ife the opposite seems to have occurred: as titular head
of the 'cradle of Yoruba civilization', the Oni was just the sort of
traditional ruler the British were looking for. They treated him as
virtually an absolute monarch within his own domain, upheld his
authority at almost every turn, and shook their heads indulgently
when he quietly failed to democratize the Ife Native Authority over
the years.[108]

In these circumstances, the men who held the office of Oni under
British rule succeeded in consolidating and extending their authority
well beyond its uncertain nineteenth-century confines. By 1909 Oni
Ajagun had succeeded in driving the Modakekes out of the town
altogether, forcing them to disperse to Odeomu, Gbongan, and
smaller villages towards Ibadan. Ademiluyi, his successor, appears
to have worked actively to extend his rights over Ife land. In 1912
he asserted that anyone who planted tree crops in Ife was expected
to pay special tribute to the Oni.[109] Although his own representative
to the West African Lands Commission effectively denied this—
'The Oni has no control over the lands, but he has control over his
father's land—the family land'[110]—the Oni's interest in the matter
did not wane. In 1921 the Ife District Officer reported that the Oni
was anxious to alter his position in Ife from a ceremonial and religious one to that of 'territorial overlord'.[111] He was usually the final
arbiter of land disputes among Ife families. In one case the chiefs

[107] Akinyele, pp. 79, 115–19; G. D. Jenkins, 'Politics in Ibadan', Northwestern
University Ph.D. thesis, 1965, chs. 3, 8, 9.
[108] See, for example, reports on Ife affairs in Oyo Province, Annual Reports.
[109] WALC, *Papers*, p. 204.   [110] WALC, *Minutes*, question 13,456.
[111] Oyo Province, Annual Report, 1921.

pointed out to the disputants that they must abide by the Oni's decision because 'the Oni is the owner of the land in Ife'.[112] The present Oni, Sir Aderemi Adesoji, who was crowned in 1930, was one of the first landowners in Ife to give out part of his own lineage land to immigrant tenant farmers, and he gained many more tenants by exercising his traditional prerogative to take over disputed land in order to avoid disturbances.[113]

In about 1950 a group of Ife families approached the Oni and asked him to allocate unoccupied rural land to them in the traditional manner, so that they could farm there and place tenants on the land. Their request was evidently motivated by the sharply rising cocoa prices of the late 1940s; at least some of them were educated men, engaged in non-agricultural occupations, who had hitherto shown little interest in farming. In searching for 'unoccupied' land to grant these families, the Oni passed over the large holdings of the royal and chieftancy lineages in Ife (e.g. those of the Ademiluyi, Omishore, Otutu, and Abeweila families) and turned instead to the southern and eastern extremities of Ife territory, where the families of several hunters (e.g. Timi, Agbedegbede, Ologbenla, and Adesunmakin) were receiving *ishakole* from large numbers of tenant farmers.[114] The Oni called a number of these hunters together and told them that, since they had no right to appropriate large areas of rural land to themselves, they must give up part of their lands. Subsequently he sent several chiefs to the area to allocate land claimed by the hunters to nearly a hundred Ife families.[115] The government evidently supported the Oni's move. In 1950 the District Officer reported, 'There is a powerful group of hunter families who have arrogated landowners' rights where only hunting rights exist, and if Native Law and Custom is correctly followed these families should be dispossessed.'[116] Although the hunters were not dispossessed entirely, in the series of legal disputes which ensued the courts ultimately supported the Oni.[117] Thus, the Oni of Ife was able, in 1950,

[112] Ife Customary Court Records, 420/29.
[113] 'Shoko Ademakinwa vs. Obutu, Land Dispute—Matter of', IFEDIV 1/1/332 (NAI); also interviews in Abanata.
[114] Some chieftancy families had permitted hunters to settle on their lineage lands in the past, and these hunters often showed land to immigrant farmers in the area. However, they did so on behalf of the landowning family who received most of the *ishagi* and *ishakole* paid by the tenants. I encountered such cases in Omifunfun, where the Bale was originally a hunter engaged by the Otutu family, and in Shekunde.
[115] Ife Customary Court Records 105/68.
[116] Ife-Ilesha Division, Annual Report, 1950, IFEDIV 3/9 (NAI).
[117] Ife Customary Court Records 105/68 and Supreme Court Case 44/64; inter-

to do what the Bale of Ibadan had failed to do in the 1930s—
namely, to set aside the claims of self-made landowners in cocoa-
farming areas in the name of customary law and chiefly prerogative.

The different experiences of the hunter-landowners in Ife and
Ibadan illustrate yet another way in which the needs and opportunities generated by the spread of cocoa farming in Yorubaland
tended to modify, without completely overthrowing, established
patterns of social and economic activity. Just as relations between
land-holders and land-users became more economically oriented
than they had been in the past, while retaining some of their older
characteristics, so new avenues were opened for the accumulation of
wealth and power, but not always at the expense of existing ones.
The extent to which families were able to establish control over large
areas of good cocoa land and to use that control to increase their
wealth and extend their influence in a community depended in part
on the existing political situation within that community. In Ibadan,
where the authority of traditional government was weakened by the
colonial administration's local version of Indirect Rule, the landowners amassed property and advanced their interests more easily
than in Ife, where the hunter-landowners' position was successfully
challenged with the help of traditional authorities whose power had
been greatly strengthened by colonial policy.

In Ondo, to carry the comparison one step further, lineage rights
to rural land have not been firmly established and men wishing to
acquire land in cocoa-farming areas have simply bought it—either
by purchasing established cocoa farms or by obtaining grants of land
from a local chief in exchange for a substantial 'present' of cash.
Thus, in recent years a number of men who have acquired considerable wealth in other occupations have invested it in land and/or
cocoa farms without having to seek the sanction of traditional
authorities.[118] Indeed, in Ondo even more than in other Yoruba
towns, wealth has been an important means to both landownership
and chieftancy titles.[119] Until the recent advent of stranger cocoa
farmers, there has been little basis for conflict between Ondo land-

---

views with Chief Orafidiya and Mr. Odutalayo. Tenants were sometimes caught
between rival claimants to a piece of land. In the first case cited here, a group of tenants
paid *ishakole* to two families—one the descendants of a hunter and one which had
been allotted land by the Oni—from 1951 until 1963.

[118] I have met or heard about several such men in the course of my fieldwork.
Cf. S. M. Essang, op. cit., which shows that licensed buying agents are some of the
largest cocoa farmers in the Ondo area.

[119] Lloyd, p. 107; interview with Bishop T. O. Olufasoye in Ondo.

owners and the Oshemawe and chiefs. Whether the system of tenancy and lineage landownership now emerging will generate such conflict in the future remains to be seen.

Conclusion

In general, the spread of cocoa cultivation in Western Nigeria modified the distribution of rights to rural land and methods of exchanging such rights in various Yoruba states rather than engendered a complete break with the past. The fact that uncultivated land was usually available to farmers wishing to plant cocoa no doubt helped to prevent a sharp polarization of interests between landholders and land-users, and permitted both groups to adapt established practices to new economic opportunities and constraints. Thus, large numbers of stranger farmers have been readily absorbed into some parts of the cocoa economy, although their presence has to some extent sharpened the distinction between landlord and tenant and thus facilitated the sale of established cocoa farms. However, these two groups have not so far crystallized into distinct socio-economic classes; individual landowning families may be unpopular among their tenants, but one does not get the impression that they are in a position to exploit their tenants economically. Similarly, in conflicts with traditional political authorities over the control of unused forest land, landowning families have not always gained the upper hand.

CHAPTER V

Farm Owners, Farm Workers, and the Distribution of Farm Incomes

UNLIKE land, labour has generally been a factor of production in relatively short supply in the cocoa economy. This has been somewhat puzzling to outside observers, who have by and large attributed it to the fact that Yoruba farmers could usually obtain land to farm on their own, instead of having to work for others, and that cocoa farmers had therefore to rely on migrant labourers from other parts of Nigeria where agricultural opportunities were less favourable than in the cocoa belt. On the other hand, C. D. Forde reported as early as 1938 that 'in the main cocoa-growing areas hired labour is employed on cocoa farms to a somewhat surprising extent; farms in which no such labour is employed being very much in the minority'.[1] And Forde went on to say that, in some areas, 'all the hired labour appears to be local'.[2] In short, there is some confusion in the literature over just who works for whom and why. In this chapter I shall attempt to trace changes over time in the sources of cocoa farmers' labour and the terms on which farm labourers have been employed, relate these changes to the economic requirements of cocoa production and to fluctuations in farmers' incomes, and examine their implications for the distribution of income and the character of social relations between farm owners and farm workers.

The Supply of Farm Labour

From the beginning of the colonial period in Western Nigeria until World War II (and again in the 1950s), both official and private employers voiced repeated complaints about the scarcity of labour in Western Nigeria. The Lagos government found difficulty in obtaining sufficient labour for public works projects in the 1890s[3] and in 1901 Governor Macgregor warned the Colonial Office that it

---

[1] C. D. Forde and R. Scott, *The Native Economies of Nigeria*, vol. i of M. Perham, ed., *Economics of a Tropical Dependency*, p. 91.

[2] Ibid.

[3] A. G. Hopkins, 'The Lagos Strike of 1897', *Past and Present*, 35 (Dec. 1966).

would be expensive to hire workers for railway construction because 'more labour is now needed in this country for economic purposes than was ever the case before'.[4] Similar complaints are scattered throughout official correspondence during the next forty years. Farmers faced the same problem. At least one observer has associated the failure of European-owned plantations in West Africa with the high cost of labour.[5] In 1903 African farmers in Abeokuta declared that their chief problems were 'labour and price': agriculture was not so profitable as it had been, they maintained, because farmers could no longer rely on slave labour and had no alternative source of supply.[6] A decade later, the newly established Southern Nigeria Department of Agriculture reported that 'nearly all the farmers complained that the scarcity of labour prevented their giving better attention to the requirements of their crops'.[7] Even in the depressed conditions of the 1930s, the Director of Agriculture wrote that labour was so scarce in Southern Nigeria that labourers 'are in a position to more or less impose their own terms' on farmers.[8]

Most observers have attributed the scarcity of labour in the colonial period to the growth of income-earning opportunities in agriculture, trade, and government employment *combined* with the ready availability of uncultivated land in Western Nigeria. As Allan McPhee expressed it, 'There is no local labour market [in British West Africa], for each native who feels inclined to work can get a farm of his own, and naturally he prefers to work for himself than to toil for others.'[9] Consequently, it has been argued, traditional institutions such as domestic slavery declined very rapidly after the advent of colonial rule, and many of 'the freed slaves stayed in agriculture', where 'it seems likely that they became the independent cocoa farmers in the early colonial period'.[10] Deprived of such traditional sources of labour, farmers were forced to rely primarily on their own efforts and those of their immediate relatives. As late as 1962, Lloyd maintained, 'There is still a very small demand for agricultural land, for although many men have the capital to develop farms they find

[4] 'Correspondence Relating to Railway Construction in Nigeria', Great Britain, Parliamentary Papers, Cd. 2787, 1905.
[5] See, e.g., A. McPhee, *The Economic Revolution in British West Africa*, p. 131.
[6] *Lagos Gazette*, 5 Dec. 1903.
[7] Department of Agriculture, *Annual Report*, 1911.
[8] Director of Agriculture to Chief Secretary, Lagos, 18 Nov. 1938, in 'Report of Commission of Enquiry into the Marketing of West African Cocoa', CSO 26/34883, vol. i (NAI).
[9] McPhee, p. 42. Cf. Hopkins, 'The Lagos Strike', and Cd. 2787.
[10] Hopkins, 'The Lagos Strike', pp. 143–4.

it difficult to employ labour—for men can still get land for their own farms and are not forced by landlessness to work for hire'.[11] Consequently, there is said to have been little use of wage labour in the cocoa belt until the 1930s, when people from other parts of Nigeria began to migrate seasonally into the forest areas in search of employment. In the 1950s Galletti, Baldwin, and Dina stated that 'in the main cocoa-producing area there is a certain amount of movement of the local labour. But it is not nearly so important to the local economy as the labour moving in from outside the cocoa-producing areas both seasonally and semi-permanently. This has become in every area a greater source of labour power than the local labourers willing to work for wages.'[12] Lloyd is of the same opinion: although 'the Yoruba farmer may work as a labourer for a few days to earn a little ready cash most agricultural labour comes from the far north or from Kabba Province'.[13]

The evidence I have collected suggests a somewhat different set of conclusions concerning the sources of cocoa farmers' labour and changes in the relative importance of different sources over time. I did find that the importance of hired labour has increased over time, relative to 'family' and other traditional sources of labour, but I also found that the use of hired labour dates back to the earliest days of cocoa growing in Nigeria; that it increased steadily in areas of early cocoa development (not suddenly, with the advent of migrant workers in the 1930s), and that even today a large part of the labour employed on cocoa farms is supplied by local, not immigrant, workers. I have also encountered evidence that in some areas domestic slavery declined only gradually during the early decades of colonial rule, and am inclined to think that for some early cocoa farmers (especially in the interior) slaves provided an important source of agricultural labour.

Among the descendants of early planters whom I interviewed in 1966, only a few mentioned relatives as a source of labour on their own farms, but roughly half of them said that their fathers were helped on their farms by children and/or other kinsmen. Of course, it is possible that some informants did not mention family labour because they took it for granted. However, a number specifically said that their fathers had enjoyed the assistance of their children, whereas

---

[11] P. C. Lloyd, *Yoruba Land Law*, p. 329.
[12] R. Galletti *et al.*, *Nigerian Cocoa Farmers*, p. 206.
[13] Lloyd, p. 329.

nowadays their own children were educated and no longer engaged in farming. More recently, migrant farmers who began growing cocoa in Ife after World War II also relied heavily at first on kinsmen or men from their home towns for extra farm labour. Many of my informants said that they had got their start in cocoa farming by working for or with their fathers, uncles, or older brothers, who did not pay them but helped them to start their own farms. Today, however, their children have moved on to farm for themselves or engage in non-agricultural occupations. As one informant put it, 'In the past, sons worked for their fathers, but today we have schools and civilization, and now the fathers work for their sons.' Even so, the proportion of farmers who said that they currently receive help from sons or junior brothers was higher in the immigrant village of Abanata (in Ife) than in Araromi-Aperin, where most of the cocoa was planted long ago. In Ondo a number of the immigrant farmers I interviewed were in the process of establishing their own farms, with assistance from kinsmen for whom they had worked in the past. Some continued to help on their fathers' or brothers' farms in Ife, especially at harvest time.

In principle, early cocoa farmers could also obtain assistance on their farms through several other 'non-market' mechanisms, including mutual assistance groups (*owe* and *aro*), debtors (*iwofa*), and slaves.[14] In fact, few of my informants said that their forebears had actually made use of *owe*, *aro*, or *iwofa* over any length of time. Mutual assistance arrangements were usually employed only for heavy one-shot tasks such as clearing forest land or building a house, and only men with money to lend could obtain the services of *iwofa*.

On the other hand, several of my informants mentioned slaves as a source of labour on their families' early cocoa farms. Although in Lagos colony and the neighbouring Egba and Ijebu states domestic slavery declined rapidly after the imposition of colonial rule,[15] further inland it seems to have lingered for several decades. Except in Lagos colony, slavery was not officially abolished in Southern Nigeria until 1916, and as late as 1921 the Resident of Oyo Province noted that there were still a number of people who 'consider themselves

[14] These institutions are described in several sources, including Johnson, *History of the Yorubas*; N. A. Fadipe, *Sociology of the Yoruba*, ed. F. O. and O. O. Okediji; and Chief J. A. Ayorinde, 'Western Nigeria Village Social Organization', mimeographed (1966?).

[15] Hopkins, 'Economic Imperialism', *Economic History Review*. 21, 3 (Dec. 1968); Agiri, 'Kola in Western Nigeria'.

domestic slaves [and] insist on paying manumission fees'.[16] In 1923 there were said to be 'hundreds' of slave descendants in Ondo town, and periodic disputes were reported concerning redemption fees or dowry payments to the owners of female slaves.[17] At the same time J. A. Obisesan noted in his diary that his family's 'personal retainers are going one by one' and wondered who would replace them 'in this age of freedom and enlightenment', without wars or slave raids.[18] Thus the transition from slavery to an agricultural population composed of independent farmers and wage labourers probably occurred more gradually in Oyo and Ondo Provinces than it did further south, and some cocoa farmers may have continued to use slave labour as late as the 1920s.

However, farmers have also used hired labour from the earliest years of cocoa cultivation, and have come to rely increasingly on hired workers as the availability of labour from other sources has declined. In the course of my fieldwork, I found that the majority of farmers I interviewed employed labourers, and a large number said that the earliest cocoa planters in their families had also hired farm workers. In the Ibadan area most of my informants employed labourers in 1966, and nearly half of them said that their fathers had done so. In Ondo, where cocoa farming began later than in Ibadan, three-quarters of the first-generation planters were said to have hired labour and nearly everyone does so today. Similarly, all of my informants in the Ife area said they used hired labour. The widespread use of hired labour has also been documented by other students of the cocoa economy, including C. D. Forde (quoted above) and Galletti, Baldwin, and Dina, who found that in 1951/2, about 40 per cent of the total man-hours worked on cocoa and food farms in their sample households were supplied by hired labourers.[19] However, as I pointed out above, most of these observers associate the development of wage labour in the cocoa economy with the advent of migrant workers from outside the cocoa belt, and state (or imply) that most of the non-family labour employed by cocoa farmers is supplied by immigrants.

In fact, local labour supplies may have been more important than

[16] Oyo Province, Annual Report, 1921, CSO 26/06027 (NAI). Cf. Ife Division, Annual Report, 1917, OYOPROF 4/6, 355/1917, and McPhee, p. 257. Lloyd (p. 256) also cites cases of slaves who continued to live with their former masters.
[17] Ondo Province, Annual Report, 1923, CSO 26/11874, vol. i (NAI).
[18] J. A. Obisesan, Diary, 16 Feb. 1921.
[19] Galletti et al., p. 668.

these statements indicate. Forde found widespread use of local labour in Ibadan, although not in Colony Province.[20] The information I collected in group interviews suggests that a majority of farmers in the Ife and Ibadan areas employ other Yorubas on their farms, although these data do not distinguish clearly between local and migrant Yoruba labourers. However, when I began in my sample villages to interview farmers at length about their occupations, I discovered that a number of those who had described themselves simply as 'farmers' in response to the census questionnaire *also* worked as farm labourers, or had done so in the past. Conversely, two-thirds or more of the labourers I interviewed had farms of their own. (See Table V.1.) Although the importance of local labour supplies may have increased during and after the Nigerian civil war, which interrupted the flow of migrant labourers, especially Ibos, into the cocoa belt, it seems likely that farmers have worked for each other for a long time.[21]

TABLE V.1

Labourers in Four Villages

Village	Per cent of farmers who also work as labourers	Per cent of labourers who have farms of their own
Araromi-Aperin	49	65
Abanata	20	75
Orotedo	62	67
Omifon	19	100

Source: Based on detailed interviews with a sample of farmers and labourers in each village.

The reason why Yorubas resident in the cocoa belt have been willing to work as farm labourers (or even to have remained in a condition of slavery for several decades after the beginning of colonial rule) is, I think, related to their need for financial resources or other assistance in getting established as cocoa farmers. As I pointed out

[20] Forde and Scott, p. 91.
[21] Although he recognizes the existence of local labour supplies, Lloyd appears to assume that the temporary character of local labourers' contracts with their employers meant that they made up a minor part of the total hired labour force. (p. 329). Such an assumption is not warranted, however, since *most* labourers work on temporary contracts.

in Chapter III, migrant farmers from the savannah often began by working for several years on other men's farms—either for cash wages, which they later invested in cocoa farms, or for subsistence and support while they planted their first farms. Similarly, in the early decades of cocoa growing, many young men worked for their fathers, brothers, or 'masters', who, in turn, later helped them to establish their own farms. One of my informants, whose father had employed many slaves, pointed out that his father had helped many of his slaves to start their own farms: 'that was his way of paying them'. Eventually, as cocoa growing spread, more and more farmers could afford to hire farm workers, and the relative importance of non-market methods of employment declined. However, the terms on which hired workers were employed also reflected 'traditional' practices and labourers' concern with economic security and their future, as well as with short-run monetary rewards.

The Terms of Employment for Hired Labour

Most hired labourers today work for cash wages, calculated on a daily or task basis, or by the year. As far as I can tell, these have been the predominant methods of labour employment since the early years of cocoa farming. The remuneration of labourers with a share of the crop—a common practice in other cocoa-producing areas of West Africa—occurs infrequently in Nigeria. Usually farmers employ sharecroppers, or 'caretakers' as they are often called, when they cannot or do not wish to *manage* their own farms.[22] Women who inherit cocoa farms, for example, often employ caretakers to maintain and harvest the farm in return for a share of the crop. Similarly, a farmer who owns cocoa farms at some distance from his residence or who is primarily engaged in some other occupation may also hire caretakers to look after his farms. In 1961 the Ondo Customary Court concluded that a cocoa farm had been sold to its present user on the grounds that the original owner, who had been ill for some time, 'never gave this farm to any caretaker with whom he and his brother could have been sharing the net proceeds'.[23] Among my

[22] Polly Hill has criticized use of the term 'caretaker' to denote farm labourers employed under the *abusa* system—i.e. for one-third of the crop—in Ghana. In Nigeria, however, the term seems more appropriate, since most sharecroppers assume complete responsibility for the farms they work in situations where the farm owner is unable or unwilling to do so. P. Hill, 'Systems of Labour Employment on Gold Coast Cocoa Farms', *W.A.I.S.E.R. Conference Proceedings*, Mar. 1956, p. 57. Sharecropping is also prevalent in Ivory Coast. M. Dupire, 'Planteurs autochtones et étrangers en Basse-Côte d'Ivoire orientale', *Études Éburnéennes*, 8 (1960).

[23] Ondo Grade B Customary Court Records 89/C1/61.

informants, those who presently employ sharecroppers are either relatively well-to-do farmers with large, scattered holdings, or civil servants and businessmen, whose time is primarily taken up with non-agricultural occupations,[24] and who do not want to take the time to supervise labourers directly.

In the past, sharecropping contracts often provided that the farm owner and caretaker each received one-half of the net proceeds of the farm, after deducting expenses. Since the use of pesticides and insecticides has become widespread among cocoa farmers, it has become common to divide the proceeds into three parts—one for the owner, one for the caretaker, and one for 'chemicals'. In practice, whichever party handles the purchases of chemicals probably earns more than one-third of the value of the crop. In some cases, farm owners are now commuting their third of the crop into a cash payment agreed upon in advance. This system attributes all the risk of a poor crop or gain from a good one to the caretaker, and thus increases his incentive to manage the farm well. In the long run, this is to the owner's advantage as well, since a farm properly cared for will usually yield more and the caretaker's 'rent' may be reassessed from year to year.

Most hired labourers, as distinct from sharecroppers, work under the direct supervision of their employers. Basically, there are two different types of agreement between farmers and farm workers: 'annual contracts', under which a labourer engages to work for one employer for a year (or major portion thereof) in return for food, lodging, and a sum of money paid at the end of the labourer's period of service; and 'casual contracts', under which a labourer undertakes to perform a specific task—for example, harvesting cocoa or weeding a farm—for which he is paid as soon as the work is completed.[25] His remuneration may be calculated on either a daily or a piece-rate basis. Details of each type of contract vary: in some cases an annual

[24] Also, men who have retired from active work sometimes employ caretakers. Caretakers or sharecroppers should not be confused with tenants, discussed earlier in this book. A tenant obtains the use of a piece of land, usually in exchange for gifts and/or *ishakole*; he farms it for himself and is considered the owner of whatever he plants on the land, including tree crops if that was part of the original bargain. A sharecropper works on someone else's farm. Thus, it can happen that a tenant employs a caretaker.

[25] Galletti *et al.* refer to 'permanent' and 'semi-permanent' labourers, by which they mean men paid on an annual or a monthly basis. Since many of these labourers are migrants who do not settle in the cocoa belt, the term 'permanent' seems misleading. They also divide casual labourers into those paid by the day, by the 'task' of 200 heaps, and by the 'contract' of variable extent. See pp. 211–14.

worker's wage may be reckoned on the basis of a daily or monthly rate, so that the worker is penalized for idleness, or a casual worker may agree to accept payment after the cocoa harvest. However, the two contracts are quite distinct and involve rather different advantages and disadvantages for employer and worker.

Annual contracts. The status of a labourer employed on an annual contract is similar to that of a junior member of the employer's household. The employer provides the necessities of life—food, shelter, sometimes even work clothes—and the tools or equipment needed for farm work. He also serves as the labourer's chief contact with the local community. The labourer may in turn be asked to perform any kind of task at any time. He is treated as an economic and social dependant of his employer. I found, for example, that annual labourers, like sons or junior brothers of the head of a household, refused to be interviewed unless the head of the house was present and then often let the latter answer most of my questions.

Annual contracts provide the labourer with a measure of social and economic security but relatively low wages. During the 1960s annual labourers appear to have earned between £15 and £36 per annum, depending on the worker's age and ability.[26] In Ondo I met a number of employers who said they paid their annual labourers on the basis of daily or monthly rates. The ranges cited were one to two shillings per day, or £1. 15s. to £2. 5s. per month. If a labourer worked thirty days a month for ten months, these daily rates would yield annual earnings of £15 to £30; the monthly rates, annual earnings of £17. 10s. to £22. 10s. These wages are considerably lower than those a labourer can earn on daily or task contracts.

Farmers, on the other hand, generally stated that they prefer to hire labourers on annual rather than casual contracts because such labourers are 'always available' (so that farm tasks such as planting food crops or spraying cocoa trees can be done on time) and can be asked to do any kind of work. Economically, such contracts involve not only a low effective daily rate, but are easily financed, since the labourer is paid after the cocoa harvest, when the farmer is most likely to have cash on hand. Labourers who have to be paid upon completion of their tasks impose a financial burden on their employers, as Galletti *et al.* pointed out: 'this demand [by labourers] for ready money rather than excessive rates of wages or genuine

[26] The average figure derived from responses of 47 informants in four sample villages was £24. 16s.

shortage of labourers seems to cause the farmers' difficulties'.[27] Thus if a farmer is likely to need more than a small amount of labour during the season, it is usually cheaper and more convenient for him to employ annual labourers than to borrow money to pay casual labourers who may not be available when he needs them most.

Casual contracts. These pay much better than annual contracts, on a daily basis, and leave the labourer free to move from employer to employer, so that he is likely to accumulate a higher income over the year than he would on an annual contract, unless demand for labour is very low. (Some labourers move from village to village during the farming season, and are employed almost continuously.) Table V.2 summarizes the information I collected (from both farm

TABLE V.2

Agricultural Wage Rates Reported by Informants
(*casual contracts*)

Task	Shillings per *igba*	Shillings per day
Clear bush	8·65	—
Make heaps	8·08	—
Weed food farms	10·28	—
Weed cocoa farms	5·41	5·08
Spray cocoa farms	—	5·24
Pluck cocoa	—	4·74
Other	4·71	3·96

Notes: Figures are weighted averages of all informants' responses, from both group and individual interviews. Only responses referring to the period 1965/6 to 1970/1 are included. Yams are planted in heaps of earth which stand about two feet high. One *igba* is 200 yam heaps or approximately one-fifteenth of an acre.

owners and farm workers) on rates paid for different tasks. Workers paid on a daily basis, usually for spraying or harvesting cocoa, typically earn about five shillings a day, although responses varied from one to ten shillings per day. Women, who assist at the cocoa harvest by breaking open the pods, removing the beans, and carrying them to the place where they will be fermented and dried, are usually paid less—about three shillings per day.

For other tasks—notably clearing and preparing ground for cultivation, or weeding cocoa and/or food farms—labourers are usually paid by the job. The rate for a given area of land varies widely,

[27] p. 210.

depending on how overgrown the site is and on the relative bargaining positions of employer and labourer(s). The rates quoted to me were said to be typical of the informant's experience, rather than based on specific transactions, and thus may contain elements of wishful thinking. However, the results suggest that, if anything, such tasks pay even better than daily-rated ones: most informants agreed that a labourer could easily handle the basic task unit (the *igba*) in a day, except when clearing heavy forest. Indeed, some enterprising labourers said that they could do two or more *igba* in a full day's work.[28] For example, one Igbirra farmer at Omifon, who was establishing his own cocoa farm, said he employed labourers to weed the farm for him at a cost of £2. 10s. for two to three weeks' work. He paid them with money which he himself earned by working on other farmers' food plots, where he could earn as much as 10s. 6d. in a day by making heaps. Similarly, an Ibadan farmer at Araromi-Aperin used money he earned cutting palm fruit (anything from 12s. 6d. to £1. 10s. per day) to hire labourers (at 10s. to 15s. per week) to clear the ground, make heaps, and plant food crops for him.

As these examples suggest, casual contracts also have some advantages from the employer's viewpoint. If labourers are available they can of course be hired to do only limited amounts of work, which may be all a poor farmer can afford. If the farmer has no concurrent source of cash income from which to pay his labourers, or enjoys considerable influence in the community, he may be able to persuade them to wait for their money until after the harvest. J. A. Obisesan, as a member of the landowning Aperin family in Ibadan, seems, for example, to have had little difficulty getting people to work for him during the depression, although his financial resources were almost non-existent.[29] One of my informants said that he often employed his tenants as labourers on his own farms. Usually he paid them after the harvest but 'if they needed money' he paid them as soon as their work was finished. In one village an influential man had done some of his neighbours a favour by taking over their outstanding obligations to pay back wages to a group of 'Agatu' labourers;[30] on the

---

[28] Cf. Galletti *et al.*, p. 212. In 1938 Forde reported that in Ibadan labourers 'are employed on the "Egba" system [*sic*], being paid from 6d. to 8d. for clearing, hoeing or harvesting an area equivalent to 200 yam heaps . . . This is approximately a day's work though a good worker can hoe or reap up to 300 and even occasionally 400 in the course of a day' (Forde and Scott, p. 91).

[29] Obisesan, Diary, 1930s.

[30] The term 'Agatu' is loosely applied to a variety of peoples from the Niger–Benue confluence by their Yoruba employers. In addition to Agatus proper, I have

strength of his public position, he persuaded the labourers to accept his promise to pay them at the end of the farming season. He subsequently defaulted on his promise and, as a result, 'Agatu' labourers were boycotting the village of the farmers involved.

In a tight labour market, however, workers are in a relatively good bargaining position and may successfully refuse to work on annual contracts. Certainly, much of the available evidence suggests that most labour in the cocoa economy is hired on a casual basis. Galletti, Baldwin, and Dina found, for example, that only 10 per cent of the households (and about the same proportion of the labourers) they interviewed employed annual labourers.[31] The results of my own interviews yielded what at first appeared to be a very telling piece of evidence on this point. In my 1966 interviews with descendants of early planters in Ibadan and Ondo, and again in talking with individuals or groups of farmers in several Ife and a few Ondo villages in 1970/1, most of my informants said that they employed labourers on an annual basis whereas relatively few mentioned casual contracts. In Ibadan and Ondo the reported incidence of annual contracts was higher among second- than among first-generation cocoa farmers, suggesting that the relative importance of such contracts had increased over time. However, most of these people were asked only whether they employed labourers at any time and, if so, in what manner they paid them. In the village studies I made in 1970–1 I asked farmers for particulars about the labourers they had employed most *recently*. In this case most of the employers said that they had last employed labourers on a daily or task basis, whereas less than half mentioned annual contracts. My interviews with labourers yielded similar information. (See below, Tables V.9 and V.10.) Thus it would appear that the form of my question in the group interviews had led

---

heard it used to refer to other Idoma-speaking peoples (e.g. Oturkpos) and to Igaras, and it may be used for other groups as well. According to R. G. Armstrong, the term 'Igara' is also misused by the Yorubas to mean Igala, in which case some of the labourers described by Yoruba farmers as Agatus may also be Igalas. I never met any Igala labourers in my own fieldwork; all the 'Gara' labourers I encountered were Igaras from the Midwest State. See Armstrong, 'The Idoma-Speaking Peoples', in C. Forde *et al.*, *Peoples of the Niger–Benue Confluence*, Ethnographic Survey of Africa: Western Africa, Part X (London, 1955).

[31] p. 206. Their evidence on the importance of casual contracts is not very useful for our purposes, since they report the number of times such contracts occurred in their records—not the number of farmers or labourers using this system. Thus, presumably, if one farmer or one labourer were involved in half a dozen casual contracts during the course of a year, this fact would be recorded half a dozen times, whereas a farmer or labourer involved in an annual contract would appear only once. Ibid., p. 213.

farmers to express their preference rather than their practice; in actuality, most cocoa farmers could only get labourers by the day or by the job.

However, my results are consistent with an alternative explanation. Both the Galletti study and my village surveys were made at times when the demand for labour in the cocoa belt was especially high relative to the supply. In 1951/2 the cocoa price reached an unprecedented height; at £170 per ton, it was nearly half as high again as the previous year's price and ten times the level of prices prevailing during World War II. Conditions of employment in cocoa farming were so favourable that labourers recruited by the Public Works Department for road work in the cocoa area 'merely took advantage of the transport arranged for them and as soon as possible departed to a farming settlement'.[32] Under these circumstances, it is hardly surprising that labourers preferred short-term engagements and employers were willing to provide them. 1970/1 was also a year of relatively favourable cocoa prices; after falling steeply for most of the 1960s, the Marketing Board price of cocoa was increased substantially in 1969/70 and again slightly in 1970/1, thus putting farmers in a better position to hire labourers than they had been for a decade.[33] Moreover, the supply of migrant labour was reduced in the late 1960s and early 1970s, owing to the virtual disappearance of Ibo labourers from the cocoa-farming area after 1966. In 1970/1, although a few Ibos had begun to return to the Western State after the end of the civil war, far fewer farmers were employing Ibos than had done so in the past. Officials in the Ministry of Agriculture opined that the resulting labour shortage had forced farmers to hire more Yorubas, who insisted on better terms than farmers had formerly accorded their Ibo labourers. However, the increase in labourers' wages would be quite consistent with the change in labour market conditions, without the implied influence of ethnic bias.

[32] Galletti et al., p. 211, n. 1.
[33] See Appendix III. The cost of living for low-income families in Ibadan rose 26 per cent between 1960 and 1969, so that the purchasing power of the value of a ton of cocoa was lower in 1969/70 than it had been at the end of the 1950s. However, it was higher, even allowing for the rising cost of living, in 1969/70 and 1970/1 than at any time from 1961 on. It is impossible to estimate changes in farmers' average real incomes (as opposed to gross receipts), owing to the lack of data on changes in average yield. Helleiner uses the term 'real producer income' to refer to the value of total marketing board purchases, deflated by an index of consumer prices. See G. K. Helleiner, *Peasant Agriculture, Government and Economic Growth in Nigeria*, Table II-B-1.

The evidence presented so far may simply reflect a tendency for most labourers to be employed on a casual basis during periods of high cocoa prices and/or limited labour supply, when workers are in a favourable bargaining position *vis-à-vis* their employers. At other times, when the market for cocoa was depressed and/or labour unusually abundant in the cocoa belt, more workers may have been employed on annual contracts. Forde reports, for example, that in 1938, when the Nigerian economy was still suffering from the effects of the depression (the price of cocoa had risen the year before and then dropped sharply again), most farm labourers in the Agege and Abeokuta areas were employed on an annual basis.[34] 1966 was also a year of relatively low cocoa prices; the Marketing Board price fell from £116 in 1964/5 to £61 the following year. Thus the impression I gained in 1966—that my informants were more likely than their fathers had been to employ labourers on annual contracts—may have reflected actual economic circumstances rather than mere wishful thinking.

Agricultural Wage Rates and Labourers' Share in the Gains from Cocoa Growing

If, as the historical evidence cited in the first section of this chapter suggests, the supply of farm labour has tended to grow more slowly than the demand for it, one would expect the terms on which farm labourers are employed to become more favourable over time, although they might tend to fluctuate with cyclical variations in the market for Nigerian cocoa.[35] I do not have enough evidence on

[34] Forde and Scott, pp. 91–2.

[35] Technically one would expect to find a positive association between labourers' earnings and the market price of cocoa if (1) the supply curve of farm labour were relatively constant, compared to the demand schedule, and (2) wage rates were determined by market rather than by institutional forces. The latter assumption seems justified for agricultural labour. Since World War II, the combined influence of trade unions and public opinion has served to raise wages in the public and industrial sectors above a market-clearing level, so that there is now an excess supply of labour for unskilled and semi-skilled jobs, at least in urban areas. Cocoa farmers, however, still complain '[we] cannot find workers when we want them' or cannot afford to hire them under present conditions. Also, since the supply of farm labour depends largely on alternative income-earning opportunities in agriculture, in the short-run it should shift to the right when agricultural markets are depressed, to the left when demand for agricultural commodities is high, thus reinforcing rather than offsetting cyclical variations in demand. Cf. C. R. Frank, 'Urban Unemployment and Economic Growth in Africa', *Oxford Economic Papers*, 20, 2 (July 1968), and S. S. Berry, 'Economic Development with Unlimited Supplies of Labour: Some Further Complications Suggested by Contemporary African Experience', ibid., 22, 2 (July 1970), and below, p. 142, n. 39.

long-term trends in the relative importance of annual and casual
contracts to test the validity of this proposition for the terms on
which labourers were employed, but there is some information on
changes in agricultural wage rates over time.[36] This evidence is
presented in Fig. 7 and Table V.3. In general, the *Bluebook* rates are
consistent with the few data on wages actually paid by farmers which
I have been able to put together from other sources. The discrepancy
between daily rates and the daily equivalent of task rates is consistent
with Galletti's findings in 1951/2 and mine in 1970/1: task rates are

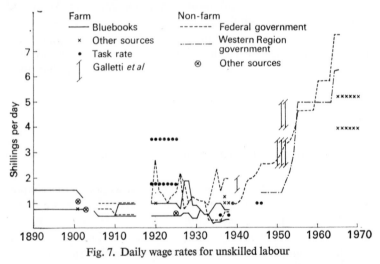

Fig. 7. Daily wage rates for unskilled labour

decidedly higher. However, since the official data give rather wide
ranges of rates instead of annual averages, it is quite possible that
they disguise year-to-year fluctuations within those ranges, which the
other available data are too scanty to reveal.

Additional information on the market for unskilled labour may
be obtained from the wage rates paid by the government. As Fig. 7
shows, the government wage rate for unskilled labour fell somewhat
from the 1890s to the period 1905–14, which may have contributed
to the spread of cocoa growing by increasing the number of people

[36] The colonial government published data on wages in their annual *Bluebooks*,
which generally include both the government rates for unskilled labour and one or
more figures for unskilled farm labour. Unfortunately the *Bluebooks* do not state the
source of their data on agricultural wage rates. We do not know, therefore, whether
they refer to wages paid by farmers or by the Department of Agriculture; to Lagos
Colony only or to all of Southern Nigeria; or, if they are wages paid by farmers, how
representative a group of farmers supplied the government with this information.

willing to work for farmers in the decade preceding World War I. During the war the colonial administration's staff and budget were considerably reduced and publication of the *Bluebooks* ceased. From 1919 on, however, there is some information not only on wage rates for unskilled labour in both government and agricultural employ- ment, but also on prices of domestic staple foodstuffs and of imported

TABLE V.3

Monthly Wage Rates (Long-term Contracts)
(£. s. d.)

Date	Farm	Non-farm
1902		£1. 6s. 0d. (Ibadan)[a]
1905	£7. 4s. 0d.–£9. 0s. 0d.	—
1914		£1. 5s. 0d.–£1. 10s. 0d. (Ibadan)[a]
1919		£1. 5s. 0d.
1920		£2. 0s. 0d.–£2. 2s. 0d.
1921		£2. 18s. 4d.
1922		—
1923		£1. 5s. 0d.
1924		£1. 16s. 8d.
1925		£2. 0s. 0d.
1926		—
1927		£1. 0s. 0d.–£2. 5s. 0d.
1928		£1. 5s. 7d.
1929		£1. 11s. 3d.
1930		£1. 9s. 5d.
1931		18s. 4d.–£1. 7s. 6d.
1932		£1. 0s. 7d.–£1. 6s. 7d.
1933	10s. (Ife)[b]	£1. 0s. 9d. (PWD only)
1934	12s. 6d. (Ife)[b]	18s. 0d. ,,
1935		16s. 11d. ,,
1936		16s. 8d. ,, £3. 0s. 0d. (Ibadan)[c]
1937		15s. 11d. (PWD only)
1938	10s.–15s. (Egba)[d]	16s. 7d. ,,
1939		—
1940	15s. (Ife)[b]	
1940–9	15s.–18s. (Ibadan)[e] 10s. (Ife)[e]	
1951/2	£1. 10s. 0d.–£2. 0s. 0d. (Ilesha)[f] £2. 10s. 0d.–£3. 0s. 0d. (Ibadan)[f] £1. 0s. 0d.–£1. 10s. 0d. (Ife)[f] 16s. 8d.–£3. 3s. 4d. (Ondo)[f]	

Notes and Sources: All data from *Bluebooks*, except as follows:
[a] Mapo Hall records.   [d] Forde and Scott.
[b] Ife Customary Court Records.   [e] My interviews.
[c] Oyo Province, Annual Report, 1936. [f] Galletti *et al.*

consumer goods. Thus we can trace roughly the progress of real as well as money wages.

During the interwar period, government money wage rates for skilled labour tended to reflect the state of Nigeria's foreign trade, as one would expect of a government whose financial policy aimed at budget surpluses and whose revenues came mainly from customs duties. Real wages were less volatile: in the early 1920s the government money wage rate fluctuated with import prices, so that the real wage in terms of imported commodities remained roughly constant.[37] Real wages rose in the late 1920s and fell during the depression, though by considerably less than the decline in money wage rates.

By 1940, however, colonial economic policy began to reflect the combined impact of African nationalist pressure and Keynesian economic theory. With the passage of the Colonial Development and Welfare Act in 1940, the British departed officially from 'the old principle that a Colony should have only those services which it can afford to maintain out of its own resources', and proposed to subsidize 'active development of the natural resources of the various territories so as to provide their people with improved standards of life'.[38] The Act specifically provided for the payment of adequate wages in government-sponsored projects and, in Nigeria, the central government's minimum wage rate began a stair-like climb which has yet to be reversed. During the 1940s import prices rose also because of wartime restrictions on output and shipping in the United Kingdom, so that real wages of government employees probably fell slightly. However, they rose substantially during the economic boom of the early 1950s, and since Independence the Nigerian governments have faced continued pressure at least to maintain the standard of living of their unskilled employees.[39]

[37] In terms of domestic foodstuff prices, the real wage rose in 1920 and declined thereafter.
[38] 'Statement of Policy on Colonial Development and Welfare', Great Britain, Parliamentary Papers, Cmd. 6175, 1940.
[39] The relative importance of general economic conditions, trade union activity, and political circumstance in determining the wage rates of government employees and other urban workers since 1940 has been the subject of considerable debate. See W. M. Warren, 'Urban Real Wages and the Nigerian Trade Union Movement, 1939–60', *Economic Development and Cultural Change*, 15 (Oct. 1966); P. Kilby, 'Industrial Relations and Wage Determination: Failure of the Anglo-Saxon Model', *Journal of Developing Areas*, 1 (July 1967); J. F. Weeks, 'A Comment on Peter Kilby', ibid. 3 (Oct. 1968); Kilby, 'A Reply to John F. Weeks's Comment', ibid.; R. Cohen, 'Further Comment on the Kilby/Weeks Debate', ibid. 5 (Jan. 1971); Weeks, 'Further Comment on the Kilby/Weeks Debate: An Empiricial Rejoinder', ibid.; Kilby,

Farm wage rates in Western Nigeria appear to have been more directly influenced by the fortunes of the cocoa economy than by government wage rates—at least since the mid-twenties, when Nigerian cocoa exports rose substantially, reflecting the considerable spread of planting during and after the war.[40] In the early twenties the official data suggest that agricultural money wage rates were constant, implying that the real wage moved counter-cyclically. If that is true, it is not surprising that farmers complained of acute labour scarcity in 1919–20.[41]

In subsequent periods of sharply rising cocoa prices, however, money wage rates also rose sharply and real wages in agriculture appear to have remained constant or increased. Moreover, during the brief boom of 1936–7, when the cocoa price jumped by almost 60 per cent above that of the previous year, wage rates in some areas were higher than those given in the *Bluebooks*, which suggests that competition for unskilled labour increased substantially at the time. In Ibadan the District Officer remarked that 'labourers were getting as much as £3 a month at the cocoa and transport depots. Labour for Government or Native Administration for roads or buildings at the rate of 7d. or 8d. a day was quite out of the question.'[42] Two years later the Registrar of Cooperative Societies wrote that farm wage rates had increased by as much as 50 per cent in 1937.[43]

During periods of falling prices, on the other hand, farm wages appear to have been somewhat stickier. In the major price slump of 1928–33 money and real wages both declined, though the drop in real wages was mitigated by falling prices of both domestic and imported consumer goods. In 1937/8, however, wages failed to decline with the price of cocoa. According to one observer, owing to the resulting high labour costs in addition to rising import prices and the reimposition of a tax on cocoa trees, cocoa farmers' standards of living were even lower in 1938 than they had been in the early 1930s.[44]

'Further Comment on the Kilby/Weeks Debate: Final Observation', ibid. Since individual authors' conclusions often rest heavily on their choice of indicators or base periods, it is difficult to draw a single conclusion from this debate. Weeks is probably right that 'economic forces set the limits for political action' ('Further Comment', p. 170), but that does not deny the importance of political action in effecting particular wage awards.

[40] Annual export volume averaged 17,422 tons between 1915 and 1921; 37,385 tons in the next six years.

[41] Department of Agriculture, *Annual Report*, 1920–1.

[42] Oyo Province, Annual Report, 1936.

[43] Registrar of Cooperative Societies to Chief Secretary, Lagos, 5 Mar. 1938, in 'Cocoa Agreement, 1937: Miscellaneous', CSO 26/25807, S. 8 (NAI).   [44] Ibid.

Indeed, agricultural wage rates appear to have changed little from 1937 to the mid-1940s; since import prices rose during this period, however, the real wage tended to decline. Much the same thing happened in the late 1950s and early 1960s, although some of my informants said that money wage rates also fell towards the end of this period. As I suggested earlier, some of this apparent stickiness may have masked a shift from casual to long-term contracts, which would have entailed an effective reduction in the wage rate.

In general, these data indicate that farm owners and farm workers have shared the vicissitudes of the cocoa market. Labourers do not appear to have suffered direct economic exploitation at the hands of farm owners; on the contrary, as something of a scarce commodity, farm workers have usually participated in the gains from high cocoa prices. This is indeed what we would expect in view of the fact that many farm labourers are also farm owners who regard their periods of labour service as opportunities to accumulate savings (and, in the past, experience in cocoa cultivation) rather than their only means to a subsistence income. Even for those workers who have no alternatives, and in times of general distress, farm workers appear to have been assured a measure of economic security, albeit a low wage, through the possibility of working on an annual basis.

Ethnic Affiliation, Economic Opportunity, and the Distribution of Income

So far I have presented evidence which suggests that farm labourers as a group have participated in the gains from cocoa production, particularly in periods of rising cocoa prices. However, as we have seen, the farm labour force includes a substantial proportion of farm owners, who work part time as labourers on other farms. Thus the possibility arises that landless labourers—most of whom are non-Yoruba migrant workers—form a distinct sub-group within the labour force, whose economic prospects and social position are inferior to those of resident Yoruba farmer-labourers.[45]

My evidence on labourers' ethnic backgrounds and terms of employment is unfortunately not as direct as I would like, because most of my information comes from farmers rather than from labourers themselves. Since I set out to study the development of

---

[45] Landless is not really an appropriate term to describe these workers, since most of them have access to farmland in their home communities and some grow their own foodstuffs in the cocoa belt.

cocoa farming I selected areas to study on the basis of the history of cocoa farming there and simply interviewed the labourers whom I happened to meet in the four sample villages. As a result, the group of labourers I talked to may include an unduly high proportion of resident relative to migrant workers and cannot be considered representative of the population of cocoa farm labourers. Also, I did not have the time or resources to record specific transactions on a regular basis throughout one or more farming seasons. Consequently the best I can do is to look for patterns in farmers' responses to questions about whom they hire, for what purposes, and on what terms and, when possible, check these against the responses of the appropriate groups of labourers. I shall then propose interpretations of these patterns, more to suggest lines for further investigation than to offer a definitive analysis.

The earliest *migrant* labourers employed on Yoruba cocoa farms were probably other Yorubas who lived in areas where cocoa was not yet established or could not be grown. Cocoa farmers near Lagos began to employ labourers from 'the interior' around the turn of the century and continued to do so for decades.[46] A number of my informants in Ibadan and Ondo said that their fathers had employed Ekitis. Few early cocoa planters in Ondo employed Yorubas from savannah communities, but several had done so in Ibadan. (See Table V.4.) In 1921 an observer reported that in Ilesha many people used hired labourers to clear their farms—'usually small boys from the Ekiti country'—and that labour was scarce 'even at one shilling a day'.[47] By the 1930s northern Yorubas were beginning to plant cocoa for themselves in southern Oshun and Ife Divisions, and friends and kinsmen followed them to gain experience and accumulate savings by working for local farmers.[48] In 1936 there were labourers from northern Ibadan, and from Ekiti and Ilorin Divisions in Ife, and some migrants from the savannah went as far as Ondo in search of employment.[49]

By the 1930s one also begins to encounter references to non-Yoruba

---

[46] See Chapter II above, especially citations of J. B. Webster's work on the Agege planters and A. G. Hopkins's unpublished research on the same subject.

[47] Oyo Province, Annual Report, 1921.

[48] Informants in Aba Iresi, where the first immigrant planted cocoa in 1929, pointed out that at first people from Iresi worked for Ife farmers, since none of the Iresis had any money yet to pay labourers.

[49] A. F. B. Bridges, 'Intelligence Report, Ondo District', 1935, CSO 26/30172 (NAI); Oni of Ife to District Officer, Ife, 15 July 1936, in 'Agricultural Department, Miscellaneous Correspondence', IFEDIV 1/1/112 (NAI).

TABLE V.4

Sources of Labour: Farmers' Responses
Number of employers (% employers)

A.1966

	Ibadan		Ondo	
	a	*b*	*a*	*b*
Oyo Yoruba	9 (23%)	15 (32%)	— (—)	1 (2%)
Eastern Yoruba	13 (33⅓)	2 (4)	16 (53%)	7 (14)
All Yoruba	21 (54)	20 (43)	16 (53)	8 (16)
North	5 (13)	13 (28)	5 (16⅔)	2 (4)
Niger–Benue Confluence	10 (26)	27 (57)	12 (40)	14 (27)
East	— (—)	1 (2)	6 (20)	34 (67)

B. Area notes, 1966 and 1970/1

	Ibadan	Ife	Ondo
Yoruba	20 (43%)	13 (54%)	8 (16%)
North	13 (28)	2 (8⅓)	2 (4)
Niger–Benue Confluence	27 (57)	13 (54)	14 (27)
East	1 (2)	17 (71)	34 (67)

C. Village Studies, 1970/1

	Araromi-Aperin	Abanata	Orotedo	Omifon
Yoruba	26 (81%)	12 (55%)	6 (54%)	6 (50%)
North	14 (44)	— (—)	— (—)	— (—)
Niger–Benue Confluence	14 (44)	10 (45)	4 (29)	10 (83)
East	— (—)	5 (23)	7 (50)	6 (50)
Unknown	3 (9)	4 (18)	5 (36)	2 (16⅔)

a First-generation planters. *b* Second-generation planters.

labourers working on cocoa farms. Hausa labourers were reported to be working in Otta District as early as 1926/7,[50] and in Ibadan and Ife by the early 1930s.[51] Ibos were employed in Ondo in the 1930s; according to one source, they originally sought employment on rubber plantations and timber concessions there and then moved into cocoa.[52] Also, I have found reference to Igbirras

[50] 'Assessment Report, Otta District, Abeokuta Province', 1926–7, CSO 26/20629, (NAI).

[51] Obisesan, Diary, 18 Jan. 1933; Ife Customary Court Records 1/33.

[52] This information was supplied by Chief J. A. Ayorinde. Ibo labourers in Ondo are also mentioned by Bridges, 'Intelligence Report', and Forde and Scott, p. 88.

and other peoples from the vicinity of the Niger–Benue confluence working on cocoa farms in Ife and Ondo in the 1930s.[53]

Non-Yoruba labourers may well have been employed in the cocoa belt before the 1930s. A number of first-generation planters in Ibadan and Ondo were said to have employed Hausa, Ibo, and/or 'Agatu' labourers.[54] However, the importance of non-Yoruba migrant labourers does seem to have increased after 1930. According to Chief Ayorinde, Hausas gradually replaced Ekiti labourers in the Ibadan area. In the 1950s, as we have seen, observers thought that most hired labour came from non-Yoruba areas and, among my informants, second-generation planters were more likely than their fathers to have employed non-Yorubas. (See Table V.4.) In particular, Ibadan farmers tended to employ Hausas and 'Agatus' in addition to other Yorubas. Further east, in Ife and Ondo, few farmers employed Hausas, but Ibo labourers were mentioned frequently. 'Agatus' were also to be found in these areas. Galletti et al. give no information for Ondo proper, but otherwise their comments on the origins of labourers in different parts of the cocoa belt are consistent with my findings. They also report finding numbers of Hausa and northern Yoruba labourers in Ilesha.[55]

From my interviews in the four villages I have information on three variables—wage rates, tasks performed, and types of contract—related to the terms on which labourers were employed. In the case of contracts I also have some evidence from group interviews on both current practice and the terms on which early cocoa farmers employed labourers. These data are shown in Tables V.5 to V.10.

On the whole, I found no evidence of outright wage discrimination

TABLE V.5

Range of Wage Rates Paid: Employers' Responses

Contract: Village	Annual (£ p.a.)	Daily (s. d.)	Task (s. d. per *igba*)
Araromi-Aperin	—	3/0– 7/6 [21]	8–20/0 [18]
Abanata	15–35 [9]	6– 7/6 [35]	1/6– 7/6 [20]
Other Ife	15–40 [21]	2/0–10/0 [13]	1/4– 5/0 [2]
Orotedo	15–30 [4]	3/0– 8/0 [12]	2/0–15/0 [8]
Omifon	22/10–36 [4]	4/0– 6/0 [7]	2/6–15/0 [16]

Note: Figures in brackets are numbers of responses in each category.

[53] Bridges, 'Intelligence Report'; Ife Customary Court Records 52/36.
[54] See above, p. 136, n. 30.   [55] Galletti, *et al.*, pp. 207–9.

in the sense that workers of different ethnic groups received different rates of pay for the same type of work and contract. Most farmers reported hiring labourers from more than one ethnic group, but made no distinction among ethnic groups when asked what wages they paid. There was no systematic variation from one part of

TABLE V.6

Range of Wage Rates Paid: Labourers' Responses

Contract: Labourer's Area of Origin	Annual (£)	Daily (s. d.)	Task (s. d. per igba)
Yoruba	18–25 [2]	1/6–8/6 [15]	1/0– 7/0 [8]
Hausa	—	10/0 [1]	10/0–30/0 [3]
Niger-Benue Confluence	—	5/0–20/0 [6]	2/6–20/0 [18]
Ibo	20/10 [1]	—	—

Source: Based on interviews in Araromi-Aperin, Abanata, and Orotedo.

TABLE V.7

Tasks Performed: per cent of Employers' Responses

Village: Task	Araromi- Aperin	Abanata	Orotedo	Omifon
Clear bush	25	14	8	33⅓
Make heaps	25	14	21	25
Weed cocoa	47	73	64	83
Spray cocoa	—	55	21	25
Harvest cocoa	50	55	64	33⅓
Other	34	18	21	8⅓

TABLE V.8

Tasks Performed: per cent of Labourers' Responses

Labourers' Area of Origin: Task	Yoruba	Hausa	Niger-Benue Confluence	All non- Yoruba
Clear bush	3	—	18	12
Make heaps	10	25	45	37
Weed cocoa	20	100	55	62
Spray cocoa	10	—	—	—
Harvest cocoa	20	25	45	37
Other	53	25	36	31

TABLE V.9

Contracts: per cent of Employers' Responses

A. 1966

| | Ibadan | | Ondo | |
	1st generation	2nd generation	1st generation	2nd generation
Traditional	31	—	10	—
Annual	46	64	$66\frac{2}{3}$	82
Casual	8	30	30	16
Other (caretakers)	—	4	—	10
No information	28	13	13	—

B. Area Notes, all years

	Ibadan	Ife	Ondo
Traditional	—	—	—
Annual	64	92	82
Casual	30	62	16
Other	4	8	10
No information	13	—	—

C. Village Studies, 1970/1

	Araromi-Aperin	Abanata	Orotedo	Omifon
Traditional	—	5	—	—
Annual	9	50	29	$33\frac{1}{3}$
Casual	90	86	71	100

TABLE V.10

Contracts: per cent of Labourers' Responses

Labourers' Area of Origin: Contract	Yoruba	Hausa	Niger–Benue	Ibo
Annual	$6\frac{2}{3}$	—	—	100
Daily	43	25	54	—
Task	37	100	100	—
Other	$6\frac{2}{3}$	—	—	—

the cocoa belt to another in wage rates quoted for the same task, although the ethnic composition of the labour force does appear to vary from one place to another.[56] (See Tables V.4 and V.5.) Among the labourers I interviewed, daily and task rates cited by non-Yorubas tended to be somewhat higher than those given by Yorubas.[57] (See Table V.6.) This discrepancy may simply reflect the fact that, as strangers in these villages, the non-Yoruba labourers misunderstood the question or were more suspicious of my activities than were the local people; in either case, they may have tended to give their asking price rather than what they were actually paid. If my information is accurate, however, it suggests that, far from being discriminated against, non-Yoruba migrant workers who specialize in farm labour and can move easily between employers and villages may have a better bargaining position, *vis-à-vis* the farmers, than do resident Yorubas who are obviously hard up for cash. Non-Yoruba labourers were also more likely than their Yoruba counterparts to be employed on a task than on a daily basis, which also suggests that their bargaining position was good.[58]

I did not find differences in the types of work performed by hired labourers which could be clearly related to ethnic differences. The farmer in Araromi-Aperin who told me that he never hired Hausas to pluck cocoa 'because they didn't know how to do it properly' was unusual. In general, farmers in the four sample villages hired labourers primarily to weed cocoa farms and to pluck cocoa. Over half of the farmers who employed labourers said that their labourers performed these two tasks, whereas no other task was mentioned by more than one-third of the farmers in any village. (See Table V.7.) The exceptions to this pattern were in Omifon, where only one-third of the employers used hired labour to harvest cocoa, and Abanata, where more than half of the employers hired labourers to spray their cocoa trees. Both these exceptions can be explained in terms of the development of cocoa farming in the areas involved. Most of my informants in Omifon had planted their cocoa farms after 1963, so

[56] In general, farmers expressed little open ethnic prejudice with respect to their labourers. Some made no attempt even to describe the ethnic affiliations of their labourers, saying merely that they employed 'anyone who was available'.

[57] In the four sample villages I interviewed 46 labourers: 30 Yorubas, 4 Hausa, 1 Ibo, and 11 men from the area of the Niger–Benue confluence, including Igbirras, Idomas, and Igaras.

[58] Among the labourers I interviewed, all the Hausas and 'Agatus' said they worked on a task basis, whereas only one-third of the Yoruba labourers mentioned such contracts. Half the 'Agatus' also mentioned daily rates, as did 40 per cent of the Yorubas.

that many were bearing little or no fruit at the time of my interviews, and therefore little labour was needed for harvesting. The proportion of farmers who said they hired labour to clear uncultivated land for establishing new farms was also highest in Omifon, the most recently established of the four villages. In Abanata, where most cocoa farms were planted in the 1950s, the trees were in or near their period of peak yields, when potential returns to spraying are likely to be greatest,[59] whereas in Araromi-Aperin (where most cocoa farms are older) or in Orotedo and Omifon (where they are younger) spraying is probably less profitable. Thus, the fact that farmers allocated less labour to harvesting cocoa in Omifon and more labour to spraying in Abanata is probably due to economic rather than ethnic considerations.

Among the labourers I interviewed in these villages, the Yorubas were most likely to be engaged on food farms or on other tasks not directly related to cocoa growing, such as cutting palm fruit, whereas weeding cocoa was the task mentioned most frequently by non-Yoruba workers. (Table V.8.) However, this probably does not indicate a general pattern, since in other villages some groups of non-Yorubas specialize in weeding food farms or cutting palm fruit.[60] Moreover, weeding food farms does not appear to pay any more or less than weeding cocoa (cf. Table V.2), so there is no reason to think that the Yoruba labourers of my acquaintance would be worse off than their non-Yoruba counterparts because of such a division of labour.

In the case of contracts, however, I did find variations from one part of the cocoa belt to another which appear to correspond to variations in the ethnic composition of the labour force. Both generational and geographical evidence suggest that non-Yoruba labourers are more likely to be employed on an annual basis than are Yoruba. (See Tables V.4 and V.9.) In Ibadan and Ondo both the proportion of farmers who employed non-Yoruba labourers and the proportion who employed labourers on an annual basis were higher in the second than in the first generation of farmers. Similarly, my general interviews in Ibadan, Ife, and Ondo showed a positive relationship between the proportion of farmers employing non-Yoruba labourers and that reporting the use of annual contracts. In the villages studied the incidence of Yoruba employees was markedly higher, and that of

[59] Western Nigeria Ministry of Agriculture and Natural Resources, *Tree Crop Planting Projects*, p. 13; Cocoa Research Institute of Nigeria, *Annual Report*, 1967/8.
[60] Galletti *et al.*, pp. 206 ff.; Forde and Scott, p. 83; Lloyd, pp. 88 ff.

annual contracts markedly lower in Araromi-Aperin than in the other three; among the latter, however, the relationship was not strictly inverse.

Within the non-Yoruba group further distinctions are apparent. Hausa labourers are employed more frequently in Ibadan than in Ife and Ondo, whereas Ibos were mentioned more often in Ife and Ondo than in Ibadan. In other words, Ibo labourers tend to be found in areas where labourers are most often employed on an annual basis; Hausa labourers where annual contracts are not so commonly used. This was the case in the village studies as well as in the group interviews, so that this generalization is based upon current practice as well as on farmers' general statements. Only workers from the Niger–Benue confluence were fairly evenly distributed geographically and hence were not, in my data, associated one way or the other with the use of annual contracts.

The data on casual contracts are not so clear cut. The village studies show that in 1970 *most* workers were employed on a casual basis. Galletti *et al.* came to the same conclusion in 1951/2 and, as I explained above, the importance of casual contracts may have been understated in the material I collected in 1966. Hence, we would probably not be justified in putting much emphasis on apparent variations in the importance of such contracts over time or between geographical areas. However, the apparent association between annual contracts and non-Yoruba—especially Ibo—labourers warrants some attempt at explanation.

Why should non-Yoruba workers in general, and Ibos in particular, be more likely than Yorubas (or non-Ibos) to accept work on annual contracts? Earlier in this chapter, I suggested that although annual contracts do not pay as well as casual ones, they do provide the labourer with a certain amount of security: he is guaranteed food, lodging, work clothes, and a sponsor in the community for a year or more at a time. Presumably such contracts would be relatively attractive to strangers—people who have no assured source of livelihood or assurance against illness or difficulty in the community where they seek employment. Resident Yorubas, who have their own farms and nearby kinsfolk, would be most unlikely to engage themselves as annual labourers; they prefer the higher rates of pay and greater freedom to work on their own farms (or at other occupations) afforded by daily or task contracts. Today, most stranger Yorubas in cocoa-belt communities are in a similar position. Either they are tenant farmers with their own farms to look after or, like the Ijebus, Ekitis, etc., in Araromi-Aperin, they are established residents with other occupations to take up their time and provide them with income. In the past, however, migrant Ekiti or Oyo Yorubas did tend to work on annual contracts (or for their kinsmen). This was the characteristic mode of employment at Agege, for example, and some of my informants described similar arrangements. Even today one occasionally finds a stranger Yoruba employed on an annual basis, such as an Ilorin man I met at Araromi-Aperin who was managing a farm for an absentee owner.

Among non-Yoruba labourers the tendency for Hausas to be employed on casual contracts and Ibos on annual contracts can be explained along similar lines. Most migrant Hausa labourers come to Western Nigeria for a few months during the dry season when they are not busy on their own farms at home.[61] Thus they are in the cocoa belt from around November to March, rather than for the whole growing season. Moreover, when they come, they usually lodge with resident Hausa traders, who provide them with shelter, security, and local contacts. This system has been documented in detail for Hausas living in major towns, such as Ibadan, but it exists in the rural areas as well.[62] Before the late 1920s most of the kola consumed in Northern Nigeria was imported. Domestic production began to increase in the 1920s, first around Agege, Otta, and Ijebu Remo and, later, further east in Ibadan and Ife.[63] Despite the protests of Yoruba traders, Hausa kola traders moved into the rural areas to deal directly with farmers and small-scale middlemen and women. During 'the 1930's and 1940's, scores of such communities sprang up in the Ibadan, Shagamu, Abeokuta, Agege, Ifo, Ijebu and other districts'.[64] Hausa traders established miniature 'Sabos' (strangers' quarters) in major villages, which provided not only bases for their kola-buying operations but also accommodation for migrant labourers.

I encountered such communities in Araromi-Aperin and Abanata. The 'Sabo' in Araromi-Aperin, for example, had a resident population of about thirty and migrants began arriving in October. The latter were often young men who had spent little time in the Western

---

[61] R. M. Prothero, *Migrant Labour from Sokoto Province, Northern Nigeria* (Kaduna, 1958?). I observed this pattern among Hausa labourers in Araromi-Aperin.

[62] A. Cohen, 'Politics of the Kola Trade', *Africa*, 36, 1966, and *Custom and Politics in Urban Africa*.

[63] Agiri, *passim*.   [64] Cohen, 'Politics of the Kola Trade', p. 28.

State and knew no Yoruba. Hence they relied on the resident Hausa traders to find them jobs, help them bargain over wage rates, etc., with local farmers. The fact that the earliest references I found to Hausa labourers in the cocoa belt date from the 1930s (or the late 1920s in Otta District) suggest that Hausas did not begin to seek employment on cocoa farms until Hausa kola traders had begun to establish connections in Yoruba villages; consequently, the labourers always had a base to work from and did not need the security of annual contracts.[65]

Ibos, on the other hand, appear to have had no such bases of operation in the cocoa belt. Little is known about the history or organization of the migration of Ibo farm labourers to the cocoa belt, and I was unable to collect much information because there are so few Ibo labourers there now. However, there is no reason to believe that there were groups of resident Ibos in the *rural* areas of Western Nigeria comparable to those of the Hausa kola traders.[66] There were of course many Ibos living in Yoruba towns and engaged in non-agricultural pursuits before the civil war,[67] and it may be that most Ibo farm workers aspired to join their countrymen in the towns, rather than to settle in the rural areas as farmers.[68] Whatever the reasons for it, the absence of established Ibo communities in rural Yorubaland would seem to make annual contracts more attractive to Ibo than to Hausa labourers.

The fact that I did not find a similar association between annual contracts and 'Agatu' labourers, who also do not appear to have local bases comparable to the Hausas' in the cocoa belt, does not necessarily refute this line of argument. Agatu labourers appear to be ubiquitous in Western Nigeria: I found no significant variation in the proportion of farmers employing Agatu labourers from one part of the cocoa belt to another, as I did in the case of Hausas and Ibos. Moreover, as indicated earlier, the term 'Agatu' is very imprecise and may well conceal variations in the incidence and treatment of different ethnic groups from the general area of the Niger–Benue

[65] Not all 'annual contracts' last for a year, so the fact that Hausa labourers stay in the cocoa belt for only a few months does not fully explain their association with casual contracts.

[66] I did not encounter any such groups in 1966, before Ibos began to leave the Western Region, and have found no references to them in the literature. The Ibo farmer I met in Egbejoda was a lone exception.

[67] C. Okonjo, 'The Western Ibo', in P. C. Lloyd, B. Awe, and A. L. Mabogunje, eds., *The City of Ibadan.*

[68] This was the opinion of some of my Yoruba informants, who said that Ibo labourers preferred to invest their savings in trade rather than in cocoa farms.

confluence. The evidence I have on the position of these workers compared to that of workers from other ethnic groups is insufficient to warrant any conclusions.

Conclusion

Polly Hill has characterized Ghanaian cocoa farmers as 'capitalists' and, to a considerable extent, this term also applies to Nigerian cocoa growers. The establishment of a cocoa farm is an act of capital formation, and requires financial and entrepreneurial resources as well as land and labour. The fact that farmers have often relied on non-economic institutions for help in mobilizing resources and organizing their productive activities does not alter the basic economic character of their undertakings. And, over time, their methods of farm management have become increasingly commercialized; this is particularly clear in the case of labour employment.

On the other hand, the term 'capitalist farmer' may suggest a somewhat different pattern of socio-economic relationships between farm owners and farm workers than that which obtains in the Nigerian cocoa economy. For one thing, the particular institutional relationships between farm owners and farm workers, such as the 'annual contract' or the types of 'sharecropping' arrangements found in Western Nigeria and elsewhere in West Africa, obviously derive from indigenous social and cultural systems—just as the relationships between 'landowner' and 'tenant' in the Nigerian cocoa belt retain characteristics of the traditional ties between community leaders and immigrants. However, the distinctive characteristics of Nigerian cocoa farming do not derive solely from its African setting; the distribution of economic gains and the pattern of social relations between Yoruba cocoa farmers and their employees also reflect underlying economic conditions. Given the technical requirements for successful cultivation of Amelonado cocoa and the ready availability of suitable land to most people wishing to grow cocoa, labour has been a relatively scarce factor of production in the cocoa economy. Many men have offered their services temporarily to men who could afford or could arrange to pay them, but there does not seem to have been the 'unlimited' supply of labour assumed in classical and Marxist analyses of European economic change or the more recent models of economic development deriving from the work of W. A. Lewis. Consequently, farm workers appear to have shared in the gains of the Western Nigerian cocoa economy over time, rather than to have been kept at a minimal wage by their 'capitalist' employers. Indeed, as we have seen, many farm workers in the cocoa belt are also farm owners.[69]

It cannot be said that the rural economy of Western Nigeria is an egalitarian system in which every man has equal access to the means of production or enjoys the same standard of living as his neighbours. Not only are there considerable differences in wealth and income associated with differences in landownership or the accumulation of capital, but there are also differences in occupations and the distribution of farm ownership which coincide with ethnic divisions.[70] The significance of these patterns is difficult to establish, but the evidence I have presented in this and earlier chapters suggests that it is not simply a matter of economic discrimination against ethnic minorities. Rather, ethnic ties (like those among kinsmen) appear to have afforded many individuals an alternative mechanism for mobilizing economic resources and organizing their productive activities, which has frequently contributed to their economic success. Yoruba farmers have often substituted the support and assistance of relatives and fellow townsmen for savings, purchased insurance, and hired labour in establishing and maintaining their cocoa farms. And, in so far as non-Yoruba migrant labourers have been able to rely on their 'countrymen' in Western Nigeria for support and assistance in finding jobs and maintaining themselves while they work, their bargaining position *vis-à-vis* potential employers and the terms on which they work appear to have been improved. This in turn has helped to prevent the formation of distinct social strata or classes in the rural sector based on differences in economic function and income.

[69] This pattern of income distribution is, of course, likely to last only as long as land remains relatively abundant in the cocoa belt.

[70] On the unequal distribution of income among cocoa farmers and its relationship to the marketing of cocoa, see Chapter VII, below and S. M. Essang, 'The Distribution of Earnings in the Cocoa Economy of Western Nigeria'.

CHAPTER VI

The Structure of the Rural Economy

THE establishment of thousands of new farming settlements in the
Western Nigerian forest belt, followed by the growth of farm incomes
as more and more cocoa plots matured, led to a substantial widening
of the rural market, which in turn has encouraged the development
of a more diversified pattern of production.

Historical evidence on the changing structure of production and
distribution of income is extremely limited, and I have been forced to
base much of my discussion on current information. In particular, I
shall draw on my study of current economic and social conditions in
four villages in different parts of the cocoa belt. These villages were
selected to illustrate different 'stages' in the development of the cocoa
economy.[1] The limitations of such 'cross-section' data as evidence of
long-run trends are well known, but I have tried, wherever possible,
to supplement the village studies with historical evidence. The results
can only suggest likely patterns of change.

Four Cocoa-farming Villages

Like thousands of other villages in the cocoa belt, the four I
studied were established by cocoa farmers.[2] Araromi-Aperin, the
oldest and largest of the four, was founded during the reign of Bale
Shittu in Ibadan (1914–25) by the Aperins.[3] Their interests in the
area were represented by a member of the family named Motosho,
who became the first *bale* of Araromi and took charge of allocating
land to potential tenants and receiving *ishakole* from them.[4] Cocoa

---

[1] See above, p. 13, n. 23.

[2] This point has not been emphasized in the literature. Galletti *et al.* (*Nigerian Cocoa
Farmers*) make no mention of the effects of cocoa farming on the over-all pattern of
settlement in Western Nigeria or even on the establishment and growth of the villages
they surveyed. They imply that most villages in Yorubaland were founded by people
moving out of old Yoruba towns under the pressures of war and population growth
or 'the desire for new hunting grounds', and that villages which have grown into
sizeable settlements have done so because they were located at 'nodal points on the
old network of bush paths' (pp. 84–5). Cf. J. O. Adejuwon, 'Agricultural Colonization
in the Forest Areas of Western Nigeria', 1970 (mimeographed).

[3] Cf. pp. 117–20, above.

[4] Indeed, Motosho was inclined to treat Araromi-Aperin and its environs as his
personal domain, which led to periodic friction between him and other members of
the family. J. O. Obisesan, Diary, *passim*. The present *bale*, Chief L. O. Obisesan, is
Motosho's son.

planting proceeded rapidly during the 1920s; thereafter it became increasingly difficult for new arrivals to obtain uncultivated land there, although men who could afford it sometimes bought established farms. Most of the cocoa farmers there today are descendants of the Aperins and their tenants, who have inherited farms and/or farmland from their forebears. Subsequent immigrants have by and large *not* gone into cocoa farming—a point I shall develop below. Araromi-Aperin is twenty-one miles south of Ibadan on the (paved) Akanran road, which runs from Ibadan to Ijebu-Igbo.

Of the other villages I surveyed, Abanata, in Ife Division, was a farming camp for a couple of families from Ifetedo, until around 1945.[5] At that time immigrant farmers from savannah towns began to seek land at Abanata for growing cocoa, and today most of the population are non-Ifes. Most of the tenant farmers have obtained land from one of the Ifetedo settlers—Nathaniel Ogunwobi, the present *bale*, after whom the village is named and who manages its affairs with casual but undisputed paternalism. (*Aba* = village; 'nata' = Nathaniel; Abanata therefore signifies 'Nathaniel's village'.) In the late 1940s an Ife family also claimed ownership of farmland in the area and the resulting dispute over the right to allocate land and receive *ishakole* from stranger farmers was eventually brought before the Oni for settlement. He, exercising his traditional prerogatives, assumed control of the disputed area, and has received *ishakole* from the strangers farming thereon ever since. A few of the strangers regard Olusoji—a member of the Ife family—as their landlord rather than Ogunwobi, and have settled together with Olusoji on the western edge of Abanata. The half-dozen houses comprising their residences are referred to as Aba Soji [Olu]soji's village). Most of the strangers now living in Abanata settled there between 1945 and 1960; today newcomers can no longer obtain uncultivated forest land in Abanata. Some farmers are still extending their cocoa plots, however, and the farms are likely to continue to yield well for some time. Abanata is five miles from the main paved Ife–Ondo road, on a poorly maintained dirt road which is motorable during the dry season.

[5] Ifetedo is today a sizeable town on the border between Ife and Ondo. It was founded in 1931 by a group of people from Okeigbo who had quarrelled with the Ondo authorities over taxes. Since the people of Okeigbo are Ifes, many of whom had established farms in Ife territory long before 1931, the founders of Ifetedo were not 'strangers' as indicated by Galletti *et al.*, p. xxvii. Many of the villages in the eastern part of Ife Division were originally founded by farmers from Ifetedo and Okeigbo.

Orotedo and Omifon, in the southern part of Ondo Province, have been settled mostly within the last ten to fifteen years, by groups of migrant farmers from northern Yorubaland and from Okitipupa Division, south of Ondo. Vacant land is still available in this area and settlers are still arriving. The first settlers at Orotedo arrived in the mid-1950s. They included a couple of men from Ondo and several Ikales. Later, in 1963 or 1964, a group of immigrants from Okuku, in northern Oshun Division near the Kwara State boundary, acquired land and planted cocoa at Orotedo. There are also a few farmers from other savannah communities, most of whose cocoa farms, like those of the Okukus, have not yet begun to bear. All of the farmers at Orotedo obtained permission to farm there from the Oloja of Oro, whose son also farms at Orotedo and represents the Oloja's interest there. As pointed out in Chapter IV, the terms on which the northern Yorubas hold their land are apparently still uncertain—a fact which has generated considerable tension in the community.

Similarly, immigrant farmers at Omifon have also gone to a subordinate town—Odigbo—rather than to Ondo itself for permission to plant food and/or tree crops. Omifon is actually a loosely organized collection of farming camps or hamlets strung out along the main road from Ode Ondo to Ore. I conducted most of my interviews in one of these camps, which was inhabited primarily by Isanlu and other Igbomina farmers, many of whom have relatives farming at Ife (and a few at Ilesha). Some of these immigrants actually own cocoa farms at Ife, but most of them are sons or *aburos*[6] of migrants farming at Ife, who were unable to get uncultivated land there for themselves and hence moved on to Ondo. Thus they are second-generation migrant farmers from northern Yorubaland. Like their predecessors, they usually spent some time working for kinsmen who were already established as cocoa farmers and who are now helping the Omifon settlers to start farms of their own. Since most of the Isanlus' cocoa farms at Omifon were not yet bearing at the time of my visits, the farmers there continued to visit their relatives in Ife regularly, to help with the farm work and receive such 'assistance' as they might require for their own maintenance.

In three of the four villages I conducted a house-by-house census

---

[6] *Aburo* means any relative, other than one's own child, younger than oneself—e.g. junior siblings, cousins, nieces and nephews, etc. It is commonly translated 'junior brother' in English.

to collect basic information on the age, sex, ethnic background, and occupations of every resident.[7] This information is summarized in the following paragraphs, as background for my subsequent discussion of the effects of cocoa growing on the structure of the rural

TABLE VI.1

Counted Village Populations by Age and Sex

	Age	Males		Females		Total	
		No.	%	No.	%	No.	%
I. Araromi-	0–5	78	8·4	71	7·6	149	16·0
Aperin	6–10	65	7·0	68	7·3	133	14·3
	11–15	54	5·8	47	5·0	101	10·8
	16–20	13	1·4	30	3·2	43	4·6
	21–30	48	5·1	70	7·5	118	12·7
	31–40	45	4·8	58	6·2	103	11·1
	41–50	38	4·1	40	4·3	78	8·4
	51–60	25	2·7	9	1·0	34	3·7
	61–70	16	1·7	6	0·6	22	2·4
	70+	9	1·0	4	0·4	13	1·4
	Unknown	52	5·6	83	9·0	136	14·6
	Totals	443	47·6	486	52·1	930	100·0
II. Abanata	0–5	65	13·1	53	10·7	116	23·8
	6–10	50	10·1	43	8·7	93	18·7
	11–15	17	3·4	23	4·6	40	8·1
	16–20	8	1·6	35	7·1	43	8·7
	21–30	37	7·5	64	12·9	101	20·4
	31–40	24	4·8	11	2·2	35	7·1
	41–50	21	4·2	8	1·6	29	5·8
	51–60	3	0·6	2	0·4	5	1·0
	60+	3	0·6	1	0·2	4	0·8
	Unknown	12	2·4	16	3·2	28	5·7
	Totals	240	48·3	256	51·6	496	100·1
III. Orotedo	0–5	39	12·1	30	9·3	69	21·4
	6–10	19	5·9	18	5·6	37	11·5
	11–15	11	3·4	14	4·3	25	7·7
	16–20	18	5·6	21	6·5	39	12·1
	21–30	40	12·4	33	10·2	73	22·6
	31–40	17	5·3	12	3·7	29	9·0
	41–50	9	2·8	3	0·9	12	3·7
	51–60	6	1·9	2	0·6	8	2·5
	60+	1	0·3	—	—	1	0·3
	Unknown	18	5·6	12	3·7	30	9·3
	Totals	178	55·3	145	45·0	323	100·1

[7] Cf. Introduction, p. 15, n. 25 above.

economy. I also carried out longer interviews with selected individuals in all four villages which I will cite in more detail below.

Table VI.1 summarizes my information on the age and sex structure of the village populations. In Araromi-Aperin and Abanata women are in the majority, whereas the reverse is true in Orotedo. All three villages have a high proportion of young children under 11 years of age: they comprise 30·3 per cent of the population in Araromi-Aperin, 32·9 per cent in Orotedo, and 42·5 per cent in Abanata. In Araromi-Aperin and Abanata the age group between 11 and 20 is proportionately much smaller, especially in the case of young men; in Orotedo, on the other hand, this is not so noticeable. There are relatively more old people in Araromi-Aperin than in either Abanata or Orotedo.

The differences in the age and sex composition of these village populations appear to be associated with differences in their histories of settlement and in the economic opportunities now available there. Table VI.2 shows the 'ethnic' composition of the present village populations, and Tables VI.3 and VI.4 present data on the length of residence of present inhabitants of each village. In the older communities (Araromi-Aperin and Abanata) nearly one-third of the present population was born in the village; in Orotedo the proportion is much lower. Most of the people born in the villages are still children: 61 per cent of those born in Araromi-Aperin, 88 per cent

---

Notes to Table VI.1:

Araromi-Aperin. The census covered all but 4 of the households in Araromi. Two of these households had at least 10 inhabitants between them. It is possible that some household heads under-reported the number of children in their houses; checking the information from detailed interviews against the census data for the same households shows that there were more children listed in detailed interviews but omitted in the census that there were children listed in the census but omitted in detailed interviews. But the effect is small. If other men tended to understate their children at the same rate as those who answered a long questionnaire, the population figure should be increased by only 12 or 13 persons. In view of these various possible sources of under-reporting, it seems reasonable to estimate the population of Araromi at a little over 950 persons.

Abanata. Because of prolonged absence of a few migrant farmers from Abanata, the census could cover only 92 per cent of the Yoruba households in Abanata. At an average occupancy rate of 7·5 persons per household, we may estimate that the Yoruba population was under-counted by about 45 persons, which would bring the estimated Yoruba population to about 540. I was not able to obtain a count of the Hausas living in Abanata, but there appeared to be no more than 50 (probably less), so that the total population is probably under 600.

Orotedo. I was not able to obtain census information from 8 households (or 12 per cent of the households in Orotedo), most of which were composed of Ikales. At an average occupancy rate of 6, we may estimate that the population was under-counted by about 50 people, bringing the estimated total to *c.* 375.

TABLE VI.2

Counted Village Populations by Area of Origin[a]

	Araromi-Aperin	Abanata	Orotedo
Local[b]	591	35	29
Northern Yoruba[c]	66	415	151
Other Yoruba	199	38	134
⌈ of which Ijebu ⌉	⌈ 80 ⌉	⌈ — ⌉	⌈ 1 ⌉
| Ijesha-Ekiti |	| 56 |	| 1 |	| — |
⌊ Ikale ⌋	⌊ — ⌋	⌊ 18 ⌋	⌊ 118 ⌋
Non-Yoruba[d]	48	4	9
Unknown	28	4	—
Total	932	496	323

[a] An individual's area of origin is defined as his birthplace or, in the case of one of our villages, his father's birthplace.
[b] Local means the city-state in which the village is located: Ibadan for Araromi-Aperin, Ife for Abanata, and Ondo for Orotedo.
[c] All Yoruba communities located in savannah areas.
[d] See notes to Table VI.1.

TABLE VI.3

Number of Persons Born in Each Village

	Araromi-Aperin	Abanata	Orotedo
Total (% village total)	271 (29%)	137 (28%)	45 (14%)
of which, aged 0–5	96	75	37
6–10	69	45	6
11–15	57	12	1
16–20	15	5	—
21 and over	23	—	—
Unknown	11	—	1

TABLE VI.4

Length of Residence in Village of Persons Born Elsewhere

Length of residence (years)	Araromi-Aperin	Abanata	Orotedo
0–5	237	104	155
6–10	108	89	96
11–15	61	52	15
16–20	55	29	2
21 and over	137	32	2
Unknown	63	54	8
Total persons born elsewhere (% village population)	661 (71%)	360 (73%)	278 (86%)

Note: Of persons born elsewhere, some were children whose parents were already living in these villages at the time of their birth. There were 71 of these in Araromi-Aperin, 48 in Abanata, and 35 in Orotedo.

of those born in Abanata, and 93 per cent of those born in Orotedo
are under the age of 11. In Araromi-Aperin, however, there are
some adults who were born in the village and have lived there all
their lives.[8] As one would expect from the villages' dates of establishment and settlement, Araromi-Aperin has the highest proportion
of long-term residents: of those not born in the village, nearly 40
per cent have lived there for more than 10 years and 21 per cent
for more than 20 years.[9] In Abanata, on the other hand, less than
10 per cent of the 'non-natives' have been there for more than 20
years, although almost one-third of them have been there for 11
years or more, reflecting the influx of northern Yorubas in the 1950s.
In Orotedo, 4 of the non-Ondos claimed to have been farming there
before 1955; otherwise, the present inhabitants all came after 1955
and most of them after 1960.

The recent establishment of Orotedo and the fact that it is still
growing, with continued arrivals of men looking for uncultivated
forest land, seem likely to account for two of its distinctive demographic features: the excess of men over women and somewhat lower
proportion of dependants—both children and old people—relative
to the rest of the population. Also the relatively high proportion of
young adults, especially men, in Orotedo (Table VI.5) reflects the

TABLE VI.5

Young Men as a Proportion of the Total Population (%)

Age	Araromi-Aperin	Abanata	Orotedo
11–20	7·2	5·0	9·0
21–30	5·1	7·5	12·4
Total	12·3	12·5	21·4

fact that opportunities for establishing one's own farm have attracted
young men and, often, their wives in recent years. To Araromi-
Aperin and Abanata, where good cocoa land is scarce and expensive,
few young people now come to plant cocoa. On the other hand, the
proportion of recent arrivals in these two villages is strikingly high.

[8] A substantial proportion of persons born outside these villages, who have lived
there less than 10 years, are also children whose parents were already settled in the
village at the time of their births. In such cases, the mother usually went to her home
town to give birth and later returned to her husband's house in the village.

[9] Among the adult Yoruba residents the proportion of long-term residents is considerably higher; over 60 per cent have lived there continuously for 10 years or more
and nearly 40 per cent for more than 20 years.

TABLE VI.6

Occupations of Adult Men

	Araromi-Aperin		Abanata		Orotedo	
	No.	%	No.	%	No.	%
Farmer	111	57	70	73	58	64
Farm and household labourer	5	3	6	6	25	27
Trader						
(a) Produce*a*	49	25	2	2	3	3
(b) Other*b*	23	12	5	5	1	1
Traditional crafts and services*c*	26	13	4	4	2	2
Modern crafts and services*d*	30	16	12	13	3	3
Clerk, teacher, and student	20	10	6	6	3	3
Other labourer*e*	20	10	—	—	—	—
Total occupied men	195		96		91	
Total occupations	284		105		95	

Notes: Totals do not add up to 100 per cent because all occupations reported by each person are included and a number of people practise more than one occupation. Adults are all persons aged 16 and over. Percentages refer to proportion of occupied adults.

a Produce buyers deal in cocoa, palm kernels, and kola.
b Other traders include sellers of cooked foods (most of whom also prepare the food to sell), cloth, provisions (tinned food, sugar, flour, matches, plastic- and enamelware, etc.), kerosene and petrol, patent medicine, livestock, and water.
c Traditional crafts and services include: mat maker, blacksmith, barber, carver, cloth dyer, drummer, butcher, washerman, herbalist, basket maker, soda maker, nightwatch, hairdresser, hunter, painter, weaver, shoemaker, dancer, native doctor, goldsmith, medicine seller, and baker.
d Modern crafts include: driver, mechanic, tailor, seamstress, carpenter, contractor, bricklayer, tinker, nurse, miller, photographer, bicycle repairer clinic attendant, and pools agent.
e Other labourers worked for the state government—mostly the Ministries of Public Works and of Agriculture and Natural Resources.

In Araromi-Aperin over half of the persons born elsewhere had come during the last ten years, which suggests that economic opportunities were not altogether lacking even there. I shall return to this point in the next section.

The decline of *agricultural* opportunities in older cocoa-growing areas is further reflected in the structure of occupations in the three villages. In Araromi-Aperin three-fifths of the adult men are engaged in farming (including farm labourers), whereas in Abanata 80 per cent and in Orotedo over 90 per cent of the men farm or work for other farmers (Table VI.6). Even more strikingly, nearly all the women in Orotedo said that they helped their husbands with farm work,

TABLE VI.7

Occupations of Adult Women

	Araromi-Aperin		Abanta		Orotedo	
	No.	%	No.	%	No.	%
Farmer	44	20	1	1	—	—
Farm and household labour[a]	5	2⎱	57	47	68	96
Palm produce[a]	112	52⎰				
Trader						
(a) Produce	21	10	25	21	1	1
(b) Other	100	46	25	21	8	11
Traditional crafts and services	17	8	—	—	—	—
Modern crafts and services	7	3	7	6	2	3
Clerk, etc.	3	1	2	2	1	1
Unemployed	8	4	8	7	—	—
Total occupied women	216		121		71	
Total occupations	317		125		80	

Notes: See notes to Table VI.6.

[a] In Abanata and Orotedo a number of women said that they helped their husbands on the farm, which included making palm oil and cracking palm kernels. In Araromi-Aperin, on the other hand, few women did any farm work *except for* making palm oil, etc., and helping break open cocoa pods at the time of harvest.

although Yoruba women normally do very little farming (Table VI.7). In Abanata and Araromi-Aperin, however, where most of the cocoa farmers have for some time earned enough from their bearing cocoa farms to hire labourers, only half of the women do any agricultural work at all—even when making palm oil, which is traditionally women's work, is included.[10] For similar reasons, a majority of the children aged from 5 to 15 in Araromi-Aperin and Abanata go to school, whereas only one-third do so in Orotedo—in spite of the fact that Orotedo has a primary school, whereas Abanata does not. A correspondingly higher proportion of the children in Orotedo were described as helping their parents with farm and household tasks than in either Abanata or Araromi-Aperin (see Table VI.8).

[10] The customary division of labour between men and women in the Yoruba economy—whereby men bear primary responsibility for agricultural production and women tend to specialize in trade and agricultural processing—obtains in cocoa farming as well. Women who have acquired cocoa farms, through inheritance or purchase, do not work them themselves, but employ caretakers and/or labourers. Other women work on their husbands' farms or even hire themselves out for wages, but, except in recently developed areas such as Orotedo, the only task they perform is that of breaking open pods, removing the beans, and carrying them home to ferment and dry. The cocoa pods are actually harvested by men. Cf. Galletti *et al.*, p. 202.

TABLE VI.8

Occupations of Children Aged 5 to 15 (per cent)

	Araromi-Aperin	Abanata	Orotedo
In school	70	62	39
Employed	18	12	34
Farm and household tasks	9	6	34
Trade, crafts, or services	9	6	—

On the whole, Araromi-Aperin is economically more developed than the other two villages. It boasts a four-day market, three primary schools, several churches, mosques, storehouses, and shops, a community palm-oil mill, an abattoir, a rest house, and a Hausa quarter or 'Sabo',[11] whose residents specialize in kola marketing. The main road to Ibadan is paved, and lorries stop in Araromi every hour. By contrast, although lorries visit Abanata daily, there are not nearly so many of them as in Araromi-Aperin—at most, half a dozen or so during the dry season. There is no regular market in Abanata, and only three or four traders dealing in manufactured items, although a number of men and women deal in produce or foodstuffs in addition to their farming activities. There is one church and one mosque (both well-built, brightly painted structures), but no schools or other public buildings, though there are several privately owned storehouses. Orotedo, like Abanata, is five miles from a main road but, since the dirt road to Orotedo does not lead on to any larger communities, lorries hardly ever come there, except during the cocoa harvest. There are no markets and no shops in Orotedo; the people must go to the main road or further to buy goods, although occasionally itinerant pedlars visit the village. Orotedo has a primary school, however, and several churches and mosques.

The Changing Structure of Rural Economic Activity

The opening up of extensive forest areas for cocoa growing, which was followed by the growth of farm income as more and more cocoa trees reached maturity, led to substantial changes in the character of rural settlements and the structure of rural economic activity. For one thing, as farmers moved into the forests to plant cocoa, they

---

[11] Cf. A. Cohen, *Custom and Politics in Urban Africa* and p. 153 above.

not only built new farm hamlets but began to spend increasing amounts of time there. Before the introduction of cocoa, most Yoruba farmers lived in towns and either walked to and from their farms each day or built huts near their farms, where they stayed for brief periods during the height of the farming season. These farming hamlets were not permanent communities; P. C. Lloyd has described them as 'merely place[s] where people sleep whilst on their farms,' without 'recognized chiefs' or important political or social activities.[12] As cocoa led people to establish farms further and further from town, and also lengthened the duration of the farming season, many settlements developed into sizeable villages with an economic life and political structure of their own. As early as 1929 the Resident of Oyo Province commented, 'There is a strong tendency to establish farm markets to trade in and for people to establish themselves in the farming areas under more permanent conditions.'[13] Today one finds many large villages in the cocoa-farming areas whose residents have erected permanent dwellings—often plastered with cement and roofed with iron—and live there most of the year. Many of these communities have permanent market-places, schools, mosques, churches, shops, and co-operative marketing societies. They have their own leaders and tend to be largely self-governing. Most village residents retain ties with their home towns (whether or not these lie in the same city-states as their farms) and visit them for major religious or family ceremonies, but their family and social lives as well as their economic activities are centred in the village, and they think of themselves as rural rather than urban dwellers.[14]

The development of rural economic activity associated with the formation of permanent rural communities in the cocoa belt has been intensified by the growth of farm income resulting from cocoa production itself. Rising farm incomes led, of course, to increased consumption of imported goods—a fact which some economists have interpreted to mean that the desire for imported commodities constituted the principal incentive for increased agricultural production

[12] Lloyd, *Yoruba Land Law*, p. 54. Other descriptions of Yoruba towns say little about the changing character of related rural settlements. See, e.g., A. L. Mabogunje, *Yoruba Towns* (Ibadan, 1962), and *Urbanization in Nigeria* (New York, 1968); N. C. Mitchel, 'Yoruba Towns', in K. M. Barbour and R. M. Prothero, eds., *Essays on African Population* (London, 1961); Galletti *et al.*, p. 85.

[13] Oyo Province, Annual Report, 1929.

[14] I am indebted for this point to Gavin Williams, who found a strong sense of rural identity accompanied by a tendency to disparage urban ways among many of the farmers he interviewed in Ibadan villages.

for export.[15] In addition, however, as cocoa farmers' earnings grew, their demand for domestically produced goods and services also expanded, creating increased opportunities for the growth of internal trade and the diversification of domestic production. The dearth of evidence on trends in domestic production and trade makes it difficult to trace the extent to which local producers exploited these opportunities but, as I shall argue below, we can discern at least some of the resulting changes in the structure of rural economic activity.

Certainly, the growth in consumption of imported goods was one of the most obvious (and easily documented) effects of expanded cocoa production. Although we have no way of estimating what proportion of total imports into Lagos were ultimately sold in the cocoa belt, there is ample contemporary commentary on the growing demand for imported goods in major cocoa-producing areas. In inland towns European firms tended to follow the cocoa tree, rather than vice versa. In 1927, for example, the District Officer at Ife reported that in the preceding three years nine European firms had opened stores at Ife 'where none before existed,'[16] and by 1930 several firms were also established in Ondo. In Ibadan, where cocoa growing had spread widely before World War I, not only were firms doing a large volume of business in imported goods by the 1920s, but they found that their sales fluctuated with annual variations in the cocoa price. In 1923, for example, an official noted that 'the Native customer is now purchasing more and more of the cheaper grades of cloth, the demand for the better class cotton goods having fallen off considerably, showing that the spending power of the native has been greatly reduced, chiefly due to the low prices ruling for produce during the year.'[17] Two years later John Holt's agent in Ibadan reported that reviving produce prices had led to an increase in his firm's sales of finer grades of cloth, tinned meat, fish, biscuits, flour, rice, cigarettes, and, inevitably, corrugated iron sheets.[18]

Indeed, the corrugated iron sheets came almost to symbolize the prosperity associated with cocoa. One of my informants, who had left his home town (Ondo) in 1910 and worked for many years as a tailor in Ibadan and Ilesha, said that when he left home all the houses had thatched roofs; when he returned in the late 1920s many

[15] See, e.g., G. K. Helleiner, *Peasant Agriculture, Government and Economic Growth in Nigeria*, pp. 11 ff.
[16] Oyo Province, Annual Report, 1927.
[17] Ibid., 1923.   [18] Ibid., 1925.

houses were roofed with iron sheets and people told him that the money to buy them had come from cocoa. On hearing this, the man decided to settle down in Ondo and become a cocoa farmer. British officials also associated iron roofs with cocoa and prosperity. One District Officer declared that the effect of the growing cocoa trade in Ilesha could be seen 'in the number of corrugated roofs and cemented walls'.[19] In Ilorin it was rumoured that people were hesitant to put iron roofs on their houses for fear the British would raise their taxes.[20] And one official lamented that Ife had not been the same since cocoa growing caught on there: 'With the insane early prices of this commodity, its quiet, ceremonial loving people were swept from their normal lives in the rush to earn more . . . simple grass roofs disappeared and an ill-pleasing zinc town with little respect for arrangement took its place.'[21] By the 1950s iron roofs and cemented walls were common in rural communities as well as in the towns.[22]

The effects of increased incomes on cocoa farmers' consumption of domestic goods and services and, hence, on internal trade and production are more difficult to trace. This is particularly true in the case of foodstuffs. During the colonial period it was widely believed that as farmers took up cocoa they reduced their output of food crops—a practice considered dangerous by colonial administrators. In 1917 an official complained of 'a growing tendency to neglect foodstuffs' in favour of cocoa among farmers in the Akanran area south of Ibadan;[23] twenty years later the same unfortunate propensity was attributed to farmers in Ibadan, Ife and Ilesha.[24] Official reports indicate that by the 1920s non-cocoa-growing areas, such as Oyo Division and Ilorin Province, were exporting foodstuffs to the cocoa belt—a pattern of regional specialization and exchange which has persisted to the present day.[25] Similarly, the growth of the cattle trade between Northern and Western Nigeria since the time of World War I has been linked to the growing demand for beef in

[19] Ibid.
[20] Ilorin Province, Annual Report, 1926.
[21] J. A. Mackenzie, 'Report on the Native Organization of Ife District', 1934, CSO 26/29829 (NAI).
[22] Galletti et al., pp. 275–6.
[23] Ibadan Division, Annual Report, 1917.
[24] Oyo Province, Annual Report, 1938. Cf. A. McPhee, The Economic Revolution in British West Africa, p. 43.
[25] See, e.g., Galletti et al., pp. 60–3; A. M. Hay and R. H. T. Smith, Interregional Trade and Money Flows in Nigeria, 1964 (Ibadan, 1970), pp. 27 ff.; R. Güsten, Studies in the Staple Food Economy of Western Nigeria, pp. 189 ff.

Yorubaland.[26] Most of these descriptions of internal trading patterns fail to distinguish between urban and rural areas within the cocoa belt; it is possible that rising food imports reflect the expansion of urban centres, such as Ibadan, as much as they do rising agricultural incomes. In 1966, for example, R. Güsten found that whereas Ibadan and Lagos imported large quantities of foodstuffs from other areas both within and outside the Western Region, a rural area east of Ibadan (including parts of Ibadan, Oshun, Ife, and Ilesha Divisions) imported only 10 per cent of its estimated total consumption of food-stuffs.[27] He concluded that 'this agricultural area can still support both its rural and its urban population. This agrees with the generally known fact that most cocoa-farmers, in extending their cocoa-plantations, do not abandon food crops.'[28]

Güsten's rural area happens to include savannah as well as forested terrain and his findings do not preclude the possibility that the cocoa farmers themselves do not grow much food, relying instead on specialized food crop growers within the sample area.[29] More generally, however, the fact that the cocoa belt as a whole imports food-stuffs need not imply that cocoa has supplanted food crop production in these areas; it may instead reflect increased consumption, owing to growing population or to higher incomes or both. Indeed, studies of the production and consumption patterns of individual farming households indicate that most cocoa farmers do grow food crops and that they also often sell a substantial part of what they grow, either to traders or, often, to their wives, who process raw foodstuffs and sell the resulting products. At the same time, few families store enough food to last them the year; instead, they purchase the greater part of the foodstuffs on a daily basis. Thus, the fact that cocoa farmers do not 'subsist' on the food crops they grow themselves does not necessarily mean that they do not produce enough to satisfy their own needs; instead, it may simply reflect the great extent to which they are involved in market transactions.[30]

[26] A. Cohen, *Custom and Politics*, p. 105; F. A. Okediji, 'The Economic History of the Hausa–Fulani Emirates of Northern Nigeria, 1900–1939', Indiana University Ph.D. thesis, 1971, ch. 6.

[27] Güsten, p. 182.   [28] Ibid., p. 180.

[29] In parts of the cocoa belt, such as Ife, there are settlements of Igbirra and other non-Yoruba farmers who specialize in the production of food crops. Lloyd also points out that Urhobo palm-oil makers are diligent food crop farmers as well. *Yoruba Land Law*, pp. 88, 179.

[30] According to Galletti *et al.*, 'The Yoruba cocoa-farming family does not store and consume its own crops. It prefers to sell its produce at the time of harvest and buy its needs from day to day in the market. It appears to have much confidence in the

It is tempting to argue from the above information that the spread of cocoa cultivation and resulting growth of farmers' incomes are responsible for the extensive commercialization and specialization in the production, processing, and exchange of foodstuffs at the village and household level. However, there is considerable historical evidence that widespread local trade in domestic goods and specialization by women in food processing and trade were prevalent in Yoruba economic life before the advent of cocoa. The extent of such activities may well have increased with spreading cocoa cultivation, but it is impossible to prove this from available historical or statistical evidence.[31]

We can, however, learn something about the probable long-run diversification of village economic life in the cocoa belt by comparing communities at different stages of development today. In my four survey villages, differences in the length of time that cocoa has been grown in each community are apparently asssociated with differences in the structure of economic activity. To be sure, there are other differentiating features: in particular, Araromi-Aperin's size and the fact that it is located on a paved and well-travelled road connecting two urban centres help to account for the extent of commercial development there. However, the construction of the road itself owes a good deal to (a) the extensive development of cocoa production in the area *before* 1936, and (b) the influence of the Aperin family in the political structure of Ibadan, which is in turn associated with their position as landlords to hundreds of tenant farmers in the cocoa-growing area south of Ibadan. Moreover, evidence on the history of settlement and immigration in each of these villages tends to confirm the importance of rising incomes from cocoa in determining their present economic structures.

As I mentioned earlier, one of the most striking differences which

---

market's regulation of supplies and prices' (p. 598). G. O. Okurume found that, although the over-all level of food crop production may or may not have fallen in cocoa farming areas, there has apparently been a tendency to substitute food crops such as cassava and cocoyam with relatively low labour requirements for yam and maize (*The Food Crop Economy in Nigerian Agricultural Policy*, CSNRD Report No. 31 (E. Lansing, Mich., 1969), pp. 81 ff.).

[31] Proponents of the vent-for-surplus model have cited the continued production of foodstuffs by growers of cocoa and other export crops as evidence that the growth of export production entailed a sacrifice of leisure rather than a reallocation of labour from alternative productive activities. As I have argued above, they are no doubt partly right; the evidence is simply insufficient to warrant firm conclusions. However, in so far as this argument implies that food crop production was the only significant alternative to growing crops for export, it gives a misleading picture of the structure and complexity of rural economic life in Western Nigeria.

emerged from the three village censuses is the relatively high proportion of people engaged in non-agricultural pursuits in Araromi-Aperin; 40 per cent of the adult men there did no farming at all, compared to 21 per cent in Abanata and 9 per cent in Orotedo. (See Tables VI.6 and VI.7.) Moreover, more men in Araromi-Aperin combined farming with non-agricultural pursuits. Out of the total number of occupations reported by adult men in each village, 59 per cent were non-agricultural in Araromi-Aperin, compared to 28 per cent in Abanata and 13 per cent in Orotedo.

Similarly, the adult women of Araromi-Aperin were more likely to trade or engage in some form of craft or processing activity than was the case in either of the other villages, although there were also marked differences between Abanata and Orotedo in this respect. Nearly three-quarters of the women in Araromi-Aperin were engaged in trade, foodstuff processing, craft or non-domestic service occupations, compared to 57 per cent in Abanata and only 16 per cent in Orotedo. However, the women of Araromi-Aperin also frequently combined non-agricultural pursuits with some type of farm work, so that the proportion of women's *occupations* which were non-agricultural was actually lower there than in Abanata. This is partly due to the fact that a number of women in Araromi-Aperin had inherited cocoa farms from their fathers, whereas in the other two villages most of the original planters (all male) were still living. In addition, more than half of the women in Araromi-Aperin engaged in the manufacture of palm oil and cracked palm kernels for sale; most of these did no other kind of farm work. In Abanata and Orotedo, however, many women said that they 'helped their husbands on the farm'; often with harvesting and other tasks in addition to processing palm fruit. Evidently, farmers in Araromi-Aperin either earned enough from their mature cocoa farms to hire whatever labour they needed in addition to their own, or had farms so old as to require little care. Men who were establishing their first farms or waiting for partially immature cocoa plots to bear were more likely to require their wives' assistance. This was especially obvious in Orotedo, where most cocoa farms were not yet bearing and where nearly all the women did farm work and nothing else.

Araromi-Aperin not only had a smaller proportion of farmers and farm workers than did the other two villages, but it was also characterized by a distinctive pattern of occupational specialization by ethnic group. Abanata and Orotedo were, as we have seen, settled

TABLE VI.9

Occupational Specialization by Ethnic Group[a]

Village Ethnic group[c]	Occupations[b]						
	Farmer	Farm labourer	Trade	Modern craft and service	Traditional craft and service	Clerical	All occupied persons
Araromi-Aperin							
Ibadan	75	74	51	71	46	57	61
Ijebu	3	2	14	5	19	—	8
Ijesha-Ekiti	5	7	6	8	9	4	7
Northern Yoruba	10	14	6	8	7	13	8
Other Yoruba	2	3	5	3	16	13	6
Non-Yoruba	—	—	16	3	2	13	9
Abanata							
Ife	4	5	4	16	—	—	5
Northern Yoruba	90	90	89	68	100	87	88
Other Yoruba	5	5	7	16	—	12	7
Orotedo							
Ondo	9	9	15	20	—	25	9
Ikale	28	30	23	80	—	75	30
Northern Yoruba	38	40	31	—	50	—	38
Other Yoruba	24	17	31	—	—	—	20
Non-Yoruba	2	4	—	—	50	—	3

[a] Based on census information for persons aged 16 and over. All reported occupations for each person are included. Persons of unknown age, occupation, or ethnic group are excluded. Figures are expressed as percentages of each occupational category.
[b] See Tables VI.6, VI.7.
[c] Based on area of origin. Cf. Table VI.2.

primarily by people from other city-states who came there to plant cocoa. Consequently, the overwhelming majority of inhabitants are strangers, most of whom are engaged in farming. In Abanata especially, there are few occupational differences among ethnic groups (see Table VI.9), except that relatively fewer northern Yorubas are engaged in 'modern' craft and service occupations (e.g. tailoring) than is the case with the Ifes and other Yorubas. In Orotedo the practice of modern craft and 'clerical' occupations is confined to Ondos and Ikales, and Ondos and 'other Yorubas' are over-represented among the traders, but on the whole the number of people engaged in any non-agricultural occupation is so small in Orotedo that little significance can be attached to these differences.

In Araromi-Aperin, however, there are fairly marked variations in the occupations of different ethnic groups. Basically, the Ibadans (and Northern Yorubas) tend to engage in farming and related activities, whereas the other strangers are predominantly occupied with non-agricultural pursuits. Within the latter group, the Ijebus tend to concentrate on trade and traditional crafts and services (principally butchering) whereas the Ijeshas and Ekitis are more diversified in their activities. The high proportion of 'other Yorubas' in traditional craft and service occupations reflects the presence in Araromi-Aperin of a group of Akoko palm-wine tappers, who stayed for a few months and then moved on to tap in another village. (Most of the non-Yorubas are Hausa kola traders.) Furthermore, information collected in longer interviews with a sample of adult men indicated that whereas most of the Ibadan farmers grow cocoa, most non-Ibadans engaged in farming grow food crops only:

Area of origin	Cocoa and other crops	Food crops only
Ibadan	18	2
Non-Ibadan*	3	11
	21	13

* 13 Yorubas and 1 Isoko. From interviews with 34 farmers in Araromi-Aperin.

The reasons for these occupational differences among ethnic groups in Araromi–Aperin appear, from my evidence at least, to be primarily historical and economic. Most of the Ibadan cocoa farmers I interviewed had either acquired farmland at Araromi–Aperin before the 1930s or had inherited cocoa farms from their fathers. On the other hand, most of the non-Ibadans I interviewed said that they had come to Araromi–Aperin *after* 1940, to trade or to seek work as craftsmen or labourers, *not* to grow cocoa. In fact, a majority of these strangers came from other Yoruba communities *within the cocoa belt*, and pointed out that if they wished to grow cocoa they would return home, where land was more readily available.[32] As Table VI.9 indicates, most of them were engaged primarily in non-agricultural occupations; they grew foodstuffs only for themselves and their families.[33] The same was true of the few Ibadans who had moved to Araromi-Aperin in the last twenty years, and of the Hausas, who had come to Araromi-Aperin to buy kola, not to plant tree crops for themselves. They had all been attracted to Araromi-Aperin by the prospect of a good market afforded by the community's size, accessibility, and location in a prosperous cocoa-farming area.

From the foregoing evidence, it seems plausible to argue that in Araromi-Aperin, where cocoa farming developed extensively in the 1920s, the growth of farm incomes associated with increased cocoa production generated a sustained increase in demand for consumer goods. This growth of demand was sufficient to attract a substantial number of traders and craftsmen to the area, who were able to support themselves largely or even entirely by providing non-agricultural goods and services for the local market. In Abanata and Orotedo, on the other hand, cocoa has been grown for a shorter period of time and neither village has yet reached Araromi-Aperin's stage of development. However, the effects of rising incomes from cocoa cultivation are beginning to be felt in Abanata, where cocoa was planted extensively in the 1950s. Thus, despite its relatively poor location, Abanata supports a proportionately larger non-agricultural population than does Orotedo: one-fifth of the adult men and over half the adult women in Abanata do no farm work at all, compared to 9 per cent of the men and only 4 per cent of the women in Orotedo; similarly, 30 per cent of the men and 50 per cent of the women of Abanata engage in trade, craft, or service occupations on a part- or full-time basis, whereas only 12 per cent of the men and 16 per cent of the women do so in Orotedo. Thus, in these villages at any rate, the early development of cocoa growing does appear to be positively associated with the diversification of local economic

---

[32] Some actually owned cocoa farms at home, individually or together with kinsmen.

[33] Some of the more prosperous traders (chiefly Ijebus and Hausas) did not even bother to do that. Of 22 strangers whom I interviewed in Araromi-Aperin, only 14 farmed. Of the remainder, 6 were traders or craftsmen and 2 were labourers whose employers provided them with food and shelter.

activity. Although it is always risky to extrapolate trends from cross-section data, it seems likely that the degree of occupational diversity will rise in Orotedo as more cocoa farms mature. It may also increase further in Abanata, especially if the road is improved.

Economic Inequality and Rural Social Stratification

Although the spread of cocoa cultivation and subsequent diversification of economic activity in the rural sector has entailed a general rise in rural incomes, there is no reason to believe that the gains from cocoa farming and related pursuits have been equally distributed among the rural population. In the preceding chapters I argued that most participants in the cocoa economy have shared in these gains to some extent, and that the development of cocoa farming has not led to the emergence of either a landowning class or a landless agricultural proletariat. However, it has created unprecedented opportunities for the accumulation of agricultural capital in rural Yorubaland and hence for a potentially unequal distribution of income among farmers themselves. In the remainder of this chapter, I shall consider the extent to which this potential has been realized, and the implications of economic inequality for the stratification of rural society.

Although I was not able to undertake any systematic collection of data on household incomes, there is good evidence in the literature on the Western Nigerian cocoa-farming sector that individual (or household) incomes are fairly unequally distributed. Galletti *et al.* found considerable inequality in the distribution of incomes among the 187 families for which they collected detailed budget data; their findings are summarized in Table VI.10. Nearly twenty years later S. M. Essang used information on sales of cocoa to estimate the incomes of 160 cocoa farmers and 60 licensed buying agents; he also found incomes to be unequally distributed within each group, although the range was much wider for the licensed buying agents.[34]

Neither Galletti *et al.* nor Essang discuss in detail the historical reasons for the unequal patterns of income distribution they observed. Essang presents evidence to show that, as of 1970, income was closely correlated with access to government services—such as agricultural credit, subsidized farm inputs, and extension services—

[34] S. M. Essang, 'Distribution of Earnings in the Cocoa Economy of Western Nigeria'.

TABLE VI.10

Distribution of Net Household Receipts in Galletti's Study

Farming		Home industry		Trade		All sources	
(187 families)		(55 families)		(163 families)		(187 families)	
% families	% net receipts	% families	% net receipts	% families	% net receipts	% families	% net receipts
21	5	49	6	64	6	25	6
18	8	22	16	16	9	23	11
21	15	16	27	16	21	31	27
25	31	9	32	2	13	18	33
11	24	2	15	2	51	3	23
5	16						

Source: Galletti *et al.*, pp. 452 ff.

and with the holding of political office, but he is careful to point out that his evidence does not warrant simple conclusions about cause and effect. Indeed, he argues that all of the variables are probably mutually interacting and reinforcing.[35] Galletti *et al.* found that 'it was not possible in the time available to study in detail the accounts of every family and to ascertain why some were poor and some much better to do'.[36] However, they hypothesize that 'the principal reason is undoubtedly that the inequality of resources and opportunities is much greater than the inequality of family size, so that some have too little land and capital to make more than a bare living, while others are more abundantly provided with resources through inheritance and the seizing of opportunities in the past, so that they can devote much land to farming for profit rather than subsistence and can engage in trades requiring capital.'[37]

The only data which Galletti *et al.* collected on 'resources and opportunities' pertain to the distribution of land-holdings among their survey families. In general, they concluded that land was also unequally distributed and that this fact accounts for much of the observed inequality of income distribution.[38] However, the force of

[35] Ibid., pp. 74–5.   [36] Galletti *et al.*, p. 592.

[37] Ibid. In view of their own data on the extent to which cocoa farming households market their food crops, it is not clear what they mean by 'subsistence' farming.

[38] Ibid. Despite all this evidence on economic inequality, the main interpretive thrust of *Nigerian Cocoa Farmers* is to depict the economic position of the 'ordinary cocoa farmer'. See, e.g., pp. 457–8.

their argument is somewhat diminished by the ambiguity of their concept of 'land-holdings'. Throughout their discussion of land-holdings they frequently confuse land and improvements on the land (such as cocoa trees); moreover, they do not adequately take into account the existence of multiple rights in a given piece of land. Thus, at one point they distinguish between land 'owned' by a household (i.e. 'land which the family effectively occupies (whether it cultivates it or not) or has as against other families even of the same *ebi* an exclusive right to enter upon for farming or building'[39]) and land 'enjoyed', in the sense that the household enjoys the produce thereof. According to this classification, we might expect that land held by a lineage would be 'owned' by that lineage but 'enjoyed' by the tenant farmers growing food or tree crops thereon. However, the authors appear to consider at least some tenant cocoa farmers (e.g. in Ibadan) 'owners' of the land they farm, although elsewhere they state that land 'held by survey families on temporary grants or leases [which they would call "enjoyed but not owned"] was mainly taken for cocoa growing . . .'[40]

Moreover, the terms 'ownership' and 'enjoyment' are never explicitly related to the concept of 'land-holdings'. It is never stated for example, whether their oft-quoted finding that 50 per cent of the families in six survey villages 'held' only 14 per cent of the cocoa farms, while at the other end of the scale, 2 per cent of the families 'held' 18 per cent of the acreage under cocoa, refers to 'ownership' or 'enjoyment' of the farms in question.[41] The same ambiguity arises in the case of food farmland, which is arbitrarily defined to include fallow and forest—i.e. some of it is uncultivated land which may be suitable for cocoa as well as for food crops.

Because Galletti *et al.* do not relate land-holding to land use in their discussion, it is not clear what their data on the distribution of land-holdings imply about the distribution of income among farming families. If their figures represent current usage (or 'enjoyment') of cultivated land, it would be reasonable to argue that the inequalities they found in land-holdings are associated with the unequal distribution of farm income, although we would still be left with the question of causation. However, if their data refer primarily to ownership rights, then the apparent relationship may not be nearly

---

[39] Galletti *et al.*, p. 136.
[40] Ibid., p. 138. Here the authors refer mainly to Ife and Ilesha.
[41] Ibid., p. 147.

so significant. In fact their data on land-holdings appear to consist of some unspecified amalgamation of ownership and usage which is not susceptible of easy interpretation one way or the other.

As we saw in Chapter IV, under the Yoruba system of multiple rights in a given piece of land, the fact of rural landownership (or, more accurately, membership in a landowning group) often bears little relationship to an individual's income or wealth. For one thing, control of a certain area of rural land by one lineage need not imply that members of that lineage will ultimately farm the land or enjoy the resulting income. Also, as was pointed out in Chapter IV, the relative abundance of uncultivated land in the forest belt of Western Nigeria meant that most farmers could gain access to as much cultivable land as they could use. Consequently, a man's income from farming was more likely to depend on his ability to mobilize labour and working capital and to invest them successfully in establishing or otherwise acquiring new farms, than on his or his family's ownership of rural land. Thus, in some areas of Ife especially, I encountered tenant farmers who had larger plots of cocoa and food crops and were obviously more prosperous than some of their neighbours who owned the land they farmed on.

To be sure, access to labour and capital is likely to be greater for members of large and/or wealthy lineages: we have seen how, for example, kinsmen often helped one another mobilize resources for investment in cocoa farms. In the case of landowning lineages, members could (especially in the past) draw on their tenants for labour or other services, in addition to the (often nominal) payment of *ishakole*. In some of the newer cocoa-growing areas the practice of requiring labour services from tenants is declining, but the amount of *ishakole* is more substantial. In my survey villages, members of landholding lineages with many tenants did generally have larger farms than their neighbours. (See Table VI.11.)

At the same time, the prosperity and power of a lineage often owe as much to the foresight and abilities of its individual members as vice versa. This can be seen not only from the history of land acquisition and development of tenancy in the cocoa-farming areas, but also in the differences in farm size and farm income which often exist among individual members of the same landowning lineage. In Araromi-Aperin, for example, I interviewed five members of the Aperin family who owned farms near Araromi-Aperin. The present *bale* of the village had about twenty-five acres of cocoa and other

TABLE VI.11

Area Farmed by Informants in Four Villages

Acres	Araromi-Aperin		Abanata		Orotedo		Omifon	
	No.	%	No.	%	No.	%	No.	%
Less than 1	5	14	—	—	—	—	—	—
1–5	7	20	17	59	5	36	6	46
6–10	6 [1]	17	9 [1]	31	2 [1]	14	4	31
10–20	4 [1]	11	1 [1]	3	4 [1]	29	1	8
More than 20	5 [3]	14	1 [1]	3	1	7	2 [2]	15
Unknown	8	23	1	3	2	14	—	—

Source: Based on interviews with 37 farmers in Araromi-Aperin, 29 in Abanata, 14 in Orotedo, and 13 in Omifon. Figures in brackets are numbers of land-owners in each category.

crops which he had inherited from his father (the original *bale*). A younger son of the original *bale* had thirteen farms, eleven of which he had purchased after the cocoa trees had been established. Another young man had about eighteen acres, part of which he had planted himself, while the fourth member of the family interviewed, a man, had only eight acres (four at Araromi-Aperin and four at another village), although he had been one of the original settlers at Araromi. The fifth was a wife of the present *bale* who had inherited ten acres of cocoa plus some uncultivated land on which she had planted nine more acres of cocoa; she had also purchased a three-acre farm of mixed tree crops. (She was also educated, a successful trader, an Aladura prophetess, and an influential figure both in her husband's house and in the community.) Since she had several co-wives, none of whom had achieved comparable economic success, it appears that her position owed something to individual achievement as well as to her family connections.

So far I have argued that the extent of an individual's farms is likely to depend both on his initial access to land, labour, and capital and on his skill in putting these resources to productive use. In addition, it is important to remember that the inequalities in farm size and farm income observable in rural Yoruba communities today (or at the time of Galletti's study, in the early 1950s) reflect several decades of cocoa production and related economic activities. Especially in the older cocoa-growing areas, today's distribution of income has been influenced not only by the historical distribution of productive resources and by individuals' skills in exploiting them, but also by patterns of reinvestment of farm earnings and by inheritance.

Once a cocoa plot reaches maturity, the farmer can usually finance annual operating expenses out of the proceeds and have some income to spare, which he may choose to save and invest in additional cocoa farms. Some farmers have, indeed, built up extensive holdings in this way. However, I do not think that the accumulation of agricultural capital (in the form of established tree crops) has yet led to the formation of a distinctive class of 'capitalist' farmers whose mode of economic activity is noticeably different from that of their poorer neighbours or whose existence as a group tends to be perpetuated over time.

For one thing, there are no technical economies of scale in West African cocoa production; in general, the farmer with fifty acres cultivates his land with much the same tools and techniques as does the farmer with five.[42] Recent improvements in technique—such as chemical sprays and improved varieties of seed—are equally effective on small farms and large. In my survey villages I found no evidence that farmers with large holdings were more likely to use chemicals than were men with small farms. In so far as farmers with large holdings have found it easier to obtain chemicals on credit, they may have been able to pursue more systematic programmes of pest and disease control on their cocoa farms. Just what effect this would have on yields is not clear, however; it would probably require detailed observations of a number of farms for several years to find out.[43] Also, as Essang's study suggests, differences between large and small farmers' access to credit and purchased inputs probably have as much to do with their contacts outside the rural sector as with the extent of their cocoa farms *per se*.

Although a farmer with large holdings can usually *finance* hired labour more easily than his poorer neighbours, and thus may enjoy

[42] Cf. S. S. Berry, 'Cocoa in Western Nigeria, 1890–1940'.
[43] See above, p. 80, n. 46.

certain 'pecuniary' rather than technical economies of scale,[44] he is likely to encounter increasing difficulties in *supervising* large numbers of labourers, especially if he owns several farms in different locations. If he can call on reliable kinsmen to manage some of his distant farms, this may not be a serious problem. If not, however, he must employ caretakers or let out his farms to sharecroppers—an arrangement which, as we saw in Chapter V, is not necessarily more profitable than direct supervision of annual or casual labourers by the farmer himself. Moreover, such methods of employment are not confined to farmers with large holdings, but are used by anyone who does not wish to manage a cocoa farm himself. This includes many women who inherit cocoa farms and men who are involved in other occupations or are too old or ill to manage their farms; many of them may have very small holdings. In short, the chief difference between farmers with large and those with small cocoa farms lies in their command over financial resources, not in their methods of production or farm management. Wealthy farmers do not, therefore, constitute a group whose mode of economic organization is markedly different from that of their less fortunate neighbours, although in so far as they can obtain cash or credit on better terms, they may enjoy lower unit costs, *ceteris paribus*.

In the long run, the distribution of tree crop holdings has been affected by patterns of inheritance as well as by economic opportunities and constraints. Under the Yoruba system of inheritance *per stirpes*, tree crop farms which are considered the individual property of the man who plants them tend to become group property over time.[45] Although joint inheritors may sometimes divide the property into individual shares, this is by no means the rule; often, one of the original farmer's children manages the farm on behalf of himself and his co-inheritors. In some cases the proceeds of the farm are also spent collectively—for example, on improvements to the family house or on school fees for a few promising grandchildren. Alternatively, the annual income from the farm may be divided among the heirs, often at a family meeting called for this purpose.[46] In the long run the resulting individual shares of the income may be very small indeed: a businessman and customary court judge whom I met in Ife

---

[44] The classic discussion of technical *vs.* pecuniary external economies is T. Scitovsky, 'Two Concepts of External Economies', *Journal of Political Economy*, 62, 2 (Apr. 1954).

[45] Lloyd, *Yoruba Land Law*, pp. 296 ff.

[46] In such cases it is the earnings from a farm, rather than the farm itself, which tend to become 'fragmented' over time.

said, for example, that his share of the annual income from his grandfather's farm amounted to £8 or £10, out of a total of £120 or more. In such cases, the system of inheritance *per stirpes* appears clearly to work against the concentration of agricultural income in a few hands. Even in the case of joint family expenditures, the effect of the system is probably to strengthen kinship ties rather than to create class distinctions.

A final characteristic of the cocoa economy which has perhaps helped prevent economic inequality from giving rise to a rural class system is the relatively low degree of occupational specialization. Both my own and others' data indicate that it is common for men and women in rural Yoruba communities to pursue more than one occupation at a time. In my sample villages census findings showed that this practice was much more widespread in Araromi-Aperin than in the other villages, but in longer interviews with a sample of adult farmers, I found evidence that some secondary occupations were probably not reported in the census, especially in Abanata. This was particularly true of farmers who also worked part-time as farm labourers, but frequently did not mention farm labour as a separate occupation in reply to questions asked during the census.[47] Thus the apparent difference between Araromi-Aperin and Abanata in this respect may be exaggerated.

Furthermore, in long interviews with a sample of adults in each village, I also found a high degree of occupational mobility. Seven of the adults whom I interviewed at length in Araromi-Aperin had lived there and done the same kinds of work all their lives. Otherwise, everyone said he had had at least one previous occupational experience in another community, and roughly one-third of my informants in each village had had more than one occupation prior to their present one. In some cases, previous occupational experience simply involved the same kind of work at another location, but in many cases, people had switched from one type of occupation to another. (Also, in the case of immigrant farmers from the savannah, who had been farmers at home as well as after moving to the forest belt, their move entailed a shift from growing only food crops to growing cocoa and other tree crops as well as foodstuffs.) Table

[47] Cf. Chapter V, above. In the census I simply asked people to state their present occupations, whereas in the longer interviews I asked a number of questions about current and previous occupations which tended to elicit fuller information than the brief census inquiry. Galletti *et al.* (pp. 199 ff.) also report that a number of their informants pursued more than one occupation.

VI.12 shows the previous occupations of my informants, listed according to their occupations at the time of my study. All reported occupations of each informant are included: the figures in Table

TABLE VI.12

Occupational Histories of Male Informants in Four Villages

Village	Previous occupations		Present occupations			
			Farmer	Trader	Labourer	Craft and service
Araromi-Aperin	Farmer	10	7	4	4	2
	Trader	11	13	9	1	—
	Labourer	7	7	2	3	2
	Craft, service	8	6	—	1	4
	Clerical	6	9	1	—	—
	None[a]	7	7	4	1	1
Abanata	Farmer	25	23	5	3	1
	Trader	4	3	2	—	—
	Labourer	8	8	—	—	1
	Craft, service	5	5	—	—	4
	Clerical	1	1	—	—	—
Orotedo	Farmer	13	10	—	3	2
	Trader	3	3	—	2	2
	Labourer	2	1	—	1	—
	Craft, service	5	5	—	—	—
	Clerical	1	—	—	1	—
Omifon	Farmer	9	9	—	—	1
	Trader	—	—	—	—	—
	Labourer	4	3	—	2	—
	Craft, service	6	6	—	—	3
	Clerical	—	—	—	—	—

Source: same as Table VI.11.

[a] Seven persons who had lived in Araromi-Aperin and done the same kinds of work there all their adult lives.

VI.12 show the number of persons currently in each occupational category who pursued various types of occupation in the past. For example, in Abanata 29 of my informants were farming at the time of my study; 23 of these had also farmed at some time in the past.

In addition, 3 had formerly been traders, 8 had worked as labourers, 5 were once engaged in a craft or service occupation, and 1 had gone to school. Those who were pursuing second or even third occupations at the time of my survey are also listed as traders, labourers, etc., who were formerly farmers, traders, etc. In all, 25 persons said they had been farmers at some time in the past; the total number reported in that row exceeds 25, however, because several were following more than one occupation at the time of my survey.

The evidence presented in Table VI.12 indicates a fairly high degree of mobility among occupational categories. In Omifon and Abanata a bare majority of persons in all occupational categories had done the same kind of work in the past as they were currently engaged in. Elsewhere this was true of only a minority—37 per cent of those interviewed in Orotedo and 31 per cent in Araromi-Aperin. In Araromi-Aperin especially, the occupational histories of farmers showed considerable diversity. In the other three villages 70 per cent to 80 per cent of persons farming at the time of my study had done some farming in the past, whereas this was true of less than half of the farmers in Araromi-Aperin. Correspondingly, over half the farmers in Araromi-Aperin had previously been traders, compared to 23 per cent in Orotedo, 10 per cent in Abanata, and none in Omifon.[48] Moreover, about one-fourth of the farmers I interviewed in Araromi-Aperin had gone to school and some had been employed as clerks—usually in commercial establishments. In the other villages farmers were more likely to have practised a craft or worked as labourers if they had done anything besides farming on their own.[49]

The extent to which individuals combine different types of occupation at one time makes it difficult to relate occupation to household or individual income, unless one has a detailed breakdown of receipts from different sources. Galletti et al. collected such data for 187 households and found that the distribution of net receipts from non-farm activities (principally trade and what they call 'home industry') was considerably more unequal than that of receipts from farming (Table VI.10). Thus, although successful traders earned far more than even the most successful farmers, the vast majority of traders earned

[48] The proportion of former traders would probably have been lower in Orotedo also, if I had been able to include a proportionate number of northern Yorubas among my informants. See above, Introduction, p. 13, n. 23.
[49] In other occupational categories the differences between villages were less pronounced. Most labourers had also farmed, and the same was true of traders. Craftsmen were the least mobile group—in the sense that once they had learned a craft they generally continued to practise it, at least on a part-time basis.

less than most farmers.[50] Clearly, then, there was no simple association between occupation and household income at the time of
their study. Traders, for example, did not constitute a wealthier or
necessarily more powerful group than did farmers in their survey
villages.

Moreover, my own evidence suggests caution in drawing conclusions about the long-run direction of occupational movement. The
relative diversification of economic activities in Araromi-Aperin,
where cocoa has been cultivated for longer than in the other villages,
does *not* reflect a uniform tendency for farmers to use their agricultural earnings to move into non-agricultural occupations. On the
contrary, the most common previous occupation among the farmers
I interviewed in Araromi-Aperin was trade—not farming. Some
people continued to trade as well as to farm at the time of my survey
but, as we saw in the previous section, a good proportion of the
traders in Araromi-Aperin were immigrants from other city-states,
rather than local farmers who had capitalized on the growing rural
market.[51] Similarly, although the desire to save and invest in one's
first cocoa farm has been an important incentive for aspiring farmers
to work for a time as agricultural labourers, men do not always stop
working for wages when their cocoa farms begin to bear. Part-time
wage labour continues to be one source of ready cash income, especially for farmers who cannot obtain sufficient credit in advance of
the cocoa harvest to meet their needs, and a number of men combine
agricultural labour with farming or other occupations during the
course of the year. To be sure, well-to-do farmers do not hire themselves out to their neighbours, but the fact that many farmers seek
temporary wage employment helps to blur another potential class
distinction in rural Yoruba society—namely that between farm
owners and farm workers.

[50] 64 per cent of households with one or more members engaged in trade earned
less than £20 from a year's trading, whereas only 5 per cent of the households had net
farm receipts of less than £20.

[51] This is not to deny that many cocoa farmers have invested part of their profits
in non-agricultural activities (especially on behalf of their children), but simply to
emphasize that the flow of resources has not been all in one direction. The tendency
I noted among early cocoa planters to invest earnings from trade, crafts, or wage
employment in cocoa farms is not just a thing of the past. Cocoa farms are still an
attractive asset to Yorubas in all walks of life, and resources continue to flow into
agriculture from commerce, crafts, and the public sector, as well as vice versa. The
implications of these flows for the future growth and structure of the cocoa economy
will be discussed in Chapter VII.

Conclusion

The growth of cocoa production in Western Nigeria has, over the long run tended to widen the rural market and encourage the expansion and diversification of rural economic activity. Income and the ownership of productive resources are not equally distributed among individuals or households in cocoa-farming villages, and the extent of inequality may well have increased over time. To date, however, economic inequality has not been associated with a clear-cut division of rural society into self-perpetuating socio-economic classes. Within most cocoa-farming villages differences in income often do not coincide with differences in occupation or 'ownership' of productive resources. Although economic success and failure tend, here as elsewhere, to be self-reinforcing, they are not invariably so. In the long run, individuals or households often move from one socioeconomic position to another.[52]

The reasons for the relative openness of rural society in the cocoa belt have been discussed at various points in this and preceding chapters, but it may be useful to summarize them here. Broadly speaking, they involve both the economic and technical requirements of cocoa cultivation *vis-à-vis* relative availability of different factors of production, and some features of the institutional context in which the growth of cocoa production has occurred. From an economic standpoint, the relative abundance of uncultivated forest land has meant that landowners have not been in a position to extract most of the potential agricultural surplus in the form of rents, and that farm workers, most of whom have access to farmland of their own, have shared in the gains as well as the losses of the cocoa-producing sector as a whole. Access to credit or other forms of working capital has always been a condition for successful entry into cocoa farming, and farmers with ample financial resources can afford more purchased inputs—including labour and, today, chemicals—for maintaining their mature farms on an annual basis. However, as I argued in Chapter III, because of the availability of alternative institutional mechanisms for the effective mobilization of working capital cocoa planting has not been confined to farmers with previously accumulated savings. Moreover, the tendency for

[52] Cf. Polly Hill, *Rural Hausa*, chs. XII and XIII, in which she argues that economic groupings within a Hausa village remained stable in the short run, *but* 'it does not follow that there is sufficient longterm stability to justify regarding the community as . . . "class-stratified" in any conventional understanding of this term' (p. 175).

successful farmers (or those with greater access to financial resources) to accumulate larger and larger farm holdings through planting, purchase, or pledging has probably been mitigated somewhat by the absence of economies of scale in cocoa production and the difficulty of supervising a large, scattered labour force. Also, in so far as the development of cocoa growing has helped to strengthen certain established, non-economic institutions in rural Yoruba society, it has probably helped to preserve practices—such as inheritance *per stirpes*—which have also worked against the concentration of agricultural holdings and income in the long run. Thus, the internal structure of rural society in the cocoa belt does not altogether conform to economic differences; ties of kinship, ethnic affiliation, and other forms of customary obligation have remained important factors in rural economic and social life, and tend to offset the polarization of interests between rich and poor in many cocoa farming communities.

CHAPTER VII

Cocoa, Migration, and
Economic Development

So far this study has discussed the effects of increased cocoa production on the rural sector of Western Nigeria and emphasized the degree of economic and social mobility which characterizes rural communities. It does not follow, however, that socio-economic mobility is equally great in Western Nigeria as a whole. Cocoa farmers have always sold their output in a relatively monopsonistic market, and Essang's study shows, for example, that some of the wealthiest cocoa farmers today are men with substantial economic interests and political influence outside the rural sector. Furthermore, since World War II the role of the state in decisions affecting farmers' economic circumstances has steadily increased, so that prospects for future growth and change within the cocoa farming sector have become increasingly dependent on 'outside' political and economic developments. Therefore, in this chapter I shall look briefly at relationships between the cocoa-farming sector of the Western Nigerian economy and at the extent to which patterns of social and economic change within the rural sector have extended beyond it.

The Role of Agricultural Exports in Nigerian Economic Development

Most discussions of the ways in which agricultural exports have affected economic development in Nigeria lay primary emphasis on their contribution to aggregate savings, investment, and foreign exchange earnings. Inter-sectoral linkage effects of increased export production have been limited—particularly in the case of cocoa, which is neither processed nor consumed in Nigeria, and which requires few purchased inputs produced in the domestic economy. It is generally recognized that rising farm incomes have served to expand the internal market for non-agricultural goods and services, but this has not always directly stimulated increases in non-agricultural production. Kilby, for example, points out that the development of domestic industries often lagged far behind the growth of domestic demand for industrial products, as indicated by import volume, and Helleiner suggests that, although cocoa farmers probably spend more than do most other Nigerian farmers on 'consumption goods furnished by Nigerian suppliers outside of their own households', their aggregate effect on non-agricultural domestic output has so far been modest.[1] He adds, however, 'Peasant agriculture has always been the principal earner of foreign exchange in Nigeria ... [and] more important still is the peasant sector's role as a source of savings.'[2]

Most writers would probably agree with Helleiner on this point, but there is considerable diversity of opinion as to the extent to which the 'savings' out of export proceeds have actually contributed to economic development in Nigeria. In particular, there has been a tendency in recent years for economists and other social scientists to question Helleiner's conclusion that 'Nigerian economic development has been aided through the device of channelling a portion of its export earnings via the Marketing Boards away from the producer to other (governmental) decision-makers.'[3] In part, their scepticism derives from a growing awareness that growth of per capita output is not a very good indicator of changes in the standard of living of the population as a whole. In assessing the pace of economic development, economists are increasingly inclined to examine the distribution as well as the growth of output and incomes.[4]

Historically, there have been at least three groups of potential savers out of agricultural export earnings: farmers,[5] traders, and government. Cocoa farmers have indeed saved and invested part of their incomes. We have already seen that the expansion of acreage under cocoa was largely self-financed as time went on, both through farmers ploughing back the proceeds of their bearing farms into the establishment of new ones, and through long-term credit arrangements between farmers and relatives or fellow townsmen who worked

for them. Farmers also spend part of their income on other types of
capital goods, such as housing, education, vehicles, and equipment
(sewing machines, grinding mills, spray pumps, etc.).[6] However,
there is little reliable evidence on the magnitude of these expenditures
or the overall rate of farmers' savings,[7] and most observers have
asserted (or assumed) that the bulk of savings out of cocoa earnings
has occurred in the public and/or large-scale private sectors.

As I pointed out in Chapter I the marketing of Nigerian exports
was essentially controlled by large-scale private enterprise before the
introduction of cocoa, and remained so until World War II. Not only
were sales overseas carried out almost entirely by large foreign-
owned firms, but the internal collection and bulking of export produce also afforded substantial opportunities for the accumulation of
capital and market power. Although the internal marketing system
does involve a large number of very small-scale traders at the village
level, it is also true, as we saw in Chapter VI, that by far the highest
incomes in the cocoa economy accrue to produce buyers; unlike
cocoa production, cocoa marketing involves substantial *pecuniary*
economies of scale and hence tends to favour a considerable degree
of market concentration. The potential economic (and political?)
power of successful African produce traders is indicated by the frequent efforts of foreign firms, often with the co-operation of the
colonial government, to limit their access to foreign markets.[8]

Relatively little is known about either the share of total export
proceeds accruing to private traders in Nigeria or their saving and
investment behaviour. Bauer's classic study, *West African Trade*,
hardly touches on the subject,[9] although his main thesis—that trade
is productive—does imply that whatever profits foreign or indigenous
traders 'ploughed back' into expanding their commercial activities
contributed to the development of the economy. He does not provide
any data on rates of reinvestment out of traders' profits and, partly

[6] Galletti *et al.*, pp. 261 ff., and my own observations.
[7] Galletti *et al.* calculated the proportion of income saved by the households in
their sample, but since the year of their study (1951/2) was one of unprecedentedly
high cocoa prices, their finding that cocoa farmers saved on the average 40 per cent
of their annual incomes is probably not representative of long-run behaviour (see
pp. 461–3).
[8] See, e. g., S. O. Adeyeye, 'The Western Nigeria Co-operative Movement, 1935–64',
University of Ibadan M.A. thesis, 1967; cf. G. B. Kay, *The Political Economy of
Colonialism in Ghana* (Cambridge, 1972).
[9] Apart from a passing, and undocumented, statement to the effect that foreigners
save a higher proportion of their incomes than do Africans. P. T. Bauer, *West African
Trade* (London, 1963), p. 32.

because of the absence of such information, most writers have assumed that most saving out of cocoa proceeds has been undertaken by
the government, especially since World War II, when the marketing
of Nigerian exports was taken over by statutory marketing boards.[10]

The effect of government tax and marketing policies on economic
development in Western Nigeria depends both on the ways in which
governments (including the marketing boards) have spent their funds
and on the effects of marketing board price policies on farmers'
decisions to produce and invest. It is by now widely recognized in the
literature on economic development that, although higher levels of
per capita income are everywhere associated with a declining agricultural share of total output and employment, efforts to accelerate the
growth of per capita income by exploiting the agricultural sector are
frequently self-defeating. If fiscal and/or marketing arrangements
depress both the incentives and the wherewithal for agricultural
expansion too severely, the economy is likely to experience shortages
of foodstuffs, raw materials, and/or foreign exchange; frequently
costs rise and rates of saving and investment are reduced in non-
agricultural sectors as well. To a considerable extent, economic
growth and a sectorally balanced distribution of income are comple-
mentary rather than competing development goals.[11]

In the literature on Western Nigeria it is frequently argued that
post-World War II policies and patterns of investment and expenditure by government and large-scale private enterprise have promoted
urban and non-agricultural expansion at the expense of agriculture,
with increasingly unfavourable economic and social consequences.[12]
Not only have the bulk of public revenues collected from the cocoa-
farming sector been used to finance urban amenities and/or non-
agricultural investment projects but those projects which government
has designed to promote rural development have frequently proved
unproductive and wasteful, or have benefited only a small minority

[10] Between 1947/8 and 1961/2 the government withdrew 32 per cent of cocoa
farmers' 'potential producer income'—defined as export proceeds less net marketing
board trading expenses plus increase in stocks. Helleiner, p. 163 and Table V-F-1.

[11] For a discussion of this well-known point with reference to rural development in
Nigeria, see J. C. Wells, 'Equity and Efficiency in Rural Development: An African
Dilemma?', Paper presented at the African Studies Association meetings, Nov.
1972.

[12] This theme runs through a number of recent articles in the *Nigerian Journal of
Economic and Social Studies* and through many of the papers presented at the Conference on Marketing Boards. For a comprehensive review of agricultural development policies in Nigeria since 1962, see J. C. Wells, *Agricultural Policy and Economic
Growth in Nigeria: 1962–68*, forthcoming. On government policies to promote industrialization see Kilby, *Industrialization in an Open Economy*.

of well-to-do farmers. Also, it has recently been argued that marketing board price policies actually depressed output and investment in
the agricultural export sector during the 1960s.[13] To be sure, there
was a correspondingly rapid rate of industrial growth in this period,
but this was accompanied by high rates of population growth in
urban areas (accounted for, in large part, by immigration from rural
areas), which have considerably exceeded the growth of employment
opportunities in the public and large-scale private sectors.[14] As a
result, many observers have concluded that there is a growing pool
of un- or under-employed labour in Nigerian cities which is not only
economically wasteful and socially disruptive in the short run, but
tends to perpetuate the pattern of sectorally unbalanced public expenditure over time. Because urban workers appear to constitute a
greater threat to social and political stability than the more widely
dispersed rural population, Nigerian governments are further im-
pelled to concentrate public expenditure on urban amenities and to
pursue minimum wage policies which aggravate rather than reduce
the urban unemployment problem.

In addition to the tendency to finance urban and industrial development at the expense of agriculture, Nigerian governments have,
since the early 1950s, devoted a very large share of their budgets (both
current and capital) to the expansion of educational opportunities.
Nowhere has this been more pronounced than in Western Nigeria.
Between 1955 and 1962 government in the Western Region devoted
from 28 per cent to 43 per cent of total annual outlays to education,[15]
and school enrolments jumped from 456,000 in 1954 to 811,400 the

[13] D. Olatunbosun and S. O. Olayide, 'Effects of the Marketing Boards on the
Output and Income of Primary Producers', International Conference on the Marketing
Board System, Nigerian Institute of Social and Economic Research (mimeographed,
1970).
[14] On problems of rural–urban migration and urban unemployment in Nigeria,
see A. Callaway, 'Nigeria's Indigenous Education: The Apprentice System', *Odu*, 1
(July 1964), and 'Unemployment Among African School Leavers', *Journal of Modern
African Studies*, 1, 3 (Sept. 1963); P. Kilby, *Industrialization*, esp. chs. 7, 9; S. O. Falae,
'Unemployment in Nigeria', *Nigerian Journal of Economic and Social Studies*, 13, 1
(Mar. 1971); V. P. Diejomaoh and W. A. T. Orimalade, 'Unemployment in Nigeria:
An Economic Analysis of Scope, Trends and Policy Issues', ibid , 13, 2 (July 1971).
On the economics of rural–urban migration, economic growth, and urban unemploy-
ment in Africa generally, see C. R. Frank, 'Urban Unemployment and Economic
Growth in Africa', *Oxford Economic Papers*, 20, 2 (July 1968); M. P. Todaro, 'A
Model of Labor Migration and Urban Unemployment in Less Developed Countries',
American Economic Review, 59, 1 (Mar. 1969); J. R. Harris and M. P. Todaro,
'Migration, Unemployment and Development: A Two-Sector Analysis', ibid. 60,
1 (Mar. 1970).
[15] Callaway and Musone, *Financing of Education in Nigeria* (UNESCO: International Institute for Educational Planning, 1968), p. 24.

following year, when the government offered free primary education to every child in the region.[16] After 1960 enrolment dropped somewhat, but the demand for education at the primary level and beyond remained much higher than it had been in the past, and the proportion of private incomes spent on schooling probably increased.[17] Today expenditure on education is one of the major uses of cocoa farmers' savings—as is reflected, for example, in the high rates of school attendance in my sample villages. (See Table VII.1.) Further-

TABLE VII.1

Proportion of Resident Children, Aged 5–15 Years, Attending School in Sample Villages

Village	Proportion %
Araromi-Aperin	70
Abanata	62
Orotedo	39

Source: Village censuses.

more, many of the individuals whom I interviewed at length in these villages were also supporting children or siblings who attended school outside the village. (See Table VII.2.)

TABLE VII.2

Some Indications of Adult Male Informants' Investment in Education

	Araromi-Aperin	Abanata	Orotedo	Omifon
No. of informants	37	31	18	13
No. of children (all ages)	140	149	35	30
No. of children in school	50	56	7	9
No. informants who support one or more pupils	21[a]	24	10	5

Source: Long interviews.

[a] In addition, five informants had helped to send relatives to school in the past.

The rapid growth in the number of school leavers which followed the expansion of educational opportunities in the 1950s has also con-

[16] Helleiner, p. 306.
[17] Callaway and Musone estimate (p. 124) that private expenditure on primary schooling alone nearly quadrupled between 1952 and 1962 in the Western Region; it is almost certain that incomes did not rise at a comparable rate.

tributed to the problem of urban unemployment in Nigeria. Young people with a primary school education have been particularly inclined to seek employment in urban areas; their skills rarely qualify them for anything more than labourers' jobs, however, and even those are becoming increasingly difficult to obtain. Available evidence shows that unemployment rates are much higher among young school leavers than among any other group in the labour force. The Labour Force Sample Survey of 1966/7 estimated that nearly 80 per cent of the unemployed in that year had attended primary school; 70 per cent were between 15 and 23 years of age.[18] Since the numbers of primary school leavers are increasing every year, the problem of providing these young people with employment opportunities is becoming an increasingly serious one.

In short, Nigeria (like a number of other African countries) appears to have run full tilt into some major socio-economic bottlenecks which have in part resulted from the post-war 'strategy' of sectorally unbalanced growth. Urban-based industrial and commercial growth has generated incentives for the transfer of labour and enterprise out of the agricultural sector more rapidly than it has created non-agricultural employment opportunities, and most sources agree that the results are economically wasteful, socially disruptive, and likely to hinder future development.

There is less agreement in the literature on what should be done to improve the situation. Some economists tend to argue (or assume) that what the government has done, the government can and should undo. Peter Kilby, for example, states that 'the prime variables controlling the rate of [rural–urban labour] flow are economic, and are capable of being manipulated by appropriate public policies',[19] and this view is reflected in other discussions of the Nigerian situation and in economic literature on rural–urban migration throughout Africa.[20] To reverse rural–urban migration and reduce urban unemployment, these writers have proposed a variety of policies ranging from rural development to roadblocks.

Other scholars tend to see both the government and various groups of workers and producers as interdependent parts of a neo-colonial economic and political system in Nigeria whose very nature gives rise to such anomalies as economic growth with rising unemployment.[21]

[18] Falae, p. 65.
[19] Kilby, *Industrialization*, p. 278.
[20] See especially the articles by Harris and Todaro cited above.

According to this view, the concentration of resources and economic
power in the hands of an urban-based elite, which grew out of
the economic developments and policies of the colonial period,
is a self-perpetuating process which has given rise to increasing
economic inefficiency and inequality on the one hand, and to the
emergence of a class system within Nigerian society on the other.
As a result, the rural population in, for example, Western Nigeria
is increasingly assuming the position of an exploited peasantry, supporting the largely unproductive elite which controls the political
decision-making process and therefore the allocation of public funds
in the region as a whole. Because of the urban bias of government
price and expenditure policies, most farmers aspire to escape the
rural sector, and many devote their limited savings to training and
equipping themselves or their children for non-agricultural occupations. In the long run this system discourages agricultural and/or
rural economic expansion, and increases the likelihood of mounting
social and political conflict between classes. These writers tend to dis-
count the likelihood of significant change through government
policy, on the grounds that it is not in the interest of the present
governing elite, and see revolutionary upheaval as a necessary condition for progress.

Implications of the Present Study

Since my research was confined to the cocoa-farming sector of
Western Nigeria (and concentrated primarily on the production
rather than the marketing of cocoa), my findings offer only partial
insights into some of the issues discussed above. Nevertheless, I think
it is worthwhile to summarize them here, in order both to place the
conclusions of preceding chapters in a somewhat broader perspective and, as I hope, to suggest lines of further investigation into the
whole question of inter-sectoral relationships and their bearing on
general patterns of socio-economic change in Nigeria.

Rural–urban Migration. One of the main findings of this study is
that the spread of cocoa cultivation in Western Nigeria involved not
only substantial migration into uncultivated forest areas, but also

[21] See, e.g., G. P. Williams, 'Social Stratification of a Neo-Colonial Economy:
Western Nigeria', in C. Allen and R. Johnson, eds., *African Perspectives* (Cambridge,
1970) and unpublished papers based on recent fieldwork in Ibadan; J. F. Weeks,
'Employment, Growth and Foreign Domination in Underdeveloped Countries',
Review of Radical Political Economics, 4, 1 (Spring 1972).

the establishment of thousands of new settlements of a more permanent character than the traditional Yoruba farming hamlet. Given
the characteristic Yoruba pattern of residence in densely populated
towns (some of which were very large even in the nineteenth century),
the spread of cocoa farming may be said to have given rise to a kind
of urban–rural migration and to have helped create a distinctly rural
sector in Yoruba society. As we saw in Chapter III, the opening up
of forest areas for cocoa growing greatly accelerated after World
War II and, in some areas, continues today. Thus, my findings suggest that there has been a continuing flow of people from towns to
the countryside in Western Nigeria from the turn of the century
until the present time.

Further evidence of a certain amount of urban–rural migration in
recent years may be found both in the data I collected in three cocoa-
farming villages and in the available census data for Nigeria as a
whole. Table VII.3 compares evidence on the sex, age, and ethnic
background of persons who migrated to my three sample villages

TABLE VII.3

*Demographic and Ethnic Characteristics of Recent Immigrants and
Total Populations in Three Villages*

	1960–4	Date of arrival 1965–70	1960–70	Total population
I. *Araromi-Aperin*				
Number	108	237	345	932
% of total population	12	25	37	
	% of column	*% of column*	*% of column*	*% of column*
Sex: male	37	43	42	48
female	63	57	58	52
Age: 0–15	32	46	41	41
16–30	22	30	28	17
over 30	29	11	17	27
unknown	17	13	14	15
Area of origin:				
Ibadan	54	60	58	63
Ijebu	17	11	13	9
Ijesha-Ekiti	7	5	6	6
Northern Yoruba	12	5	7	7
Other Yoruba	5	11	9	6
Non-Yoruba	6	7	7	5

Table VIII.3—*contd.*

	1960–4	Date of arrival 1965–70	1960–70	Total population
II. *Abanata*				
Number	89	104	193	496
% of total population	18	21	39	
	% of column	*% of column*	*% of column*	*% of column*
Sex: male	30	50	41	48
female	70	50	59	52
Age: 0–15	20	53	38	51
16–30	60	37	47	29
over 30	15	3	9	14
unknown	5	7	6	6
Area of origin:				
Ife	2	11	7	7
Northern Yoruba	90	78	83	84
Other Yoruba	8	11	9	8
III. *Orotedo*				
Number	96	155	251	323
% of total population	30	48	78	
	% of column	*% of column*	*% of column*	*% of column*
Sex: male	48	55	53	55
female	52	45	47	45
Age: 0–15	16	41	31	41
16–30	44	43	43	35
over 30	25	10	16	15
unknown	15	6	10	9
Area of origin:				
Ondo	1	1	1	9
Ikale	41	21	28	37
Northern Yoruba	47	61	56	47
Other Yoruba	1	9	6	5
Non-Yoruba	0	4	3	3

Source: Village censuses.

during the 1960s with similar information for the total population of each village. The proportion of recent immigrants in the total population was, of course, highest in Orotedo where cocoa cultivation began in the late 1950s. However, there was almost no difference between Araromi-Aperin and Abanata in the proportion of recent arrivals among the total population, although cocoa growing developed almost thirty years earlier in Araromi-Aperin. In both cases nearly 40 per cent of the current population had moved to the village since 1960. Similarly, both Araromi-Aperin and Abanata had gained considerably more female than male residents during the 1960s, in contrast to Orotedo where males outnumbered females both among the recent arrivals and among the population as a whole. Also, the proportion of children was somewhat higher among recent arrivals in the two older cocoa-farming villages than in Orotedo.[22] This suggests that recent immigrants to the older villages were more likely to be economic dependants than people seeking opportunities for economically productive activity. However, Abanata also attracted a large proportion of young men and women during this period; in this respect, it is more like Orotedo than Araromi-Aperin, which probably reflects the fact—discussed in Chapter VI—that rural economic opportunities are not confined to agricultural production per se.[23]

The data I collected in these three villages related only to the resident population at the time of my survey; I have no information on the number of people who left these villages at different times and therefore cannot draw conclusions about net immigration or emigration.[24] The only available sources of information on net flows of internal migration in Nigeria are the national censuses, and these are subject to such large and indeterminable margins of error that one hesitates to cite them at all.[25] As is well known, for example, the

[22] The high proportion of children among immigrants who arrived since 1965 partly reflects the fact that ages are given as stated at the time of my survey. Many of the people who arrived in the early 1960s were children at that time, but had become young adults by 1970/1.

[23] Information on the ethnic backgrounds of recent immigrants shows few marked differences from the ethnic composition of the population as a whole. Although a number of non-Ibadans did move to Araromi-Aperin in recent years, as discussed in Chapter VI, Ibadans have also continued to move to rural areas in recent years.

[24] In a study of five villages in Western Nigeria (one of which was Araromi-Aperin), carried out in 1967, P. O. Olusanya concludes that the populations of all the villages had declined substantially since the 1952 census. He does not, however, appear to have allowed for the fact that village populations reported in the 1952 census frequently included populations of a number of rural settlements grouped together. Also, his figure for the population of Araromi-Aperin is substantially lower than mine. His data were collected by local schoolteachers rather than by himself; there is no discussion in his report of possible errors involved in this procedure. Unfortunately most of his other demographic and attitudinal data are presented in the form of totals for the five villages, so that it is impossible to compare differences among them or relate them to differences in ecological, economic, and other village characteristics. P. O. Olusanya, 'Socio-Economic Aspects of Rural–Urban Migration in Western Nigeria', Nigerian Institute of Social and Economic Research (mimeographed, 1969).

[25] For an attempt to estimate the margins of error involved in the two censuses, and

censuses of 1951/2 and 1963 indicate that the total population of
Nigeria nearly doubled during the intervening decade. Not only is
this finding inherently implausible, but in view of the fact that the
first census was probably an undercount and the second substantially
inflated as a result of political pressures, it is almost certainly wrong.
We do not know, however, to what extent each census was in error,
or how these errors are likely to have been distributed among different geographical areas or segments of the population. Thus, it has
been argued that another 'finding' of the two censuses—namely that
there was a net eastward movement of population in Western Nigeria
during the 1950s, *away* from the provinces with the largest urban
centres and *towards* those which are predominantly rural—is probably also an error, since it is common knowledge that the basic
direction of internal migration in recent years has been from rural to
urban areas.[26] In light of the evidence that I found of substantial
migration to the eastern parts of the cocoa belt during this period,
however, it seems that the censuses may not, after all, give such a
distorted picture of changes in the geographical distribution of the
population—however inaccurate their measurement of its over-all
rate of growth.

The foregoing discussion does not, of course, imply that there has
not also been substantial movement from rural to urban areas in
Western Nigeria in recent years, but it does suggest that patterns of
internal migration were more complex and the net movement of
people from rural to urban areas somewhat smaller than those
usually described or implied in the literature. The question then
arises how this conclusion is to be reconciled with the growing body
of evidence and argument that disparities between rural and urban
incomes and opportunities have drawn people away from rural areas
in recent years, discouraging agricultural expansion and swelling the
ranks of the urban unemployed? In part, the answer lies in the fact
that the rural–urban income gap within Western Nigeria may have
been overstated in recent studies; relatively speaking, the pull of
urban wages has perhaps been weaker in the cocoa belt than in
other parts of Nigeria or of Africa in general.

More fundamentally, however, I think that the underlying model

---

the probable rate of population growth in the intervening period, see I. I. U. Eke,
'Population of Nigeria, 1952–1965', *Nigerian Journal of Economic and Social Studies*,
8, 2 (July 1966).

[26] Unpublished papers by the staff of the Physical Planning Unit, Nigerian Institute of Social and Economic Research, and conversation with L. Green.

which economists have used to explain 'excessive' rural–urban migration and to propose remedies for it is probably not adequate to the task. In particular, the assumptions that rural–urban migration (1) is simply a response to market signals, and (2) may be taken as a proxy for rural–urban flows of all private productive resources (outside the large-scale industrial and commercial sector) are probably not justified. When we distinguish between inter-sectoral movements of labour and capital, and take into account the effects of non-economic institutions on patterns of production and investment, both the causes and the consequences of rural–urban migration and income differentials take on a somewhat different appearance.

Rural–urban Income Differentials. To illustrate the growing gap between rural and urban incomes in Nigeria, several recent studies have quoted sectoral indices of average per capita income, calculated by S. A. Aluko in 1969, which show that between 1960 and 1967, per capita income in agriculture was lower and, with the exception of mining, grew more slowly than in any other sector. For several reasons these figures tend to overstate the differences between rural and urban incomes in the cocoa belt. For one thing, they refer to Nigeria as a whole and it is generally believed that cocoa farmers' incomes are substantially above those of most of the agricultural population in Nigeria; for another, they refer only to persons employed in establishments with ten or more workers, and hence exclude the great majority of Nigerian farmers as well as a large proportion of the non-agricultural labour force.[27] Furthermore, average per capita income figures include a wide variety of returns to different kinds of employment and productive activity; it does not follow from such data that similar sectoral differentials exist in, for example, wages for labourers with comparable levels of skill. Indeed, available evidence on wages paid to unskilled labourers in government employment and in the cocoa-farming sector indicates that agricultural wages were higher than those paid by the Western Region government in the 1950s, and did not actually fall below the government minimum wage until 1964.[28] Thus, the difference between wages

[27] Diejomaoh and Orimalade, p. 147.

[28] Cf. the Kilby–Weeks debate cited in Chapter V, p. 142, n. 39, above. Both Kilby and Weeks note that agricultural wages tend to set a floor under urban wages, although they disagree about the extent to which trade union activity and political forces have raised urban wages above those in agriculture. Warren apparently considers agricultural wages irrelevant to the determination of urban wages. 'Urban Real Wages', esp. pp. 34–5.

available to workers with given levels of skill in agriculture and in non-agricultural activities in Western Nigeria was probably not so great as that between average per capita incomes in different sectors for Nigeria as a whole.

Moreover, the evidence presented in Chapter VI on the diversification of rural economic activity in the cocoa belt indicates that rural economic opportunities are not confined to agriculture. Especially in

TABLE VII.4

Occupations of Recent Immigrants and Total Adult Populations in Three Villages

	Date of arrival			Total adult
	1960–4[a]	*1965–70[a]*	*1960–70[a]*	*population*
Araromi-Aperin				
Farmer	38	17	24	37
Labourer	40	37	37	35
(of which government)	(3)	(6)	(4)	(5)
Trader	47	29	36	47
Craft and service	11	17	15	19
Clerical	3	11	8	6
Abanata				
Farmer	18	16	17	33
Labourer	35	39	36	29
Trader	41	23	34	26
Craft and service	11	23	15	11
Clerical	1	5	3	4
Orotedo				
Farmer	44	25	38	36
Labourer	55	68	62	57
Trader	5	9	7	8
Craft and service	4	5	4	4
Clerical	0	1	1	2

[a] Figures expressed as per cent of occupied persons, excluding school children, in each immigrant group.

older cocoa-growing areas, a substantial proportion of the population are engaged in non-agricultural occupations, and this is also true of people who migrated to the rural areas in recent years. (See Table VII.4.) Hence, data on wages or per capita incomes in agriculture do not necessarily reflect average wage or income levels for all rural residents. Also, as S. O. Falae pointed out in an article in 1971, the relative concentration of public amenities (water, electricity, educational, health, and entertainment facilities) in urban areas does not mean that such facilities are necessarily available to low-income families in the cities.[29] For many potential rural–urban migrants, there is no reason to assume that public services and other forms of non-cash or intangible income will necessarily be higher in the city. In short, for some groups of rural residents in Western Nigeria, the relative *economic* attractions of urban life may not have been so great in the last decade as is commonly assumed.

On the other hand, it is undoubtedly true that the terms of trade between agriculture on the one hand, and the manufacturing and distributive sectors on the other, have declined in recent years, and cocoa farming is no exception to this rule.[30] Also, as I argued in Chapter VI, the growth of trade, craft, and service production in the rural areas of Western Nigeria occurred largely in response to the growth of farm incomes, and rural non-agricultural enterprise continues to depend heavily on farmers' demand. This is reflected both in the extreme seasonality of much non-agricultural production and distributive activity in the rural areas—many of the traders and craftsmen I interviewed said they did most of their business at the time of the cocoa harvest, when farmers had ready cash—and also in the decline of trading opportunities in my sample villages in the late 1960s. According to Table VII.4, for example, people who arrived in Araromi-Aperin and Abanata after 1965 were much less likely to be engaged in trade than those who had arrived in the early 1960s, and information supplied by individual traders tended to confirm the fact that the prolonged decline in cocoa farmers' terms of trade during the 1960s had exerted a depressing effect on their businesses. Thus, even if unskilled labour did not flow from rural to urban areas in the cocoa belt at a rapid rate for much of the post-war period, the question remains whether government policies have not acted in recent years to discourage increased production and investment in the cocoa-farming sector and, by so doing, helped to create the basis for a growing future imbalance between rural and urban developments, and an eventual 'peasantization' of the rural population even in the most prosperous sector of Nigerian agriculture.

Inter-sectoral Movements of Indigenous Capital. To answer this question we need to know how government policies and movements in sectoral terms of trade have influenced patterns of saving and investment in agricultural and small-scale non-agricultural activities in both rural and urban areas. (For convenience, I shall follow Polly

[29] Falae, p. 74.   [30] Teriba and Phillips, p. 89.

Hill and refer to all these activities in combination as the 'indigenous' sector of the economy.) Since I have not studied capital formation in non-agricultural activities in any detail, the following discussion is somewhat speculative; I can suggest, but not demonstrate, the implications of my findings about cocoa farming for patterns of indigenous capital formation, economic change, and social stratification outside the rural sector.

Evidence has been presented earlier in this study to show that market information is not always sufficient to explain observed patterns of economic behaviour in the cocoa-farming sector. Over time, declining terms of trade have not always led to a reduction in the rate of investment in cocoa farms; indeed, the rate of new cocoa plantings sometimes rose in periods of declining farmers' terms of trade. This happened both because farmers were able to mobilize resources for agricultural investment through non-market mechanisms, and also because cocoa trees have such a long life that relatively short-run changes in market conditions probably do not exert a decisive influence on farmers' expectations of lifetime earnings from cocoa farms.[31] It follows that, in so far as long-run expectations and institutional factors continue to affect farmers' perceived economic opportunities and productive decisions today, a decline in farmers' terms of trade (or a growing gap between urban and rural wages) *need* not depress the rate of investment in agriculture, nor induce a net outflow of resources from the rural to the urban sector. Such changes would also depend on (1) the role of non-economic institutions in the organization and expansion of economic activities outside the rural sector, and (2) changes in farmers' perceptions of *both* short- and long-run opportunities within and outside agriculture.

Most discussions of rural–urban migration assign a largely passive, redistributive role to traditional institutions in the urban economy. Families and ethnic associations provide support for urban immigrants who are seeking employment or whose jobs in the indigenous sector do not yield a living wage; they may also provide information about job opportunities and/or contacts with potential employers. Otherwise, their economic functions are assumed to be non-existent or even counterproductive. Economists in particular have paid little attention to the role which such institutions might play in capital formation or the creation of employment opportunities within the urban indigenous sector, although evidence

---

[31] See Chapter III, above; also P. Hill, *Migrant Cocoa Farmers*, p. 181.

of such productive activity is not lacking.[32] Moreover, there seems to be a widespread assumption that inter-sectoral movements of financial and entrepreneurial resources parallel the movement of labour. Skilled workers are invariably represented as forsaking the countryside for the bright lights and well-paying jobs of the cities and, although urban immigrants' practice of remitting part of their earnings to their home communities is widely noted, economists rarely examine the extent to which these remittances are saved and invested, rather than consumed, in rural areas.

In Western Nigeria these conclusions are not obviously supported by available evidence. Since the turn of the century, men have invested money earned in urban-based, non-agricultural occupations in cocoa farms and some continue to do so. (My own evidence on this point is confirmed by a couple of studies of non-agricultural groups in the Western Nigerian economy. Essang has documented the extensive investments of licensed buying agents and professionals in the cocoa-growing areas, and Williams found, in a survey of clerks and other semi-skilled government employees, that many intended to invest in cocoa farms when they had accumulated sufficient savings.)[33] Also, many urban-based Yorubas contribute to collective investment projects in their home towns—just as migrant cocoa farmers have done. Although these bits of evidence are far from conclusive, they do suggest that we cannot *assume* that government policies and expenditure patterns have induced a net drain of capital, as well as labour, from rural to urban areas in Western Nigeria without more information.

Similarly, the extent to which cocoa farmers have invested in education for their children or other dependants and the growing pool of unemployed school leavers in Nigerian cities do not necessarily represent a permanent flight from the countryside, or a sheer waste of human and economic resources. The fact that school leavers' skills are not marketable, at least in any measurable sense, does not necessarily mean that they are not productive, from either an individual or a national point of view. Callaway has pointed out, for

[32] Examples of indigenous economic organization in non-agricultural activities are provided in, e.g., P. Hill, *Studies in Rural Capitalism in West Africa*, and A. Cohen, *Custom and Politics in Urban Africa*. Kilby (*Industrialization*, p. 278) estimates that the rate of employment grew at 4–5 per cent in the 1960s, but attributes this to increased demand alone—a sort of vent-for-surplus effect.

[33] S. M. Essang, 'Distribution of Earnings in the Cocoa Economy of Western Nigeria', Michigan State University Ph.D., 1970; unpublished findings reported by G. P. Williams.

example, that a great many of these young people eventually become absorbed into the indigenous urban sector[34] which, as I suggested above, has been inadequately studied in terms of its growth and productive potential. Furthermore education, like cocoa farming, is a form of long-term investment: it takes years to put a child through school and the potential returns also stretch over his lifetime or even beyond.[35] From an individual's point of view, relatively long periods of unemployment or under-employment may 'pay off' over his lifetime if they eventually enable him to obtain a lucrative job, or if he can use such periods to develop contacts or relationships which enhance his future access to wealth and power through channels other than wage (or salary) employment—for example, good business contacts or political connections. Furthermore, investment in an individual's education is often a collective undertaking in Western Nigeria, financed by contributions from several kinsmen or the proceeds of group-held assets (e.g. family-owned farms), or facilitated by community investment in, say, school construction. Thus, his education may be viewed as worthwhile to the institutions who sponsored him if it improves their access to external sources of wealth and influence, even if the school leaver himself never earns more than an unskilled worker—or even ends up in farming. In so far as school leavers go to the cities in search of patrons as well as jobs, their labour market behaviour cannot be explained by direct market costs and returns alone; we must also take into account the institutional and political context in which they operate.

In general, I have tried to suggest in the preceding paragraphs that the obvious short-run costs of rural–urban migration in Western Nigeria need to be re-examined in relation to institutional and long-run considerations. My evidence on patterns of resource movement into the cocoa-farming areas suggests that there is no reason to assume that urban immigrants (whether illiterate or educated) and their future earnings are necessarily lost to the rural sector, especially in the long run. Moreover, the significant roles which non-economic institutions have played in facilitating agricultural capital formation and preventing the concentration of rural assets in the hands of a few

[34] Callaway, 'Nigeria's Indigenous Education'.
[35] We know very little about the long-run effects of education on economic growth. Undoubtedly, developing countries cannot *expect* public expenditure on education to yield significant short-run increases in GDP, but the long-run social and economic consequences of education should not be ignored just because they do not necessarily take the form of increases in marketable output. Cf. W. F. Stolper, *Planning Without Facts* (Cambridge, Mass., 1966), pp. 204 ff.

suggest that we may need to investigate further the extent to which
they have functioned in similar fashion outside the rural areas. It
may well be that they have *not* served to counteract the sectoral im-
balances of government price and expenditure policies, or to promote
indigenous economic growth, inter-sectoral resource mobility, and
the distribution of economic gains across incipient class lines. However, in view of my findings on the determinants of economic change
within the cocoa-farming sector, I would be reluctant to predict
relative rural stagnation or the 'peasantization' of the rural population *vis-à-vis* the rest of Western Nigerian society from an examina-
tion of market trends and government budgets alone.[36]

The Implications of Future Land Scarcity. Before turning to the
policy implications of this study, one further aspect of the rural
economy requires comment. It has been argued above that prospects
for further agricultural expansion in Western Nigeria depend not
only on what happens to the rate of exploitation of farmers by the
rest of the economy, but also on the extent to which alternative
avenues of social and economic advancement are created or closed
over time. One such avenue which is likely to close in the foreseeable
future is the ready availability of uncultivated forest land suitable
for planting new cocoa farms. We have seen that such land has
already become scarce in some parts of the cocoa belt, but that
farmers in these areas have even in the last decade been able to
obtain additional land by migrating. When land reserves are exhausted (or become increasingly expensive) throughout the cocoa
belt, the entire cocoa-farming sector will face an unprecedented
situation, which could have far-reaching consequences for rural
economic development and social change. In the past, as I argued in
earlier chapters, the relative availability of uncultivated forest land in
Western Nigeria has helped to prevent the emergence of rural socio-
economic classes and has permitted kinship and ethnic groups
to function primarily as mechanisms for promoting agricultural

[36] Those who predict agricultural stagnation and growing class conflict in Western
Nigeria, on the grounds that the present system of export marketing and agricultural
taxation tends to siphon off surplus agricultural income for investment in the urban
sector, overlook the fact that Nigerian cocoa farmers have always depended on a
relatively monopsonistic marketing-cum-fiscal system but that this has hardly prevented rural growth and diversification in the past. The Agbekoya uprising of 1969 was
apparently a revolt against *visible* exploitation of the rural sector for outsiders'
benefits, rather than a protest against deteriorating sectoral terms of trade or unbalanced growth as such. Ayoola Commission, *Report* (Ibadan, 1969) and my own
conversations with farmers.

investment and distributing agricultural wealth and income to large numbers of people. As good cocoa land becomes absolutely scarce, especially if farmers' terms of trade also continue to fall, one would expect to find an increasingly concentrated pattern of land and tree crop ownership, as rising rents force poor tenants to mortgage their farms or sell out altogether, and increasing numbers of landless labourers are obliged to accept whatever wage they can get.

Furthermore, kinship and ethnic groups would probably become engaged in competition for control of scarce agricultural resources and start to exclude non-members from sharing in that control and its benefits, rather than facilitate the entry of more and more people into cocoa farming as they have done in the past. Under such circumstances, the traditional institutions which have so far helped to prevent the polarization of rural society into unequal and mutually antagonistic socio-economic classes could well become the chief instruments of class division and conflict. Such polarization would, of course, tend to be greater, the fewer the economic opportunities outside the rural sector.

Policy Implications

There is a growing body of literature on the successes and failures of the various rural development schemes which have been tried in Western Nigeria since World War II.[37] On the whole, evaluative studies have pretty thoroughly discredited the use of large-scale capital-intensive projects—such as the Farm Settlements or government plantations—for achieving sustained and relatively widespread increases in rural production and incomes. However, although these findings have led several economists to recommend increased reliance on market incentives (e.g. by raising marketing board prices paid to farmers) as perhaps the least expensive way to achieve given increases in agricultural output, such recommendations are usually followed by statements to the effect that a variety of government services will *also* be needed to ensure the growth and diversification of agricultural production.[38] Nigerian farmers, it is argued, respond readily enough to price incentives if it is technically and institutionally feasible for them to do so. However, most economists assume, in the

[37] See Wells, *Agricultural Policy and Economic Growth*; also several of the reports on various aspects of rural development policy prepared for the Consortium for the Study of Nigerian Rural Development.

[38] See, e.g., G. L. Johnson *et al.*, 'Strategies and Recommendations for Nigerian Rural Development', CSNRD Report No. 33 (1969).

tion c. 1920; like the Ibadan Agricultural Society, the Association sought to promote improved farming practices and produce-marketing facilities.

Balogun Ipaiye was born in Ile-Oluji.[7] During the wars he was a soldier and slave-trader, travelling to Lagos to sell his captives. According to his son, A. B. B. Ipaiye, 'the abolition of slavery met him there [Lagos]', so he turned to 'legitimate trade' in gunpowder, salt, and foodstuffs. He became a wealthy man, with considerable property in Lagos (on Ipaiye Street, Isalegangan). In 1891 he and some other Ondos in Lagos decided to follow the example of the Egbas, Ijeshas, and others and establish a farming and trading community on the route from Lagos to their home town. They obtained permission from the Oshemawe to settle on the unoccupied land between the Oni River and the Imoran–Ororun–Onikan Road and, in 1895, began to build houses at Ajebamidele.

Although he never converted to Christianity, Ipaiye was a friend of Charles Phillips, and in 1899 Phillips and his brother started a farm at Ajebamidele. They planted coffee, cocoa, rubber, yam, and corn, but the venture does not seem to have been an economic success. Ipaiye's son thought that his father did not plant cocoa until c. 1909, although he grew kola before that. Other Ondos later acquired their first cocoa seeds from Ipaiye. Ipaiye adhered to traditional Yoruba religion and was not educated; A. B. B. Ipaiye (his son) received a Christian education in Lagos, but became a Muslim in 1916 and later joined the Ahmaddiya movement. Ipaiye died in 1923.

Chief Yegbata Elisha Okelola was born in Abeokuta and sold as a slave to an Ondo chief. He bought his freedom with money earned by trading, and eventually became a prosperous Ondo farmer and rubber trader. He took his chieftancy title during the reign of Oshemawe Fidipote. He was sympathetic to Bishop Phillips's activities, publicly opposing human sacrifice as early as 1886, but was not actually baptized until 1898,[8] after he had visited his native Abeokuta and the Christian community there with the Revd. E. M. Lijadu (also an Egba). He apparently also observed cocoa farming on this trip to Abeokuta and planted a few seeds in his compound when he returned to Ondo. He never became a cocoa farmer himself, but he encouraged others to plant the crop and supplied many people with seed.

Two other early Ondo planters were: *J. Alomaja*, a cloth trader who travelled to Ejinrin, Lagos, Ibadan, and Iseyin. He saw cocoa during his travels and brought some back to plant at Ilunla, whence it spread to near-by villages; and *Fagbosiwa*, a tailor in Lagos who heard about cocoa there and obtained seeds in Porto Novo, which he planted near Ajebamidele.

[7] Many of the details given here are mentioned in Bishop Phillips's diaries. Ipaiye is also mentioned in Lijadu's diary and in P. C. Lloyd, *Yoruba Land Law*, pp. 100, 132, who states that Ipaiye was at one time a slave himself.

[8] Phillips, Diary, June 1889 and 7 Aug. 1898; cf. Great Britain, House of Commons, Parliamentary Papers, 'Correspondence Respecting the War Between Native Tribes in the Interior . . . of Lagos', C. 4957, 1887.

OKEIGBO

Moses Akinwamide was an early convert to Christianity in Okeigbo. According to Charles Phillips, he demonstrated his convictions in 1899 by throwing the appurtenances of his traditional religious practices in the river.[9] Around 1898 or 1899 he went to Lagos with other people from Okeigbo and found work on J. H. Doherty's farm at Agege. He returned to Okeigbo in 1902, bringing with him cocoa seeds and a first-hand understanding of their value, and began to grow cocoa at home. By 1909 a number of Okeigbos had had the same experience and cocoa growing began to spread rapidly in the community. Other early migrants to Agege were: *Isaac Oniwide*, who went to Lagos as a road labourer, ended up working for J. K. Coker, and became both a Christian and a cocoa farmer upon his return to Okeigbo; *Gabriel Egbaibon*, Christian, who worked for five years at Agege where, according to his son, he observed that people who grew and sold cocoa 'used money like water' and hence he decided to go home and plant it for himself; *Joshua Fagunwa*, also Christian, who worked for Doherty and brought back cocoa and kola seeds to plant at Okeigbo.

Kolajo was a hunter in Okeigbo who first saw cocoa on Gureje Thompson's farm at Ilesha *c.* 1898. He discussed the new crop with Bishop Phillips, who advised him to plant it. He then obtained a few pods from Gureje Thompson and planted the seeds in his compound. He apparently did not plant cocoa extensively until about 1909, when many Okeigbo farmers took up the crop under the influence of the returned labourers from Agege. At that time he sold seeds to other farmers from his original trees. He eventually became quite prosperous: he built a large house, where members of the Department of Agriculture staff stayed when they visited Okeigbo to demonstrate proper methods of cultivating cocoa in 1918 and after, and in 1924, bought the first lorry in Okeigbo. Kolajo was a Christian and became Balogun of the Okeigbo church; in 1901 he considered renouncing polygamy.[10]

IFE

Makinde was an Ife farmer who planted cocoa on his father's land at Ijipade *c.* 1910. He first obtained cocoa from kinsmen who had worked as labourers on J. K. Coker's farm at Agege.

Chief Lowa Omishore was a wealthy and influential trader in Ife.[11] He first acquired cocoa pods *c.* 1913 from Ibadan through an Ijesha trader who had been selling gin to Chief Omishore, who in turn retailed it in Ife. He and members of his family subsequently planted cocoa at several villages south of Ife: Oye, Oyo, and Womonle.

Abraham Osunlakun planted the first cocoa at Shekunde in 1918. He was the son of an Ife chief and had previously worked as a porter, carry-

[9] Phillips, 'Memo on Ondo Mission' (NAI).
[10] Phillips, Diary, 25 Oct. 1901.
[11] Oyo Province, Annual Report, 1925.

ing palm kernels to the railway at Oshogbo and other goods back to Ife. He learned about cocoa during his travels and brought back seeds to Ife, where he and his brothers planted them.

ILESHA

James Gureje Thompson was an Ijesha who had been a slave and lived in Sierra Leone. He later returned to Nigeria and settled in Abeokuta, where he was probably involved in repelling invasions from Dahomey. Eventually he established contacts with other Ijeshas in Lagos, including Peter Apara (see below), and became involved in the Ekitiparapo Society.[12] In *c.* 1880 he and Apara were sent by the Ijesha community in Lagos to aid the Ijesha army in their war with the Oyos. They introduced the Snider rifle to the Ekitiparapo army and remained in Ilesha to teach people how to use the weapons and to help maintain them.[13] Gureje Thompson became very influential in the conduct of Ilesha policy towards the end of the wars. He led the opposition to the peace negotiations of 1886 which Charles Phillips and Samuel Johnson conducted on behalf of the British government in Lagos.[14] He was a Christian and became Baba Egbe of the CMS church in Ilesha.

When the wars ended, the Ijeshas were forced to give up their ammunition stores, which left Gureje Thompson and Apara with nothing to do. Accordingly, they settled down to farm. Gureje Thompson first planted cocoa in 1896, using seeds he had acquired from Bishop Phillips.[15] His farm, at Etioni on the Oni River, was on good cocoa land and the crop grew well. He gave seeds to many people, including two of his Christian friends in Ilesha—*Loye* of Igangan and *Loja-Odo* of Iwara—and *Kolajo* of Okeigbo (see above), all of whom in turn helped to spread the crop. Gureje Thompson died in 1901.[16]

Peter Apara was also an Ijesha slave; he had been taken to Brazil and later repatriated to Nigeria. He settled in Lagos and became a salt trader. He met Gureje Thompson in Abeokuta, where he went to sell salt, and later went with him to teach the Ijeshas how to use Snider rifles.[17] During his sojourn in Brazil he became a Catholic, but later apparently joined the Anglican church in Nigeria. He also planted cocoa and other new crops (such as kola, orange, cassava, maize, and bamboo) in Ilesha after the wars. After Gureje Thompson's death, he established farms at Igbogi towards Oshogbo, though some of his kinsmen obtained land at Etioni near Thompson's. Apara subsequently became a church leader and a customary court judge. He died in 1922.

[12] Details of Gureje Thompson's role in Ekitiparapo political and military affairs are documented in Akintoye, *Revolution and Power Politics*; Johnson, *History of the Yorubas*; Kopytoff, *Preface to Modern Nigeria*; and Great Britain, House of Commons, Parliamentary Papers, 'Correspondence etc.', C. 4957, 1887.   [13] Johnson, p. 459.
[14] Ibid., pp. 534–5; Great Britain, House of Commons, Parliamentary Papers, 'Correspondence etc.', C. 4957, 1887.
[15] See Ayorinde, p. 19, who states that Gureje Thompson got his first cocoa seeds through the CMS agent at Ilesha, Mr. G. A. Vincent ('Daddy Agbebi'). Thompson's descendants disputed this story. Cf. Johnson, pp. 534–5.
[16] Phillips, Diary, 18 Nov. 1901.   [17] Johnson, p. 459.

APPENDIX II

Case Studies of Migration from Savannah Communities

The process by which Yorubas from the savannah areas first became involved in growing cocoa can best be illustrated by a few examples. The brief case histories which follow concern three towns or groups of settlements in the northern parts of Yorubaland. One of these—Isanlu-Isin—I visited because its people are widely reputed to have played a pioneering role in the migration to the cocoa belt. In some Ife and Ondo villages all Yoruba migrants from savannah areas are referred to as 'Isanlus', although in fact they come from many different towns. I found people from Isanlu itself in ten of the twenty Ife villages I visited and also in several places in Ondo. (There were Isanlus in: Aye-Oba, Amula Soji, Asawure, Okoro, Omidire, Omifunfun, Onigbodogi, Oniperegun, Shekunde, Aba Orafidiya. I was also told of many Isanlus in Olode and Mefoworade.) There was a sizeable group of Isanlus in Omifon—one of the two Ondo villages in which I conducted a series of detailed interviews with local and stranger farmers. Isanlu-Isin is the principal town of the Isin group which, according to the chiefs of Isanlu, includes seven smaller towns and eleven subordinate villages in addition to Isanlu itself.[1]

In Abanata, the Ife village which I surveyed in detail, most of the immigrant farmers came from two 'sister' towns in northern Oshun Division—Eripa and Iree—and I have compiled historical information about migration from these two communities from my interviews in Abanata. Finally, I also interviewed a group of farmers from Iresi, a town about seven miles east of Eripa and Iree. The Iresis consider themselves to have been one of the first groups to obtain land for cocoa growing in Ife Division. (Their Ife landlord supports this claim.) These three communities obviously cannot be considered a 'representative sample' of all the savannah communities from which people have gone to farm in the cocoa belt, but their experiences are similar to those described to me more briefly by farmers from other towns, and their stories may serve to illustrate the migratory process.

Isanlu-Isin[2]

According to tradition, the first *oba* of Isanlu (the Olusin) came from Ile-Ife to settle at Isanlu. He was later joined by others from Ife, Iseyin,

[1] For brevity, I shall henceforth refer to Isanlu-Isin simply as Isanlu, but should point out that it is quite different from Isanlu Makutu which is also located in Kwara State.

[2] Sources: Olusin and Chiefs of Isanlu-Isin; five farmers in Isanlu; Ogagba Bolarin in Imokore; E. Afolayan in Aye-Oba; B. A. Elujobade in Ifetedo. Some of these details were subsequently corroborated by B. A. Agiri on the basis of his research on the development of kola growing in southern Egba and Ijebu areas.

and Oyo. As the community expanded, people established the other Isin towns and villages. The people of the Isin group are part of the Igbominas, a sub-group of the Yoruba-speaking peoples.[3] Isanlu warriors fought alongside other Igbomina soldiers during the nineteenth-century wars: during the Sixteen Years War in the late nineteenth century they supported the Ekitiparapo.[4] After the wars people could move about more freely and some began to leave Isanlu for Lagos and other towns in Western Nigeria, where they traded or worked as labourers.

Sometime before 1930 a young man from Isanlu named Ogagba Bolarin followed the example of his fellow townspeople and went to Lagos in search of work.[5] At first he worked as a labourer for a produce buyer in Lagos; later he and three other Isanlus went to Otta area in Egba Division to weed farms and cut palm fruit. At Otta he and his companions saw farmers growing cocoa and making money from it. They decided to try cultivating it themselves and approached their employer for some land, which he gave them. They paid money when they were allotted land but did not pay *ishakole* to the grantor afterwards. However, they were not considered owners of the land.[6]

The village where Bolarin and his companions went to farm was Aganna, near Otta. Aganna was a centre for migrants from the northern parts of Yorubaland who came to work as farm labourers in the Otta area. At Aganna the migrants obtained shelter upon their arrival and information about jobs in the area. The present Bale of Aganna is from Ikirun.[7] After Bolarin and his companions had planted cocoa at Aganna, he returned to Isanlu and told people that there was money in growing cocoa. Some Isanlus followed him back to Aganna to grow cocoa for themselves.

The Isanlus remained at Aganna for several years, but their cocoa farms did not do very well and they found it difficult to obtain additional uncultivated land in the area. So when some of the Ikiruns at Aganna reported that there was good cocoa land available near Orile Owu (in what is now Southern Oshun Division), Bolarin and the other Isanlus decided to move there. In 1932[8] they obtained land at a village called Imokore; it turned out to be very good for cocoa and when they sent word of this home to Isanlu, more people came to join them from Isanlu and other Igbomina towns. Some, including Ogagba Bolarin, still live there.[9]

[3] Forde, *The Yoruba-Speaking Peoples of South-Western Nigeria*, pp. 71–5.

[4] Johnson, *History of the Yorubas*, pp. 438–44; S. A. Akintoye, *Revolution and Power Politics*.

[5] The exact date is uncertain. Bolarin himself said it was after the railway had reached Ilorin—1907. A junior brother of Bolarin's, whom I met independently at Aye-Oba in Ife Division, said that he had gone to work near Agege in 1919, but did not indicate whether he left Isanlu before or after his brother.

[6] Cf. Lloyd, esp. pp. 275–6.   [7] I am indebted for this information to B. A. Agiri.

[8] Bolarin's brother gave the date of the move to Imokore as November 1932. Bolarin said that this brother was the only educated member of his family and had written down the date at the time. The Olusin of Isanlu said that the move to Imokore occurred in 1933, the year that his father was installed as Isanlu, which closely corroborates Bolarin's brother's information.

[9] Ogagba Bolarin seems to have been an influential man among the Isanlus. The

Igbominas came to Imokore in such numbers that they soon exhausted the available supplies of uncultivated forest land in the immediate vicinity. By the late 1930s they began to move on to Ife, where an Isanlu man named Bajepade had obtained farmland from the Oni of Ife c. 1935.[10] Some people settled at Aye-Oba with Bajepade; others obtained land in different parts of Ife Division, especially in the forests south and east of Aye-Oba. Among the villages I visited, Isanlus claimed to have been the first strangers to settle in Omifunfun, Amula Soji, and Aye-Oba, arriving in the late 1930s and 1940s. Many people went first from Isanlu to Imokore or Aye-Oba, where they learned how to grow cocoa (often by working as labourers for a year or two) from the Isanlus already settled there, before seeking land of their own. Many later acquired land and planted cocoa in several places, using the proceeds from their first farms to develop additional ones. Today the sons of some of the early migrants have established farms in Ilesha or Ondo in addition to those their fathers planted in Ife.

Iresi[11]

Cocoa was introduced to Iresi in the 1920s. Some people started to plant it on nearby uncultivated forest land belonging to Ila, but the Ilas drove them away. One of these nearby planters, a man named Joseph Oladiran, had two brothers who were working as pit sawyers near Ife. When he told them, in 1928, that the Ilas had destroyed his cocoa farm, they offered to help him find land in Ife. They appealed to one of their Ife clients, who was sympathetic to their request for farmland but had none to spare at his own village (Ogbagba—see Map 5). He did, however, approach various Ife families on the Oladirans' behalf, and, after several months, found one —the Abeweilas—who agreed to accept the Oladirans as tenants. (The Abeweilas said that at that time the Oladirans' request for uncultivated forest land on which to plant cocoa was considered unusual; the family deliberated for some time and held a general meeting before deciding to give out part of their land.)

In 1929 Joseph Oladiran and his wife started to farm on the Abeweilas'

Olusin and chiefs of Isanlu described him as 'the man who led the Igbominas to the West'. He is a herbalist and *babalawo* as well as a farmer and blacksmith, whom people consult for guidance on dealing with illness and other problems. Isanlus whom I met in different Ife villages spoke of him with respect, which seemed to corroborate the Olusin's description. Bolarin's own account of the move from Aganna to Imokore was as follows: at Aganna some Ikirun people asked him to consult the Ifa oracle concerning their future. Bolarin learned from the oracle that the Ikiruns would go to Imokore to plant cocoa. He then asked them to let him know whether the land at Imokore was indeed good for growing cocoa. They sent word that it was, so he and his people followed the Ikiruns to Imokore, where the Ikiruns helped the Isanlus obtain land.

[10] Several sources in Ife mentioned Bajepade as the first Isanlu to have settled in Ife. He apparently worked as a labourer in Ife for several years, before approaching the Oni for land. He then became a tenant on the Oni's own family land at Aye-Oba. Interviews with B. A. Elujobade; Bale of Aye-Oba; chiefs and farmers in Isanlu.

[11] Sources: Abeweila family, Ife; Afolayan and his son, Dr. A. Afolayan of the University of Ife; Bale of Aba Iresi; Mrs. Oladiran; the Revd. G. A. Bamikole, Ijebu Ode.

land; the following year one of his brothers left his work as a sawyer and joined him on the farm. During the next few years more people came from Iresi to plant cocoa at Ife. The Abeweilas, most of whom lived and worked in Ife rather than on their farmland, put Joseph Oladiran in charge of allocating farmland to each newcomer, and the strangers' settlement was called Aba Iresi after their hometown. Later people also came from Eripa, Ikirun, and Ilorin to settle at Aba Iresi; there are now five villages on the Abeweilas' land, populated almost entirely by non-Ife Yorubas. The Abeweilas themselves had not planted cocoa before the Iresis arrived and began to do so only when they observed how much money the Iresis were earning from their cocoa farms.

By the late 1930s most of the Abeweilas' forest land had been culti- vated or allocated to potential farmers and people coming to Aba Iresi for land had to look elsewhere in Ife Division. Also some of the early settlers discovered that their plots of cocoa did not yield as well as their neigh- bours'; accordingly, they too sought better land in other parts of Ife—for example, at Bolorunduro and Ogudu. Aba Iresi became a stopping place for migrants from Iresi and neighbouring towns, just as Imokore and Aye- Oba were for Isanlus. Newcomers lodged at Aba Iresi while they looked for land of their own, or settled down there for a year or two to learn the techniques of cocoa cultivation and save money for starting their own farms, by working as labourers for the farmers already established there.[12] A number of the farmers from Eripa and Iree who eventually settled at Abanata had come there via Aba Iresi.

Eripa and Iree[13]

Like the Isanlus and people from other Yoruba towns, men from Eripa and Iree first encountered cocoa around Lagos and southern Egbaland, to which they had travelled to trade or work. Jacob Okediji, now the head of the strangers at Abanata village in Ife Division, first went to Lagos around 1920 to seek employment. At first he worked as a labourer, clear- ing farms and headloading produce at Ijoko-Ata (near Otta); later he obtained land there and planted cocoa. Like Ogagba Bolarin, he gave presents to the owner of the land but paid no *ishakole*. His cocoa did not yield well, however, so after some time he sold it and went to Ife, where his son was a school teacher at Aba Iresi. Through a half-brother who was also living at Aba Iresi, Okediji met the Bale of Abanata, who agreed to give him land. Jacob Okediji came to Abanata in 1949. At that time there were only three Ife families, a man from Erinle [14] and two brothers from Iree farming at Abanata, but Jacob Okediji sent word home that there was

[12] In 1936 the Oni of Ife wrote to the District Officer: 'We in Ife require labour from other places too, like Irehe, Iresi and Erin in Ibadan Division, Oye and Ifaki in Ekiti and Offa in Ilorin Division.' IFEDIV 1/1/112 (NAI).
[13] Sources: Interviews in Abanata; the Revd. G. A. Bamikole; M. Hündsalz.
[14] The first tenant to reach Abanata came from Erinle in 1945. Like Jacob Okediji, he had first gone to Lagos, where he rented a bearing cocoa farm at Agege. Later he went to Ife; he first obtained land at Balogun village, but his cocoa did not grow well there so he moved on to Abanata.

plenty of good land there, and before the end of the year more people began arriving from Eripa and Iree.

Most of the tenants at Abanata arrived during the early 1950s, several after spending a year or two at Aba Iresi or another Ife village such as Olode. Since then some have gone on to acquire land and plant additional farms (either for themselves or for their sons or junior brothers) at such places as Igbo Olodumare, Etioni, and Aba Ijesha.

APPENDIX III
Cocoa Statistics

TABLE 1
Volume of Cocoa Exported from Nigeria

Year	lbs.[a]	Year	tons	Year	tons
1886	2,751	1913	3,621	1942	59,937
1887	671	1914	4,939	1943	87,487
1888	3,738			1944	70,051
1889	3,044	1915	9,105		
1890	13,657	1916	8,956	1945	77,004
		1917	15,442	1946	100,186
1891	15,254	1918	10,219	1947	110,793
1892	15,820	1919	25,711	1948	91,449
1893	18,027			1949	103,637
1894	39,177	1920	17,155		
1895	48,187	1921	17,944		
		1922	31,271	1950	99,949
1896	—	1923	32,821	1951	121,478
1897	—	1924	37,205	1952	114,731
1898	—			1953	104,671
1899	157,708	1925	44,705	1954	98,373
1900	256,234	1926	39,099		
		1927	39,210	1955	88,413
****		1928	49,163	1956	117,133
	tons[b]	1929	55,236	1957	135,300
				1958	87,648
1900	202	1930	52,331	1959	142,800
1901	206	1931	52,806		
1902	307	1932	71,039		
1903	281	1933	60,737	1960	154,176
1904	531	1934	77,982	1961	183,912
				1962	195,000
1905	470			1963	175,000
1906	723	1935	88,143	1964	197,000
1907	933	1936	80,553		
1908	1,366	1937	103,216		
1909	2,241	1938	97,104	1965[c]	259,400
		1939	113,841	1966[c]	193,300
1910	2,932			1967[c]	248,200
1911	4,401	1940	89,737	1968[c]	208,900
1912	3,390	1941	104,681	1969[c]	173,600

Sources: 1886–1900, Lagos Bluebooks; 1900–64, Helleiner, Peasant Agriculture Government and Economic Growth in Nigeria, Table IVA8; 1965–9, UN, Yearbook of International Trade Statistics.

[a] Lagos only.
[b] Western Nigeria.
[c] Metric tons.

TABLE 2
Acres Planted in Cocoa (Five-year Moving Average)

Year	Ibadan	Oyo[a]	Ondo	Western Nigeria
1900	41·6	—	—	92·8
1901	45·2	—	—	98·4
1902	83·8	—	—	176·8
1903	122·6	14	—	231·8
1904	173·0	18	—	305·6
1905	194·8	19	—	322·6
1906	315·4	37	—	509·2
1907	334·0	43	—	532·2
1908	607·0	156	—	1,002·0
1909	629·6	241	—	1,025·0
1910	1,026·8	199	40·2	1,538·2
1911	1,019·2	292	41·0	1,599·0
1912	1,449·4	239	61·0	2,179·6
1913	2,219·2	363	73·6	3,122·6
1914	2,752·0	519	84·2	3,943·8
1915	2,618·4	532	84·2	3,966·0
1916	3,988·0	1,003	117·0	6,191·8
1917	4,290·6	1,224	123·0	6,859·2
1918	6,185·2	2,779	292·8	10,880·8
1919	5,940·0	3,147	369·2	11,224·4
1920	6,515·0	3,695	417·6	12,452·2
1921	5,470·8	3,738	581·8	11,329·6
1922	6,217·5	4,369	740·2	13,216·0
1923	6,119·6	4,189	1,130·8	14,159·4
1924	7,919·0	5,190	1,674·6	18,875·8
1925	9,140·6	5,932	2,360·6	22,592·2
1926	12,165·6	7,643	3,271·0	29,915·0
1927	12,369·8	8,207	4,177·6	32,594·4
1928	13,782·2	9,663	8,920·2	40,995·2
1929	12,924·6	8,904	13,072·8	43,340·6
1930	12,649·6	8,733	17,427·0	47,687·4
1931	10,337·0	7,121	21,443·2	47,285·6
1932	9,985·2	6,501	25,756·6	50,866·6
1933	7,336·8	4,231	26,288·2	46,074·4
1934	7,792·4	4,450	27,559·6	48,911·8
1935	7,122·4	4,025	27,865·4	48,061·0
1936	7,151·0	4,249	28,700·0	49,572·2
1937	6,629·2	4,255	28,510·4	48,739·6
1938	5,679·0	4,278	27,677·4	45,893·6
1939	4,550·6	3,592	26,095·6	40,651·2
1940	3,797·6	3,326	25,243·4	37,315·0
1941	2,871	2,755	23,801	32,734
1942	2,247	2,120	23,479	29,788
1943	1,669	1,583	19,388	24,182
1944	1,165	1,558	15,879	20,036
1945	900	1,437	12,292	16,044
1946	755	1,289	8,802	12,073
1947	623	1,150	4,709	7,961

Source: Western Nigeria, Ministry of Agriculture and Natural Resources, Swollen Shoot Virus Disease Survey, 1944–9, and Re-survey, 1951–2.

[a] Rounded to nearest acre.

TABLE 3

Real Price of Cocoa in Nigeria

Year	Lagos Price[a]	Lagos Price Index[b]	Consumer Price Index[c]	Real Price Index[d]	Five-Year Moving Average
1900	41·7				
1901	37·6				
1902	43·8				
1903	44·0				
1904	36·9				
1905	36·9				
1906	37·4				
1907	51·3				
1908	37·0				
1909	32·0	51·2	15·7	326·1	
1910	34·6	55·4	16·7	331·7	
1911	36·8	58·9	17·1	344·4	347·9
1912	37·5	60·0	17·7	340·0	345·7
1913	43·5	69·6	17·5	397·7	334·9
1914	34·8	55·7	17·7	314·7	294·4
1915	34·4	55·0	19·8	277·8	244·2
1916/17	22·6	36·2	25·5	142·0	180·2
1917/18	17·5	28·0	31·5	88·9	160·3
1918/19	20·0	32·0	41·1	77·8	152·7
1919/20	71·3	114·1	53·1	214·9	94·5
1920/1	19·6	31·4	78·9	39·8	94·7
1921/2	21·5	34·4	67·5	51·0	91·0
1922/3	25·2	40·3	44·7	90·2	68·4
1923/4	16·2	25·9	43·9	59·0	81·1
1924/5	29·8	47·7	46·8	101·9	109·6
1925/6	28·9	46·2	44·7	103·4	134·3
1926/7	53·2	85·1	43·0	193·4	152·7
1927/8	50·9	81·4	38·1	213·6	160·3
1928/9	36·8	58·9	39·0	151·0	175·9
1929/30	33·9	54·2	39·0	140·0	135·0
1930/1	18·4	29·4	36·0	81·7	112·9
1931	17·2	27·5	31·0	88·7	78·6
1932	17·8	28·5	27·6	103·3	87·4
1933	13·8	22·1	27·9	79·2	90·0
1934	14·2	22·7	27·0	84·1	98·4
1935	16·2	25·9	27·4	94·5	107·7
1936	22·8	36·5	27·9	130·8	107·1
1937	28·1	45·0	30·0	150·0	105·3
1938	14·3	22·9	30·0	76·3	96·0
1939/40	17·0	27·2	36·4	74·7	78·9
1940/1	14·0	22·4	46·7	48·0	54·6
1941/2	15·0	24·0	53·0	45·3	45·8
1942/3	13·0	20·8	72·4	28·7	40·3
1943/4	13·0	20·8	64·5	32·2	41·7
1944/5	23·0	36·8	77·9	47·2	54·8

TABLE 3 *continued*

Year	Lagos Price[a]	Lagos Price Index[b]	Consumer Price Index[c]	Real Price Index[d]	Five-Year Moving Average
1945/6	27·5	44·0	79·7	55·2	62·6
1946/7	50·0	80·0	101·8	78·6	94·0
1947/8	62·5	100·0	100·0	100·0	117·1
1948/9	120·0	192·0	101·5	189·2	135·6
1949/50	100·0	160·0	98·6	162·3	163·2
1950/1	120·0	192·0	129·8	147·9	191·5
1951/2	170·0	272·0	125·7	216·4	198·6
1952/3	170·0	272·0	112·5	241·8	217·7
1953/4	166·0	256·6	118·2	224·7	237·0
1954/5	196·0	313·6	121·5	258·1	229·3
1955/6	196·0	313·6	128·3	244·4	218·7
1956/7	146·0	233·6	131·7	177·7	210·8
1957/8	146·0	233·6	123·8	188·7	197
1958/9	146·0	233·6	126·1	185·2	178
1959/60	156·0	249·6	131·7	189·5	163
1960/1	148·2	214·4	143·0	149·9	147
1961/2	96·0	153·6	154·3	99·5	134
1962/3	101·0	161·6	144·0	112·2	
1963/4	106·0	169·6	142·9	118·7	
1964/5	116·0				
1965/6	61·0				
1966/7	86·0				
1967/8	91·0				
1968/9					
1969/70	147·0				
1970/1	151·0				

Notes and Sources:

Lagos Price: 1900–15 Export Unit Value (Nigeria, *Bluebooks*).
1916–30 Average Price Paid in Lagos, Nov.–Feb. (*Trade Supplement to the Nigeria Gazette*).
1931–8 Price Paid in Lagos (*Bluebooks*) for FAQ.
1939–63 Helleiner, Table II-B-1 (Bauer and Marketing Board Reports).
1964–70 Marketing Board Reports.
[b] Index of Lagos Price: 1947/8 = 100 (1939/40—63/4: same as Helleiner, Table II-B-1).
[c] Consumer Price Index: Helleiner, Table II-B-5. 1948 = 100. Calendar years.
[d] Real Price Index: Lagos Price Index ÷ Consumer Price Index.

Bibliography

I. PUBLISHED MATERIALS

Books

AJAYI, J. F. A., *Christian Missions in Nigeria, 1841–1891* (Evanston, Ill., 1965).

—— and SMITH, R., *Yoruba Warfare in the Nineteenth Century* (Cambridge, 1964).

AKINTOYE, S. A., *Revolution and Power Politics in Yorubaland, 1840–1893*, Ibadan History Series (London, 1971).

AKINYELE, I. B., *Outlines of Ibadan History* (Lagos, 1946).

ATANDA, J. A., *The New Oyo Empire: Indirect Rule and Change in Western Nigeria, 1894–1934* (London, 1973).

AYANDELE, E. A., *The Missionary Impact on Modern Nigeria*, Ibadan History Series (London, 1966).

BAUER, P. T., *West African Trade* (London, 1963).

BROKENSHA, D., *Social Change in Larteh, Ghana* (Oxford, 1966).

BUCHANAN, K. M., and PUGH, J. C., *Land and People in Nigeria* (London, 1955).

BURNS, A., *History of Nigeria*, 4th ed. (London, 1948).

CAPLOVITZ, D., *The Poor Pay More* (New York, 1967).

CAVES, R. E., and JOHNSON, H. G., eds., *Readings in International Economics*, published for the American Economic Association by R. D. Irwin (Homewood, Ill., 1968).

COHEN, Abner, *Custom and Politics in Urban Africa* (Berkeley, Calif., 1969).

CROWDER, M., *The Story of Nigeria* (London, 1962).

DAVIDSON, B., *Black Mother* (London, 1961).

DIKE, K. O., *Trade and Politics in the Niger Delta* (Oxford, 1956).

FADIPE, N. A., *Sociology of the Yoruba*, ed. F. O. and O. O. Okediji (Ibadan, 1970).

FAULKNER, W. A., and MACKIE, J. T., *West African Agriculture* (London, 1940).

FORDE, C. D., *The Yoruba-Speaking Peoples of South-Western Nigeria*, Ethnographic Survey of Africa: Western Africa, Part IV (London, 1951).

—— and SCOTT, R., *The Native Economies of Nigeria*, vol. i of M. Perham, ed., *The Economics of a Tropical Dependency* (London, 1946).

—— *et al.*, *Peoples of the Niger–Benue Confluence*, Ethnographic Survey of Africa: Western Africa, Pt. X (London, 1955).

GALLETTI, R., BALDWIN, K. D. S., and DINA, I. O., *Nigerian Cocoa Farmers*, published on behalf of the Nigerian Cocoa Marketing Board by Oxford University Press (London, 1956).

GARLICK, P., *African Traders in Kumasi* (Accra, 1959).

—— *African Traders and Economic Development in Ghana* (Oxford, 1971).

226   BIBLIOGRAPHY

GÜSTEN, R., *Studies in the Staple Food Economy of Western Nigeria*, Afrika-Studien Nr. 30 (Munich, 1968).
HABAKKUK, H. J., *American and British Technology in the Nineteenth Century* (Cambridge, 1962).
HANCOCK, W. K., *A Survey of Commonwealth Affairs*, vol. ii, Pt. 2 (London, 1942).
HAY, A. M., and SMITH, R. H. T., *Interregional Trade and Money Flows in Nigeria, 1964* (Ibadan, 1970).
HELLEINER, G. K., *Peasant Agriculture, Government and Economic Growth in Nigeria* (Homewood, Ill., 1966).
HILL, Polly, *Migrant Cocoa Farmers of Southern Ghana* (Cambridge, 1963).
—— *Studies in Rural Capitalism in West Africa* (Cambridge, 1970).
—— *Rural Hausa: A Village and a Setting* (Cambridge, 1972).
HIRSCHMAN, A. O., *The Strategy of Economic Development* (New Haven, Conn., 1958).
IDOWU, E. B., *Olodumare: God in Yoruba Belief* (London, 1962).
JOHNSON, S., *History of the Yorubas* (Lagos, 1921).
KAY, G. B., *The Political Economy of Colonialism in Ghana* (Cambridge, 1972).
KILBY, P., *Industrialization in an Open Economy: Nigeria, 1945–1966* (Cambridge, 1969).
—— ed., *Entrepreneurship and Economic Development* (New York, 1971).
KOPYTOFF, J. H., *Preface to Modern Nigeria* (Madison, Wis., 1965).
LLOYD, P. C., *Yoruba Land Law*, published for the Nigerian Institute of Social and Economic Research by Oxford University Press (London, 1962).
——*Africa in Social Change* (New York, 1968).
—— MABOGUNJE, A. L., and AWE, B., eds., *The City of Ibadan* (Cambridge, 1967).
MABOGUNJE, A. L., *Yoruba Towns* (Ibadan, 1962).
—— *Urbanization in Nigeria* (New York, 1968).
—— *Regional Mobility and Resource Development in West Africa*, published for the Centre for Developing Area Studies, McGill University (Montreal, 1972).
MCPHEE, A., *The Economic Revolution in British West Africa* (London, 1926).
MONTGOMERY, R. and SMYTH, A. J., *Soils and Land Use in Central Western Nigeria* (Ibadan, 1962).
NEWBURY, C. W., *The Western Slave Coast and Its Rulers* (Oxford, 1961).
PEEL, J. D. Y., *Aladura: A Religious Movement Among the Yoruba* (London, 1968).
PROTHERO, R. M., *Migrant Labour From Sokoto Province, Northern Nigeria* (Kaduna, 1958?).
ROWLING, C. W., *Report on Land Tenure in Ondo Province* (1952).
—— *Land Tenure in Ijebu Province* (Ibadan, 1956).
SMITH, R., *Kingdoms of the Yoruba* (London, 1969).
STOLPER, W. F., *Planning Without Facts* (Cambridge, Mass., 1966).

SzereszewskI, R., *Structural Changes in the Economy of Ghana, 1891–1911* (London, 1965).

Urquhart, D. H., *Cocoa* (London, 1955).

Walker, G., *Traffic and Transport in Nigeria*, Colonial Research Studies No. 27 (London, 1959).

Ward Price, H. L., *Land Tenure in the Yoruba Provinces* (Lagos, 1939).

Webster, J. B., *The African Churches Among the Yoruba, 1888–1922* (Oxford, 1964).

Wells, J. C., *Agricultural Policy and Economic Growth in Nigeria: 1962–68*, to be published for the Nigerian Institute of Social and Economic Research by Oxford University Press.

Articles

Ady, Peter, 'Trends in Cocoa Production in British West Africa', *Bulletin of the Oxford University Institute of Statistics*, 2, 1940.

Ajayi, J. F. A., and Austen, R. A., 'Hopkins on Economic Imperialism in West Africa', *Economic History Review*, 25, 2, May 1972.

Akintoye, S. A., 'The Economic Background of the Ekitiparapo', *Odu*, 4, 2, Jan. 1968.

—— 'The Ondo Road Eastwards of Lagos, c. 1870–1895'. *Journal of African History*, 10, 4, 1969.

Armstrong, R., 'The Idoma-Speaking Peoples', in *Peoples of the Niger–Benue Confluence*, Ethnographic Survey of Africa: Western Africa, Part X (London, 1955).

Awe, B., 'The Ajele System: A Study of Ibadan Imperialism in the Nineteenth Century', *Journal of the Historical Society of Nigeria*, 3, 1, Dec. 1964.

—— 'The End of an Experiment: The Collapse of the Ibadan Empire, 1877–1893', *Journal of the Historical Society of Nigeria*, 3, 2, Dec. 1965.

—— 'Ibadan, its Early Beginnings', in P. C. Lloyd *et al.*, *The City of Ibadan* (Cambridge, 1967).

Ayorinde, Chief J. A., 'Historical Notes on the Cocoa Industry in Western Nigeria', *Nigerian Agricultural Journal*, 3, 1, Apr. 1966.

Bascom, W., 'Urbanization Among the Yoruba', *American Journal of Sociology*, 60, 5, Mar. 1955.

Bateman, M. J., 'Aggregate and Regional Supply Functions for Ghanaian Cocoa, 1946–1962', *Journal of Farm Economics*, 47, 2, May 1964.

Berry, S. S., 'Christianity and the Rise of Cocoa Growing in Ibadan and Ondo', *Journal of the Historical Society of Nigeria*, 4, 3, Dec. 1968.

—— 'Economic Development with Unlimited Supplies of Labour: Some Further Complications Suggested by Contemporary African Experience', *Oxford Economic Papers*, 22, 2, July 1970.

Callaway, A., 'Unemployment Among African School Leavers', *Journal of Modern African Studies*, 1, 3, Sept. 1963.

—— 'Nigeria's Indigenous Education: The Apprentice System', *Odu*, 1, 1, July 1964.

COHEN, A., 'Politics of the Kola Trade', *Africa*, 36, 1, Jan. 1966.

COHEN, R., 'Further Comment on the Kilby–Weeks Debate', *Journal of Developing Areas*, 5, 2, Jan. 1971.

DIEJOMAOH, V. P., and ORIMALADE, W. A. T., 'Unemployment in Nigeria: An Economic Analysis of Scope, Trends and Policy Issues', *Nigerian Journal of Economic and Social Studies*, 13, 2, July 1971.

DUPIRE, M., 'Planteurs autochtones et étrangers en Basse-Côte d'Ivoire orientale', *Études Éburnéennes*, 8, 1960.

EKE, I. I. U., 'Population of Nigeria, 1952–1965', *Nigerian Journal of Economic and Social Studies*, 8, 2, July 1966.

ELLIOTT, C. M., 'Agriculture and Economic Development in Africa: Theory and Experience 1880–1914', in E. L. Jones and S. J. Woolf, eds., *Agrarian Change and Economic Development* (London, 1969).

ESAN, O., 'Xenos: Alejo—Some Aspects of Greek and Yoruba Hospitality', *Odu*, 3, 1, July 1966.

FALAE, S. O., 'Unemployment in Nigeria', *Nigerian Journal of Economic and Social Studies*, 13, 1, Mar. 1971.

FRANK, C. R., 'Urban Unemployment and Economic Growth in Africa', *Oxford Economic Papers*, 20, 2, July 1968.

GODDARD, S., 'Town-Farm Relationships in Yorubaland', *Africa*, 25, 1, Jan. 1965.

HARRIS, J. R., and TODARO, M. P., 'Migration, Unemployment and Development: A Two-Sector Analysis', *American Economic Review*, 60, 1, Mar. 1970.

HELLEINER, G. K., 'Typology in Development Theory: The Land Surplus Economy', *Food Research Institute Studies*, 6, 2, 1966.

HILL, P. 'Systems of Labour Employment on Gold Coast Cocoa Farms', *W.A.I.S.E.R. Conference Proceedings*, Mar. 1956.

HOGENDORN, J. S., 'The Origins of the Groundnut Trade in Northern Nigeria', in C. K. Eicher and C. Liedholm, eds., *Growth and Development of the Nigerian Economy* (East Lansing, Mich., 1970).

HOPKINS, A. G., 'The Lagos Chamber of Commerce, 1883–1903', *Journal of the Historical Society of Nigeria*, 3, 2, Dec. 1965.

—— 'The Currency Revolution in South-Western Nigeria in the Late Nineteenth Century', *Journal of the Historical Society of Nigeria*, 3, 3, Dec. 1966.

—— 'The Lagos Strike of 1897', *Past and Present*, 35, Dec. 1966.

—— 'Economic Imperialism in West Africa: Lagos, 1880–1892', *Economic History Review*, 21, 3, Dec. 1968.

—— ed., 'A Report on the Yoruba, 1910', *Journal of the Historical Society of Nigeria*, 5, 1, Dec. 1969.

—— 'Rejoinder', *Economic History Review*, 25, 2, May 1972.

KILBY, P., 'Industrial Relations and Wage Determination: Failure of the Anglo-Saxon Model', *Journal of Developing Areas*, 1, 4, July 1967.

—— 'A Reply to John F. Weeks's Comment', *Journal of Developing Areas*, 3, 1, Oct. 1968.

—— 'Further Comment on the Kilby/Weeks Debate: Final Observations', *Journal of Developing Areas*, 5, 2, Jan. 1971.

KÖBBEN, A. J. F., 'Le Planteur noir', *Études Éburnéennes*, 5, 1956.

LLOYD, P. C., 'Some Problems of Tenancy in Yoruba Land Tenure', *African Studies*, 12, 3, Sept. 1953.

—— 'Agnatic and Cognatic Descent Among the Yoruba', *Man*, N.S. 1, 4, 1966.

MABOGUNJE, A. L., and GLEAVE, M. B., 'The Changing Agricultural Landscape of Southern Nigeria—The Example of Egba Division, 1890–1950', *Nigerian Geographical Journal*, 7, 1, June 1964.

MITCHEL, N. C., 'Yoruba Towns', in K. M. Barbour and R. M. Prothero, eds., *Essays on African Population* (London, 1961).

MORTON-WILLIAMS, P., 'The Oyo Yoruba and the Atlantic Slave Trade, 1670–1830', *Journal of the Historical Society of Nigeria*, 3, 1, Dec. 1964.

MYINT, Hla, 'The "Classical Theory" of International Trade and the Underdeveloped Countries', *Economic Journal*, 68, 270, June 1958.

NWORAH, K. Dike, 'The West African Operations of the British Cotton Growing Association, 1904–1914', *African Historical Studies*, 4, 2, 1971.

SCHWAB, W. B., 'Kinship and Lineage Among the Yoruba', *Africa*, 25, 4, Oct. 1955.

SCITOVSKY, T., 'Two Concepts of External Economies', *Journal of Political Economy*, 62, 2, Apr. 1954.

STERN, R. M., 'The Determinants of Cocoa Supply in West Africa', in I. G. Stewart and H. W. Ord, eds., *African Primary Products and International Trade* (Edinburgh, 1965).

TERIBA, O., and PHILLIPS, O. A., 'Income Distribution and National Integration', *Nigerian Journal of Economic and Social Studies*, 13, 1, Mar. 1971.

TODARO, M. P., 'A Model of Labor Migration and Urban Unemployment in Less Developed Countries', *American Economic Review*, 59, 1, Mar. 1969.

UPTON, M., and PETU, D. A., 'An Economic Study of Farming in Two Villages in Ilorin Emirate', *Bulletin of Rural Economics and Sociology*, 1, 1, 1964.

WARREN, W. M., 'Urban Real Wages and the Nigerian Trade Union Movement, 1939–60', *Economic Development and Cultural Change*, 15, 1, Oct. 1966.

WEBSTER, J. B., 'Agege: Plantations and the African Church', *Nigerian Institute of Social and Economic Research Conference Proceedings*, Mar. 1962.

—— 'The Bible and the Plough', *Journal of the Historical Society of Nigeria*, 11, 4, Dec. 1963.

WEEKS, J. F., 'A Comment on Peter Kilby', *Journal of Developing Areas*, 3, 1, Oct. 1968.

—— 'Further Comment on the Kilby/Weeks Debate: An Empirical Rejoinder', *Journal of Developing Areas*, 5, 2, Jan. 1971.

—— 'Employment, Growth and Foreign Domination in Underdeveloped Countries', *Review of Radical Political Economics*, 4, 1, Spring 1972.

230 BIBLIOGRAPHY

WILLIAMS, G. P., 'Social Stratification of a Neo-Colonial Economy: Western Nigeria', in C. Allen and R. Johnson, eds., *African Perspectives* (Cambridge, 1970).

Theses and Published Papers

ADEYEYE, S. O., 'The Western Nigeria Co-operative Movement, 1935–64', University of Ibadan M.A., 1967.
AGIRI, B. A., 'Kola in Western Nigeria, 1890–1930: A History of the Cultivation of *Cola Nitida* in Egba-Owode, Ijebu-Remo, Iwo and Ota Areas', University of Wisconsin Ph.D., 1972.
BERRY, S. S., 'Cocoa in Western Nigeria: A Study of an Innovation in a Developing Economy', University of Michigan Ph.D., 1967.
CLARK, R. C., AKINBODE, I. A., and ODEBUNMI, Y. O. K., 'Case Studies of Four Nigerian Villages', University of Ife, Department of Extension Education Research Monograph, 2, 1967.
ESSANG, S. M., 'The Distribution of Earnings in the Cocoa Economy of Western Nigeria', Michigan State University Ph.D., 1970.
FASHOLA, R., 'Changing Landscape of Ifetedo Area', Original Essay, Geography Department, University of Ibadan, 1963.
HARRIS, John R., 'Industrial Entrepreneurship in Nigeria', Northwestern University Ph.D., 1967.
HOGENDORN, J. S., 'The Origins of the Groundnut Trade in Northern Nigeria', University of London Ph.D., 1966.
HOPKINS, A. G., 'An Economic History of Lagos, 1880–1914', University of London Ph.D., 1964.
IBADAN DISTRICT COUNCIL CHURCH FARM AT ERIPA, 'Judgement re Ownership of Land, *etc.*', from Lagos Supreme Court, 19 Mar. 1906, pamphlet.
JENKINS, G. D., 'Politics in Ibadan', Northwestern University Ph.D., 1965.
JOHNSON, G. L. *et al.*, 'Strategies and Recommendations for Nigerian Rural Development', CSNRD Report No. 33, 1969.
MABOGUNJE, A. L., 'Changing Pattern of Rural Settlement and Rural Economy in Egba Division, South-West Nigeria', University of London M.A., 1958.
OKEDIJI, F. A., 'The Economic History of the Hausa-Fulani Emirates of Northern Nigeria, 1900–1939', Indiana University Ph.D., 1971.
OKURUME, G. O., *The Food Crop Economy in Nigerian Agricultural Policy*, CSNRD Report No. 31, 1969.
OLATUNBOSUN, D. and OLAYIDE, S. O., 'Effects of the Marketing Boards on the Output and Income of Primary Producers', International Conference on the Marketing Board System, Nigerian Institute of Social and Economic Research, 1970, mimeographed.
OLUSANYA, P. O., 'Socio-Economic Aspects of Rural–Urban Migration in Western Nigeria', Nigerian Institute of Social and Economic Research, 1969, mimeographed.

OYEMAKINDE, J. O., 'A History of Indigenous Labour on the Nigerian Railway, 1895–1945', University of Ibadan Ph.D., 1970.

SANDERS, Dean, 'The Price Responsiveness of Nigerian Cocoa Farmers', University of Michigan Ph.D., 1968.

Official Publications

AJAYI, J. F. A., and IGUN, A. A., *Population Census of Nigeria: Lists of Historical Events for Determination of Individual Ages*, 1963, mimeographed.

AYOOLA COMMISSION, *Report of the Commission of Enquiry into the Civil disturbances which occurred in certain parts of the Western State of Nigeria in the month of December, 1968* (Ibadan, 1969).

CALLAWAY, A., and MUSONE, *Financing of Education in Nigeria*, UNESCO: International Institute for Educational Planning, 1968.

COCOA RESEARCH INSTITUTE OF NIGERIA, *Annual Reports*, 1962–9.

FAO, *Agricultural Development in Nigeria, 1964–80*, 1965.

GREAT BRITAIN, COLONIAL OFFICE, Confidential Print, CO 879/33, No. 399.

—— —— Confidential Print, CO 879/45, No. 509, 'Correspondence Respecting Native Affairs', Nov. 1895 to Jan. 1898.

—— —— Confidential Print, CO 879/62, No. 627, 'Two Journeys in Lagos Protectorate', 1900.

—— —— Confidential Print, African 1023, 'Correspondence Concerning Palm Oil Grants in West Africa'.

GREAT BRITAIN, HOUSE OF COMMONS, Parliamentary Papers, 'Report of the Select Committee on the State of the British Settlements on the West Coast of Africa', v, 412, 1865.

—— —— Parliamentary Papers, "Correspondence Respecting the War Between Native Tribes in the Interior . . . of Lagos', C. 4957, 1887.

—— —— Parliamentary Papers, 'Statistical Abstracts for the Colonies', 1890–1916.

—— —— Parliamentary Papers, "Correspondence Relating to Railway Construction in Nigeria', Cd. 2787, 1905.

—— —— Parliamentary Papers, 'Statement of Policy on Colonial Development and Welfare', Cmd. 6175, 1940.

LAGOS, *Annual Reports*, 1900–3.

—— *Bluebooks*, 1863–1905.

Lagos Gazette, 1886–1906.

NIGERIA, *Bluebooks*, 1914–38.

—— Department of Agriculture, *Annual Reports*, 1910–40.

SOUTHERN NIGERIA, *Bluebooks*, 1908–13.

Trade Supplement to the Nigeria Gazette, 1917–31.

TURNHAM, D., *The Employment Problem in Less Developed Countries: A Review of Evidence*, O.E.C.D. Development Centre Studies, Employment Series 1 (Paris, 1971).

UNITED NATIONS, *Yearbook of International Trade Statistics*, 1970.

WEST AFRICAN COCOA RESEARCH INSTITUTE, *Annual Reports*, 1957–61.

WEST AFRICAN LANDS COMMITTEE, *Minutes of Evidence*, printed for the use of the Colonial Office, 1916.

WEST AFRICAN LANDS COMMITTEE, *Papers and Correspondence*, printed for the use of the Colonial Office, 1916.

WESTERN NIGERIA MINISTRY OF AGRICULTURE AND NATURAL RESOURCES, *Tree Crop Planting Projects* (Ibadan, n.d.).

—— Western Nigeria Development Project, *Cocoa* (Ibadan, n.d.).

II. UNPUBLISHED MATERIALS

Public Record Office, London

Nigeria Correspondence, 1912–14.

Southern Nigeria Correspondence, 1900–13.

National Archives, Ibadan

(a) *Government documents*

'Agricultural Department, Miscellaneous Correspondence', IFEDIV 1/1/112.

'Assessment Report, Otta District, Abeokuta Province', 1926–7, CSO 26/20629.

BRIDGES, A. F. B., 'Intelligence Report, Ondo District, etc.', 1935, CSO 26/30172.

'Cocoa Agreement, 1937: Miscellaneous', CSO 26/25807, 58.

'Correspondence Concerning Railway Freight on Cocoa', CSO 26/16570.

DICKENSON, E. N. C., 'Intelligence Report on Ibadan Town, 1937', IBAPROF 3/4.

File on establishment of Ifetedo, OYOPROF 3/644.

File on land disputes, OYOPROF 3/1181, vols. 1–3.

—— OYOPROF 4/5/12.

Ibadan Division, Annual Reports, 1917, 1926.

Ife Division, Annual Report, 1917, OYOPROF 4/6, 355/1917.

Ife-Ilesha Division, Annual Reports, 1929, IFEDIV 1/1, 80, and 1943–55, IFEDIV 3/9.

'Ife-Modakeke Dispute Court Cases', IFEDIV 1/1/113B.

Ilorin Province, Annual Reports, 1923–33, 1937–9, 1942–4, 1952–3, CSO 26/12687, vols. i–xiii.

'Intelligence Report on Ifon and Owo Districts, Owo Division, Ondo Province', 1935, CSO 26/29956.

'Intelligence Report, Ikire District, Ibadan Division', 1934.

'Ishakole: Collection of', IFEDIV 1/1/113.

'Land Tenure in Ibadan', IBAPROF 3/0718.

The Land Tenure Question in West Africa, reprinted from *Lagos Weekly Record*, 1913, pamphlet.

MACKENZIE, J. A., 'Report on the Native Organization of Ife District—Oyo Province', 1934, CSO 26/29829.

Ondo Province, Annual Reports, 1921–49, CSO 26/03996, 11874, vols. i–xvii.

Oyo Province, Annual Reports, 1920–51, CSO 26/06027, 09723, 12723, vols. i–xxv.

'Produce Inspection and Grading of Cocoa', CSO 26/50480.

'Report of Commission of Enquiry into the Marketing of West African Cocoa', CSO 26/34883, vol. i.
'Shoko Ademakinwa vs. Obutu, Land Dispute—Matter of', IFEDIV 1/1/332.
'Travelling Commissioner's Journal and Diary, 1897–1913', ONDODIV 8/1.

(b) *Church Missionary Society, Yoruba Mission*

ADEJUMO, J. S., 'History of the Foundation of the Gospel at Ile-Ife, 1897–1939', CMS (Y) 4/1/13.
Correspondence of J. B. Wood, 1877–1893, CMS (Y) 1/7/1–8.
OKUSEINDE, J., Journal, 1892, CMS (Y).
'Papers relating to the Development of Churches and Schools in Ondo and Ilesha Districts, 1885–1907', CMS (Y) 2/2/4.
PHILLIPS, C., Diaries and Papers, 1885–1905, CMS (Y) 1/1/2, 3/1–15.

Customary Court Records

Ibadan Lands Court Records, 1937–64.
Ibadan Native Court Records, 1910–14.
Ife Customary Court Records, 1929–69, including scattered records of the Ifetedo Native Court (1933–6) and the Ife Appeals Court (1937–1949).
Ondo Grade A Customary Court Records, 1966–9.
Ondo Grade B Customary Court Records, 1958–70.

Mapo Hall, Ibadan

Bale's Letter Book, 1914–17.
Ibadan Town Council Minutes, 1903–5, 1912.
Resident's Letter Book, 1901–5.

Private Papers

John Holt Company Archives.
LIJADU, E. M., Diary, 1898–16.
OBISESAN, J. A., Diary, 1920–40.

Unpublished Papers

ADEJUWON, J. O., 'Agricultural Colonization in the Forest Areas of Western Nigeria: The Movement of Yoruba People to the Countryside', 1970, mimeographed.
AYORINDE, Chief J. A., 'Western Nigeria Village Social Organization', 1966(?), mimeographed.
WELLS, J. C., 'Equity and Efficiency in Rural Development: An African Dilemma?', Paper presented at the African Studies Association meetings, Nov. 1972.
WESTERN NIGERIA, Ministry of Agriculture and Natural Resources, Cocoa Survey Section, Original Records of the Swollen Shoot Virus Disease Survey, 1944–9, and Re-survey, 1951–2.
WESTSTEIJN, G., and GORENZ, A. M., 'Studies on the Chemical Control of *Phytophthora Palmivora* (Butl.) Butl. on *Theobroma Cacao* L. in Nigeria, VII. Returns of Fungicide Spraying', CRIN typescript, n.d.

Index